FOURTH EDITION

Children's Literature in the Reading Program

Engaging Young Readers in the 21st Century

Deborah A. Wooten
Bernice E. Cullinan

EDITORS

The International Literacy Association attempts, through its publications, to provide a forum for a wide spectrum of opinions on reading. This policy permits divergent viewpoints without implying the endorsement of the Association.

Director of Educational Resources   Shannon Fortner
Acquisitions Editor   Becky Fetterolf
Managing Editors   Susanne Viscarra and Christina M. Lambert
Digital Project Manager   Wes Ford
Editorial Associate   Wendy Logan
Creative Services/Production Manager   Anette Schuetz
Design and Composition Associate   Lisa Kochel

Cover   Lise Holliker Dykes and Tasia12

Library of Congress Cataloging-in-Publication Data
Children's literature in the reading program : engaging young readers in the 21st century / Deborah A. Wooten & Bernice E. Cullinan, Editors.
    pages   cm
  Includes bibliographical references and index.
  ISBN 978-0-87207-387-6 (alk. paper) / 978-0-87207-388-3 (e-book)
  1. Reading (Elementary)—United States. 2. Children's literature—Study and teaching—United States. 3. English language—Study and teaching (Elementary)—United States. I. Wooten, Deborah A. II. Cullinan, Bernice E.
  LB1573.C455   2015
  372.4—dc23
                                        2014047051

Suggested APA Reference
Wooten, D.A., & Cullinan, B.E. (2015). *Children's literature in the reading program: Engaging young readers in the 21st century* (4th ed.). Newark, DE: International Literacy Association.

This book is dedicated to children's literature authors and illustrators. The books you publish are our power tools that help motivate our students to read and want to read.

CONTENTS

PART I

Exploring Genres and Subgenres

PART II

Investigating Texts and Images

PART III

Motivating All Students

PART IV

Visiting a Rich Reading and Writing Classroom

PART V

Engaging With Resources in the Field

ABOUT THE EDITORS

Deborah A. Wooten is an associate professor of reading in the Theory and Practice in Teacher Education Department at the University of Tennessee, Knoxville, USA. Before joining the university faculty, she taught elementary school for 23 years. After earning her PhD from New York University, she continued to teach in the elementary classroom for 10 years to research practical new methods for using children's literature to foster connections across content areas while scaffolding students to think metacognitively.

Deborah served on the Children's Choices Project and as a committee member for IRA's Children's and Young Adults' Book Award, Lee Bennett Hopkins Promising Poetry Award, and Paul A. Witty Short Story Award. She has also served as a committee member for the USBBY Outstanding International Books List. She is an author and editor of books, chapters, and articles, including coediting and contributing to *The Continuum Encyclopedia of Young Adult Literature* (Continuum, 2005) and *Children's Literature in the Reading Program: An Invitation to Read* (third edition; International Reading Association, 2009).

With her husband, Gene; her children, Matt and Katie; and her son-in-law, Caleb, Deborah enjoys traveling and especially reading rich, thick books while sitting in the sun at the beach. She can be contacted at dwooten1@utk.edu.

Bernice E. Cullinan, professor emeritus from New York University, USA, is both nationally and internationally known for her work in children's literature. She has written or cowritten over 30 books on literature for classroom teachers and librarians, including these published by Wadsworth/Cengage Learning: *Literature and the Child* (2013), *Language Arts: Learning and Teaching* (2003), and *Language, Literacy and the Child* (1997). Bee is known for books about poetry, such as *Easy Poetry Lessons That Dazzle and Delight* (Scholastic, 1999) and *Three Voices: An Invitation to Poetry Across the Curriculum* (Stenhouse, 1995). She has written a book for parents as well: *Read to Me: Raising Kids Who Love to Read* (Scholastic, 1992).

Bee was chief editor of Wordsong, the poetry imprint of Boyds Mills Press, for which she collected and published poetry in *A Jar of Tiny Stars: Poems by NCTE Award-Winning Poets* (1996) and *Another Jar of Tiny Stars: Poems by*

More NCTE Award-Winning Poets (2009). She is a coeditor of *The Continuum Encyclopedia of Young Adult Literature* (Continuum, 2005).

Bee has served as president of the International Reading Association, was inducted into the Reading Hall of Fame and the Ohio State University Hall of Fame, and received the IRA Arbuthnot Award as an outstanding university teacher of children's and young adults' literature.

Bee and her husband, Kenneth, reside in New York City. She can be contacted at bernicecullinan@verizon.net.

CONTRIBUTORS

Marc Aronson
Assistant Teaching Professor
School of Communication and
  Information
Rutgers University
New Brunswick, New Jersey, USA

Stergios Botzakis
Associate Professor of Adolescent
  Literacy
Department of Theory and Practice
  in Teacher Education
University of Tennessee, Knoxville
Knoxville, Tennessee, USA

Lee Galda (Emerita)
Marguerite Henry Professor of
  Children's and Young Adult
  Literature
College of Education and Human
  Development
University of Minnesota
Minneapolis, Minnesota, USA

Colleen P. Gilrane
Associate Professor
Department of Theory and Practice
  in Teacher Education
University of Tennessee, Knoxville
Knoxville, Tennessee, USA

Cyndi Giorgis
Professor of Literacy Education
Dean, College of Education
University of Texas at El Paso
El Paso, Texas, USA

Erin Greeter
Graduate Student
Department of Curriculum and
  Instruction, College of Education
University of Texas at Austin
Austin, Texas, USA

Jane Hansen (Emerita)
Professor of Education
Curry School of Education
University of Virginia
Charlottesville, Virginia, USA

David L. Harrison
Poet Laureate
Adjunct Faculty Member, School of
  Education and Child Development
Drury University
Springfield, Missouri, USA

Barbara Lehman (Emerita)
Professor
Department of Teaching and Learning
The Ohio State University, Mansfield
  Campus
Mansfield, Ohio, USA

Lauren Aimonette Liang
Associate Professor
Department of Educational Psychology
University of Utah
Salt Lake City, Utah, USA

Maggie Lingle Lohr
Primary Classroom Teacher
Underwood Elementary School
Raleigh, North Carolina, USA

Miriam Martinez
Professor
College of Education and Human
  Development
University of Texas at San Antonio
San Antonio, Texas, USA

Kimberly F. McCuiston
PhD Candidate
Department of Theory and Practice
  in Teacher Education
University of Tennessee, Knoxville
Knoxville, Tennessee, USA

Anne McGill-Franzen
Professor and Director of the
  Reading Center
Department of Theory and Practice
  in Teacher Education
University of Tennessee, Knoxville
Knoxville, Tennessee, USA

Jonda C. McNair
Associate Professor of Literacy
  Education
Eugene T. Moore School of Education
Clemson University
Clemson, South Carolina, USA

Deborah Palmer
Associate Professor of Bilingual/
  Bicultural Education
Department of Curriculum and
  Instruction, College of Education
University of Texas at Austin
Austin, Texas, USA

Nancy Roser
Professor of Language and Literacy
  Studies
Department of Curriculum and
  Instruction, College of Education
University of Texas at Austin
Austin, Texas, USA

James W. Stiles
Assistant Professor
Department of Elementary
  Education and Childhood Studies
Plymouth State University
Plymouth, New Hampshire, USA

Elizabeth A. Swaggerty
Associate Professor of Reading
  Education
College of Education
East Carolina University
Greenville, North Carolina, USA

Natalia Ward
PhD Candidate
Department of Theory and Practice
  in Teacher Education
University of Tennessee, Knoxville
Knoxville, Tennessee, USA

Deborah A. Wooten
Associate Professor of Reading
  Education
Department of Theory and Practice
  in Teacher Education
University of Tennessee, Knoxville
Knoxville, Tennessee, USA

Myra Zarnowski
Professor
Department of Elementary and
  Early Childhood Education
Queens College
Flushing, New York, USA

Kids Need to Be Reading to Become Readers

I grew up on a small dairy farm in the Midwest and attended a one-room country school through sixth grade. Then, I rode a bus to a regional junior high school and high school for the remaining six years of my K–12 education. I went to college, expecting to become a vocational agriculture teacher, but graduated as an elementary school teacher. After a few years of teaching, I began and ultimately completed two graduate degrees in reading education and became a professor of literacy education, working primarily with teachers who intended to become reading specialists or college professors. This last role has occupied much of my life for the past 40+ years.

As a professor, I've lived and worked through various reform movements, such as the open classroom, direct instruction and mastery learning, competency-based teacher education, whole language instruction, minimum competency assessments, scientifically based frameworks for reading lessons, and more recently, using gains in students' test scores to gauge teacher effectiveness. Across this period, I've watched as the reading performances of fourth-grade students (but not of eighth- and 12th-grade students) have risen quite remarkably. I've also seen the reading achievement gap between majority and minority students be reduced by half, whereas the gap between rich and poor students has widened appreciably.

I've been heartened by evidence that shows we could have all children reading on grade level by the end of first grade—and that when we do so, most students remain on level throughout their school careers. I've also been disheartened because almost no school system in the United States has implemented the services demonstrated by researchers as necessary for every child to read on grade level.

I mention all of this because one thing that seems more obvious than ever before is that all children benefit from having effective teachers and a rich curriculum, but at-risk children benefit the most. Effective teachers of reading know more about effective reading instruction and act on that knowledge to produce classrooms where everyone ends the year reading at grade level. Of all the things effective teachers know, the powerful role of children's literature in developing good readers is central to their expertise.

Effective teachers of reading realize that commercial core reading programs provide too little opportunity for students to actually read, if the goal is the development of effective readers. These teachers realize that although a core program may have useful features, it cannot be considered a complete curricular framework for reading development. They also realize that students will have few, if any, experiences with selecting the texts they'll read if the core program dominates their reading instruction. Self-selection of texts to read is a potentially powerful factor in reading development, as is student access to a classroom library of wonderful books (Guthrie & Humenick, 2004). Thus, effective teachers usually either replace the core reading program with children's books or supplement it substantially with them. What worries me, though, is that too few teachers follow this model provided by truly effective teachers of reading. What worries me more is that few evaluative models of effective literacy instruction used in schools pay any attention to much of this.

It may be a lack of expertise about effective literacy instruction that leads so many teachers to simply use the core reading program alone and leads so many schools to mandate its use. If so, then this book, *Children's Literature in the Reading Program: Engaging Young Readers in the 21st Century*, edited by Deborah Wooten and Bee Cullinan, provides rich insights into the classrooms of effective teachers that address the issue of what it is that is so often ignored in the design of environments for supporting literacy development.

Topics as diverse as the powerful potential of series books, graphic novels, poetry, picture books, and nonfiction texts; stocking classroom libraries; linking children's books and children's reading and writing development; the potential of children's literature in developing the English reading proficiency of English learners and struggling readers; and reader motivation are all addressed within this volume. Each chapter provides useful and practical advice for classroom teachers who want to create more powerful literacy instruction.

At the core of this fourth edition of *Children's Literature in the Reading Program* is an emphasis on expanding reading volume and reading breadth as part of improving both literacy instruction and literacy outcomes. Children will benefit, not only as future readers and writers but also as future citizens, if the models of classroom literacy development set forth in this book are followed. However, greater expertise may be required for that to occur among educators who design literacy curricula and monitor the quality of literacy instruction. Reading this text could be a beginning for all educators but especially those interested and in charge of facilitating the development of literate young citizens.

Richard L. Allington
University of Tennessee, Knoxville
rallingt@utk.edu

REFERENCE

Guthrie, J.T., & Humenick, N.M. (2004). Motivating students to read: Evidence for classroom practices that increase reading motivation and achievement. In P. McCardle & V. Chhabra (Eds.), *The voice of evidence in reading research* (pp. 329–354). Baltimore, MD: Paul H. Brookes.

PREFACE

The first edition of this book, *Children's Literature in the Reading Program* (Cullinan, 1987), was published in 1987. It was a time when reading wars about whole language versus phonics were raging. Although there has been and always will be friction about philosophies and pedagogy, children's literature continues to flourish. Programs and initiatives come and go, but there's still a steady allegiance to infusing children's literature in reading and content area programs. Starting with elementary school, as we prepare our students for college and their future careers, we need more than ever to use compelling books that strategically usher students into higher level thinking. If third graders need to write persuasive essays, then reading the best fiction and nonfiction texts will not only prepare them with necessary reading, writing, and content skills but can also bolster motivation and engagement.

We are blessed beneficiaries of the authors and illustrators who bring children's literature into our students' lives. Children's books are not written in a vacuum but rather serve as instruments for students to expand into other books, texts, and experiences, whetting their appetites for more. As children's literature advocates, we teachers are inherently explorers looking for the right books to use with each student. Some books inspire us to physically go places we've never been, resulting in our own growth as well as journeys brought back to our students.

Deborah recently found one of those books: *The Mad Potter: George E. Ohr, Eccentric Genius* by Jan Greenberg and Sandra Jordan (2013). This photobiography tells of the infamous George Ohr, a boisterous, wild, self-aggrandizing potter from Biloxi, Mississippi, born in 1857. The arts community of his time concurred that his pottery style was vulgar and that he tortured the clay with his unconventional curves and twisted designs. Despite this criticism, he created thousands of his signature nonconformist clay works during his lifetime. Although he believed he was the greatest potter in the world, he packed up his vast collection of pottery at the ebb of his life and put it into

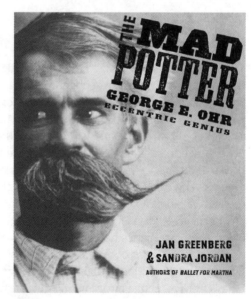

Note. From *The Mad Potter: George E. Ohr, Eccentric Genius.* © 2013 by Jan Greenberg and Sandra Jordan. Reprinted by permission of Roaring Brook Press. All rights reserved.

storage. He told his sons that one day his pottery would be worth its weight in gold. His words rang true decades after his death when he became known as a modernist virtuoso, with pieces appearing in the Smithsonian and the Museum of Modern Art.

Deborah had never heard of Ohr until she read this book. It was her ticket to more adventure. Deborah and her husband rearranged their schedules and drove 500 miles to visit the Ohr–O'Keefe Museum of Art in Biloxi. Excellent children's literature like this opens road maps so students can vicariously travel to places they've never been. And yes, she bought books at the museum, and her students marveled over photos of Ohr's pottery and the stories of his life.

This fourth edition, *Children's Literature in the Reading Program: Engaging Young Readers in the 21st Century*, sets the stage for children to be awakened with books. There are many books and teaching strategies that are designed to entice students to want to develop as skillful readers and writers. This book is attuned to teachers who say they need texts and strategies that will stretch their students in the 21st century without dimming their desire to read. Teachers are also expressing the need for fresh ways to create text sets that combine different types of genres, images, and Internet sources. Another teacher request addressed by this edition is for guidance to identify authentic, multicultural, and global books that help prepare students for our ever-growing diversified nation and world. These tools are offered here, along with sound theory and research for using children's literature and instructional strategies with students.

Overview of the Book

There were three sections in the third edition, but this fourth edition has been expanded into five. Genre/subgenre studies in the previous edition had seven chapters, whereas this edition has four. Picture books and graphic novels have a section of their own because of the emphasis on deeply understanding the richness of illustrations and text and how they work in concert with each other. A new section called "Motivating All Students" addresses multicultural and global books and ways to use them with students and has a chapter devoted to struggling readers. The book concludes with a chapter that equips teachers with valuable, readily available resources.

Part I investigates four genres and subgenres: poetry, nonfiction, picture book biographies, and series books. Chapter 1 is filled with poems and pragmatic ways to use them in the classroom, such as in teaching phonics, vocabulary development, and fluency. The nonfiction chapter is unique because the authors bring two perspectives: One is from an actual award-winning writer of children's and young adult literature who specializes in informational books, and the other is from a teacher educator who brings instructional strategies for using the books with students. Chapter 3 is an in-depth analysis of picture book biographies, along with teaching strategies such as exploring text structures by using graphic organizers and a close reading exercise. These strategies will engage students to connect to history and people who have helped shape our world today. The final chapter in this section has an overview about series books and showcases an excellent collection. It also addresses the important role these books have in promoting avid and successful readers.

In Part II, "Investigating Texts and Images," there is an overall focus on the interplay between texts and images within picture books and graphic novels. Chapter 5 addresses the elements of picture books and what they mean when understanding this literature. The author also elaborates about specific relationships that texts and images have, which can be complementary, contradictory, symmetrical, and so forth. In Chapter 6, there are intriguing conversations with teachers and students about the picture book format and the possibilities that these books offer for developing higher order thinking skills. The seventh chapter is about the richness that graphic novels bring to the learning arena, their history, and how and why to use them with students.

Part III, "Motivating All Students," begins with Chapter 8 describing the need for and importance of promoting global and multicultural books to students. The author pays close attention to guiding teachers as they evaluate books outside of their culture and offers strategies to help students think critically when reading these specialized texts. In the next chapter, you're invited into a classroom where students are learning English and Spanish through process drama using culturally conscious children's literature. Over time, the students begin to move from being self-focused to developing kinships with new perspectives. The next chapter targets ways to motivate and engage struggling readers. It provides helpful teaching tips and specially selected reading materials, such as magazines, picture books, series books, e-books, and Internet resources, that lead students to literature that they can and want to read.

In Part IV, "Visiting a Rich Reading and Writing Classroom," Chapter 11 provides invaluable ways to create robust literacy classroom environments. It details the kinds of books that need to be in a classroom library and why. Chapter 12 describes ways to use children's literature as mentor texts for upper and lower grade elementary students. Their writing examples illustrate that these students are on a journey to find their own creative voice. Chapter 13 describes a thriving reading/writing workshop environment with primary students as they develop into adept authors of informational text.

In Part V, Chapter 14 will further your awareness about the profession while providing rich resources that will support your growing interest in children's literature. This chapter provides links and information to professional organizations, children's literature awards and booklists, teaching strategies, grants, and other helpful places to visit online for ideas when using children's literature and other texts in your reading programs.

The two main purposes of this fourth edition are to provide teachers with high-quality engaging children's literature and to present rigorous activities that help students understand the craft and structure of text, analyze literature, support their work with text-based evidence, and integrate knowledge and ideas. The ultimate goal of this volume is to motivate students to enjoy learning to read and reading to learn. We invite you to fortify your reading programs with the information from this book, and we extend an invitation into the magical world of children's literature. "An RSVP from you means that you will Respond, Stretch, Venture, and Pass on the love of literacy to another generation" (Cullinan, 1992, p. xii).

Acknowledgments

Becky Fetterolf and Tori Bachman shared our vision for this new edition almost a year ago. Their support and encouragement helped make this journey a pleasure. Later, Shannon Fortner, the director of educational resources, joined the team as our new developmental editor and quickly became our closest associate at the pivotal time when chapters started arriving. She answered our numerous questions and supported us during the development of the book. We also appreciated Susanne Viscarra's dedication as managing editor and her enthusiastic shepherding of every chapter to its final stage.

We thank all of the chapter authors for contributing to this fourth edition, particularly Lee Galda, a contributor to all four editions. We feel fortunate to have chapters from other former contributors as well and by new authors joining this edition for the first time. Because of their noteworthy contributions, our readership will be enriched with a host of children's literature and cutting-edge strategies to use with it. And heartfelt thanks goes to Dick Allington for writing the Foreword for this edition. His contributions to literacy teaching and learning continue to influence our nation and beyond.

We also want to thank Mary Wooten and Jeremy Clabough, whose support and collegiality were greatly appreciated.

—*Deborah A. Wooten & Bernice E. Cullinan*

REFERENCES

Cullinan, B.E. (Ed.). (1987). *Children's literature in the reading program*. Newark, DE: International Reading Association.

Cullinan, B.E. (Ed.). (1992). *Invitation to read: More children's literature in the reading program*. Newark, DE: International Reading Association.

CHILDREN'S LITERATURE CITED

Greenberg, J., & Jordan, S. (2013). *The mad potter: George E. Ohr, eccentric genius*. New York, NY: Roaring Brook.

PART I

Exploring Genres and Subgenres

CHAPTER 1

Poetry, the Write Thing to Do

David L. Harrison, *Drury University*

I don't remember most commercials these days. Many seem to feature a talking lizard, a woman dressed in white, two characters eating in a car, or an odd-looking guru and a moronic apprentice goofing around with hamburgers. I'm not always certain what they're peddling. Back in the day, we knew our roadside slogans, radio was king, and every sponsor had a jingle. You knew what they were pushing, and their messages stuck with you.

> You'll wonder where the yellow went
> When you brush your teeth with Pepsodent!

> Halo, everybody, Halo,
> Halo is the shampoo
> That glorifies your hair,
> So Halo, everybody, Halo,
> Halo Shampoo, Halo!

> Does your husband
>   Misbehave
>   Grunt and grumble
>   Rant and rave
>   Shoot the brute some
>   Burma-Shave

Why do we remember these things forever? They rhyme. They get to the point. They're catchy. They're brief. These same traits are found in today's poems for young people.

Read Deeply, Think Deeply, Write Deeply

Poetry is more than a fun medium to read and perform. It's more than a boon for students who like books with short lines and not many words on a page. Poetry is a multifaceted teaching tool. And the structured language of rhyming verses is the easiest of all English forms to remember. They are, in short, "lessons" that stick with us.

Children's Literature in the Reading Program: Engaging Young Readers in the 21st Century (4th ed.), edited by Deborah A. Wooten & Bernice E. Cullinan. © 2015 by the International Literacy Association.

Students who are steeped in poetry develop richer vocabularies and learn to visualize the images cast by a few well-chosen words. Prereaders develop an awareness of the connections between what they hear and what they see on paper. They learn to feel the beating heart of our language. Understanding improves along with reading fluency. Poetry makes us think.

Where do we begin? One way is to help students become keen observers. Developing powers of observation can be practiced anywhere. Look around the classroom. Start a list of what your kids see, and remind them to keep posting what they observe. A table by the window? Good. Books and a vase of flowers on it? Better. Three books? Yes! Keep looking:

- What are the titles?
- What colors are the flowers?
- What kind are they?
- Does anyone observe the water stain around the vase?
- Do you see the dust on the table?
- Is it dust or pollen?

A writer could spend hours inventorying a classroom. It wouldn't be hard to write a book of poems about that table with its books and flowers. Poems come from everywhere, but what better place to begin than where students go to work each day.

In an elementary school in the Midwestern United States, I watched a fifth-grade teacher hand out an adult poem to her students and lead a critique session. These kids had become sophisticated with their understanding and use of poetic terminology. They knew what they did and didn't like in a poem and could articulate why. It was a good example of how mentor texts help students see and understand what makes some poems more appealing than others, and provide them with a strong context in which to frame their own work. Culham (2014) defines "a mentor text as any text, print or digital, that you can read with a writer's eye" (p. 31). And what do kids like? In Terry's (1974) study, she reports that students like poems about today's world written in language they understand. Students like humor, and they like poems that tell a story—poems with rhyme, rhythm, and interesting sounds. They like poems that relate to their own experiences and feelings.

Useful Strategies

"The writing teacher's real job is not to 'motivate' students but to make writing prevail" (Ponsot & Deen, 1982, p. 8). In other words, telling our students that writing is good for them and poems are fun won't likely change their prevailing attitudes. Writers say it another way: "Show, don't tell." The following strategies are meant to be helpful in showing the pleasure of writing and reading poetry. Many of them kick off with brainstorming sessions to get everyone involved.

Association

Conversations often touch on a number of subjects in a short time as we associate one thought with another. Follow a conversation long enough, and it's hard to remember where it began.

"I'm hungry."

"I can hear your stomach growling!"

"My uncle's rumbles like an elephant's!"

"Have they named the baby elephant at the zoo yet?"

"I don't know, but they named the baby lion."

"I'd love to go to Africa."

Association also works well as a writing prompt (Harrison & Cullinan, 1999; Harrison & Edmondson, 2013). Write a noun or a verb on the board and ask kids what it makes them think about. When you have several suggestions, pick one of them to start a second column. When that list is long enough, choose something from it to start a third column. In a third-grade class, I started with the noun *car*. From the first list, I chose "vacation" to start the second list, and from that one, I chose "sharing back seat" to start the third:

car	vacation	sharing back seat
fast	strange motels	licked by the dog
shiny	getting rained on	dripping ice cream
noisy	eating out	fighting with brother
vacation	museums	bored
going to school	*sharing back seat*	foot's asleep
running out of gas	taking the dog	reading stories

Pick something from the lists to work on together and rough into the beginnings of a simple poem. Don't spend much time on it now. The point is to demonstrate how quickly one can generate ideas.

Theme

Pass out books of poetry and ask students to tell what each book is about. Most collections have themes. If you're studying animals that come out after dark, you don't want to wade through 10 books looking for an owl here and a raccoon there. You need a book that has what you need all in one place.

Make a list of potential topics for a group of poems: friends, family, school, pets, and so forth. Choose one, such as *family*. Now, start a list of subjects under *family*, like this one:

parents	babysitting	sharing	homework
chores	relatives	allowance	hugs
bedtime	breakfast	siblings	love

To remind students that humans aren't the only ones with families, share mentor texts such as this poem by Jane Yolen:

Seahorse Lullaby

A bony fish, you'd think he had
Little thought of being Dad.
But with a pouch upon his tail
He carries babies without fail.
Fifteen hundred! His eyes glaze.
They're in his pouch for 40 days.
And when they're ready—he gives birth.
There's no Dad like him on Earth!!!

(Copyright © 2014 by Jane Yolen. Reprinted by permission of Curtis Brown, Ltd.)

Let students pick a family idea to write about. When all the poems are in, allowing the students time to polish their creations, bind the collection into a book and have everyone autograph it for posterity.

One Word

Every word has stories to tell. The trick in writing is to think deeply about a word until it begins to reveal itself. Write a word on the board, such as *dirt*, and have the class brainstorm about some of its stories: What is dirt? What makes it dirt instead of sand or clay? What does it taste like? Does the conversation lead to questions that can't be answered without looking up some facts? All the better! Here's what happened when poet Kenn Nesbitt thought about dirt:

My Dog Buddy

My puppy-dog, Buddy,
enjoys getting muddy.
He plays every day in
the dirt.

But I end up cruddy;
when Buddy gets muddy,
he shakes it all over
my shirt.

(Copyright © 2014 by Kenn Nesbitt. Reprinted by permission of the author.)

One Sound

There are roughly a hundred basic sounds in the English language, depending on the source. They include rimes (word families), short and long vowels, consonants, blends (combinations of consonants in which both sounds can be detected), and digraphs (combinations of consonants that together make a single, distinct sound). Poets work with these sounds, arranging them into patterns of meter and rhythm and combinations of same or similar sounds. Becoming aware of the connection between the sounds of language and how they appear in print is an essential part of learning to read, but poetry goes on from there to engage and fascinate children and offer creative outlets for self-expression (Fresch & Harrison, 2013a, 2013b, 2013c, 2013d, 2013e).

Writing poems inspired by a single sound is another opportunity to include the whole class. What makes this exercise appealing is that kids of all ages can have fun with it. Even high school students can relish the exercise of building a word list that will feed the poem they are about to write. Pick a target sound, such as the short vowel *i*, and make a list of words that feature that sound, such as this one:

big	*fig*	*pig*	*sprig*	*wig*
brig	*gig*	*prig*	*swig*	*zig*
dig	*jig*	*rig*	*twig*	

Now we have a puzzle, a word game to solve. How many words on our list are we clever enough to work into a poem? What word(s) go with what? Can a pig dig? Dance a jig? Take a swig? Can a pig be a prig? Eat a fig? Wear a wig? Brainstorm possibilities and work together to form a rough draft of a poem. Talk about ways to include more same-sound words. Here's how I started my *i* poem "Dancing Pig":

Hot diggity-dig!
I see a dancing pig.
Hot diggity-dig!

(Fresch & Harrison, 2013d, p. 44; copyright © 2013 by Shell Education. Reprinted by permission of David L. Harrison.)

The verse had a fun bounce to it but only included two words from the list: *dig* and *pig*. To work in more words, I kept repeating the stanza, each time adding another silly line. The final stanza included six *i* words:

Hot diggity-dig!
I see a dancing pig.
He isn't very big,
No bigger than a twig.
He's dancing up a jig.
Now he has a wig,
A purple piggy wig.
Hot diggity-dig!

(Fresch & Harrison, 2013d, p. 44; copyright © 2013 by Shell Education. Reprinted by permission of David L. Harrison.)

Reading to Write

As Cullinan, Scala, and Schroder (1995) point out, "Not only is poetry excellent material for reading, but it also serves as an excellent model for writing" (p. 41). Poems don't scare kids. Ask a child to write a poem, and with appropriate modeling, you'll get a poem. It might rhyme. It might not. It might be long or short, serious or funny. But it will be a poem *written* by a child. As Deen and Ponsot (1985) tell us, "The use of writing is thinking" (p. 2).

Nonfiction Poems

An important benefit of writing nonfiction poems is that it involves reading and note-taking. Your young poets can't write interestingly about their subject until they have something interesting to tell. When you introduce a new unit in science or math or social studies, tell your students that they'll be writing a poem about a favorite subject after they've read enough to decide what they like best. As the day approaches for them to make their choice, provide opportunities for them to think out loud to you or their neighbors about which way they're leaning and why. The more they read and discuss, they more they think about and absorb from their study.

> *An important benefit of writing nonfiction poems is that it involves reading and note-taking.*

Culminating a core curriculum unit by writing poems is not a new idea for many teachers. It's just such a good one that it deserves to be in this chapter as a reminder of how effective it can be to reinforce lessons learned during study.

The Wily C. vulgaris

Recently in a grocery store, I saw a couple put a watermelon into their basket, and I immediately flashed back to this strategy from Harrison and Holderith (2003):

- *Day 1:* Write "*Citrullus vulgaris*" on the board and tell the class that they should try to figure out what the words stand for by the next day but not tell anyone else. Promise to bring in a real *Citrullus vulgaris* the following day. If you want to ham it up, add that you'll be lucky if you can track one down and capture it! But if you do, you'll show it to them, and they'll study it, cut it up, eat it, and write about it!

- *Day 2:* When the kids come in, they see a large cardboard box in a corner amply covered in *alarming* signs: "KEEP AWAY!" "WARNING!" "*C. VULGARIS* EATS CHILDREN!" "RUN!!" After suitable melodrama, yank the box off the watermelon and spend the rest of the time weighing, measuring, describing, and reading and writing about the wily *C. vulgaris*. Poems generated by this exercise tend to express pleasure, such as this one by third grader Ryan Camp:

Watermelon
Heavy, plump
Slurping, slushing, dissolving
Makes me feel extremely refreshed
Citrullus vulgaris

(Harrison & Holderith, 2003, p. 29; copyright © 2003 by Scholastic. Reprinted by permission.)

The Reading of Poetry

Students learn to form mental pictures when teachers model their own associations with a poem. Reading aloud gives teachers an opportunity to demonstrate how intonation, expression, and timing play key roles in our perceptions of the poem (Robb, 2000). A poem read well leads the reader to lower his or her voice or pause or smile or look far away at the right moments. The poem becomes far more than a few lines of words arranged just so. It becomes a true expression of our language at its best.

Recordings

Juel, Griffith, and Gough (1986) report that students who enter school behind their peers in reading readiness tend to remain at the bottom of literacy development through the fourth grade. No single intervention can solve the problem, but Rasinski, Rupley, and Nichols (2008) have found that the use of rhyming poetry on a regular basis can have a significant and positive impact on students' word recognition and reading fluency. Rasinski (2003) writes, "Oral reading performance has the potential to transform a self-conscious student into a star performer—especially when he or she is coached and given opportunities to practice" (p. 23).

Being recorded has broad appeal among students of all ages and can also be helpful for struggling readers and ESL students. Harrison and Fresch (2014) posit that an important objective of creating playful little videos or CDs is to help build on students' experiences in the world beyond the classroom. Whether students write their own poems to record, read poems that they have selected, or read with a partner, recording their voices adds sizzle. When we hear our own recorded voices, we are especially attuned to what we sound like, how we read, and how we express ourselves. Here are several options on how to become your own recording studio (provided by Mary Jo Fresch):

- Video tools:
  - A video camera or flip camera
  - An iPad
  - A smartphone
  - iMovie (https://www.apple.com/mac/imovie)
  - ScreenCastle (screencastle.com) and Screencast-o-Matic (www.screencast-o-matic.com): Web-based for creation and viewing
- Free audio tools:
  - Audioboo (audioboom.com/about/education?force_mobile=true): For creating audio to share online
  - Audio Memos (imesart.com/products.php?pid=1): An iOS app for creating and sharing audio messages
  - GarageBand for Mac (https://www.apple.com/mac/garageband)
  - Hi-Q MP3 Recorder (https://play.google.com/store/apps/details?id=yuku .mp3recorder.lite&hl=en): Records audio as an MP3 file
  - iRecord (www.irecord.com): Like an old-fashioned tape recorder, just press record and talk!
  - SoundCloud (https://soundcloud.com): An online service for recording, hosting, and sharing audio tracks
  - Tape-a-Talk (https://play.google.com/store/apps/details?id=name.markus .droesser.tapeatalk&hl=en): An Android app (same as Audio Memos)

Give each reader a prop to hold when it's his or her turn to become a star. Mary Jo Fresch gives kids a star on a stick to hold. You might come up with other props. You can also give a sticker to each student who has been recorded or send home a note about the momentous occasion when the student became famous!

Poetry—Just Because It's Fun

Hansen (2009) writes,

> When children and young adolescents create their own pieces of writing, they do so under the influence of the books they have read, talked about, and appreciate. When these children write, they mentally and physically refer to the books they know—they use them as mentor texts. (p. 88)

Blasingame (2007) states, "When a young person makes a connection with an author's work, he or she will enjoy knowing more about that author's life...and will be hungry for other books by that favorite writer" (p. 104). *Poetry People: A Practical Guide to Children's Poets* (Vardell, 2007) and *Poetry Aloud Here 2: Sharing Poetry With Children* (Vardell, 2014) feature lists and biographies of contemporary children's poets and many emerging poets. In the opening poem in *Poetry Aloud Here 2*, April Halprin Wayland describes for us how to approach a poem:

How to Read a Poem Aloud

To begin,
tell the poet's name
and the title
to your friend.

Savor every word—
let
   each
      line
         shine.

Then—
read it one more time.

Now, take a breath—
and sigh.

Then think about the poet,
at her desk,
late at night,
picking up her pen to write—
and why.

(Vardell, 2014, p. ix; copyright © 2014 by April Halprin Wayland. Reprinted by permission of the author.)

Olio

An olio is an assortment of something. A miscellaneous presentation of poems is a poetry olio. At the 2014 Poetry Olio during the International Reading

Association Conference, 400 people sat one evening from 7:30 to 10:30 p.m. to hear poets present their work. Think about that. After a long day of sessions, hundreds of teachers sat for three hours listening to poetry for children!

You can hold your own poetry olio without traveling. When students know they're going to stand before an audience (e.g., classmates, other classes, an assembly, parents, a parent–teacher meeting), they *will* practice. The rules are simple: Each performer is given a fixed amount of time to present, and the poems can be original or personal favorites. That's it. What would happen, do you think, if a group of teachers modeled a segment of the olio? Does it sound like fun? It does to me.

Jam

A poetry jam combines the benefits of reading aloud and thinking fast. Seat a group of students at the front of the room and provide each with one or more books of poetry. One student reads a poem aloud. The others scramble to find a poem in their books that connects in some way with the one just read. If the first poem is about a bird, someone else may find a poem about a tree or the sky or a cracker or a birdbrain. Anything goes as long as the student can defend his or her choice. If the class groans and boos in delight, great! Someone else jumps in with a poem connected to the second poem, and so on. Students enjoy the act of "seeing" how the message, voice, tone, rhyme, or subject of one piece of writing can have a relationship with another.

With Flair

Here are four ways to read a poem:

1. Silently
2. Aloud but without expression
3. Dramatically
4. Performatively

The first two ways are the least nutritious. Poems read silently or aloud without feeling are like a diet of celery and water: No taste + no calories = no fun! Poems are most fulfilling when read aloud, but you have to put some *oomph* into the effort. Some kids (and adults) read poems aloud as though they were being punished for doing something awful. The words come out in a wooden whisper that doesn't carry six feet and isn't meant to.

We'll have none of that! We move directly to the third and fourth options. I've had the pleasure of hearing four actors and a musician, rehearsed by actress and director Julie Bloodworth, read from my work on a day in Springfield, Missouri, that was proclaimed by the city as David Harrison Day. One selection was from *When Cows Come Home*, which begins like this:

When cows come home
At the end of the day,
They chew their cuds
And gently sway
And swish their tails
In a cow-like way,
When cows come home
At the end of the day.

But when Farmer looks
The other way,
Cows take off
On a holiday!
You never saw
Such cow horseplay
When Farmer looks
The other way.

(Harrison, 2001, pp. 5–9; copyright © 2001 by Boyds Mills Press. Reprinted by permission of David L. Harrison.)

Sarah Wiggin, who played Farmer, stuck her thumbs behind imaginary coverall straps and drawled out the narrative as the three other actors, led by Michael Frizell, bent low, munching grass, chewing cuds, and uttering contented, guttural cow sounds, all accompanied by musician Ray Castrey. When Farmer looked the other way, the cows leaped straight up and jigged with exaggerated abandon. The audience went from smiles to giggles to cackles. When Farmer looked back, the chagrined cows resumed their cowlike ways. The reading was hysterical, yet the actors never moved more than a few feet throughout their dramatic presentation.

To do that poem in your class, you might have one farmer (at a time). The rest of the students can be cows so everyone gets in the "moo-ed" to lose their inhibitions. (I "herd" that groan!)

Performing

Some poets become physical when presenting their work. If the poem is about a ball game, they may run around imaginary bases. They advance on and retreat from their audience, sweeping their arms, their voices ringing over the room. Performance poets bring great energy to the scene, as though they're performing on stage.

Think of performing a poem as a miniplay, a small production. Read a selection aloud several times with your students and talk about how certain gestures, expressions, and props would help. Ask volunteers to act out the poem so everyone can see it in action and decide whether other directions are needed.

To spread excitement (and involvement), consider creating a theatrical company with stage hands, scenery designers, directors, prop makers, wardrobe designers, hair brushers, and cue card holders. Brad Pitt was known in high school for his willingness to take any job that needed doing, whether he had a role in the play or not (S. Harrison, Pitt's high school counselor, personal communication, August 13, 2014). Gather or make props for the great performance and announce a dress rehearsal that allows time for the actor(s) to practice and company members to complete their tasks. Holding a rehearsal provides an opportunity to critique, talk about speaking so others can hear, and work on stage presence. And don't forget the audience! This is a performance, so bring on the parents, other classes, and other teachers!

In Patricia Cooley's fifth-grade classroom at Komensky Elementary School in Berwyn, Illinois, two boys rehearsed and performed my poem "Brussels Sprouts" before a giggly audience of kindergartners (see Figure 1.1). For props, the poem was projected on a screen behind the players, and the boys used a bowl filled with "Brussels sprouts," "cottage cheese," "pickled beets," "cauliflower," "lima beans," and "chicken liver."

The "parent" reader kept offering the bowl to the "child" reader, who kept throwing the offending food back in the bowl and howling about not wanting it. The audience loved their performance, which brought out the ham in both boys. (You can view the video at www.reading.org/brusselssprouts.) Here's the poem:

Figure 1.1. Fifth Graders Performing a Poem for Kindergartners

Brussels Sprouts

(CHILD)
What are those
green things?

                                      (PARENT)

I don't want no
Brussels sprouts.

                                      Brussels sprouts.

                                      Any.
                                      Come on, try some
                                      Brussels sprouts.

I don't want no
Brussels sprouts!

                                      Any.
                                      These are special
                                      Brussels sprouts.

I don't want no
Brussels sprouts!

                                      Any.
                                      Just one taste of
                                      Brussels sprouts.

If I taste these
Brussels sprouts,
then can I have
something else?

                                      Sure!

Ugh!
I hate these
Brussels sprouts!

                                      Here's some yummy cottage cheese,
                                      pickled beets, cauliflower,
                                      lima beans, and chicken liver.

Please pass the
Brussels sprouts.
I don't want no
chicken liver.

                                      Any.

The Matter of Rhyme

Elementary teachers used to be told that their students weren't ready to write verse—that is, poems with rhyme and meter. Free verse (without rhyme or meter) was thought to be easier and more age appropriate. Most teachers I meet today are happy with either. Some kids come by rhyme naturally. I was one of them. Early listening experiences are predominantly to poems in verse. *The Random House Book of Poetry for Children* (Prelutsky, 1983) includes roughly 95 verse poems for every five written in free verse.

Many poets prefer to write free verse, and many write in both genres depending on the subject and the best voice at the time. If some of your students compose in verse, they're merely borrowing techniques that they hear from us. In *The Writing Thief: Using Mentor Texts to Teach the Craft of Writing*, Culham (2014) tells us that good writers of any age get better by stealing great ideas from other writers. And writing in verse has its advantages. Fresch and Wheaton (2002) point out that "when designing activities for young spellers, rhyme and word play is an effective and fun way to reinforce letter/sounds within words" (p. 114).

Poetry, the Write Thing to Do

Strategies themselves need strategies for success. To put poetry to work in the classroom and achieve best results, it's important to assemble a collection of good poetry both in the classroom and in the school library. You can find collections to support every area in the curriculum, including language arts, science, math, and social studies. Many are listed at the end of this chapter. *What Really Matters for Struggling Readers: Designing Research-Based Programs* (Allington, 2001) reminds us that as readers progress, they read not only faster and more accurately but also with better phrasing and intonation. There is a certain risk that in our eagerness to increase fluency, we may teach some readers to develop speed without comprehension. Most poems for young readers are only a few lines long. There's no rush to get to the end. Instead, we emphasize taking time to pronounce each word, to taste its meaning, to see the pictures it's helping to paint. Poetry can be sung, performed, recorded, shared, and remembered. It is an all-purpose tool in the classroom.

> *To put poetry to work in the classroom and achieve best results, it's important to assemble a collection of good poetry both in the classroom and in the school library.*

Writers know that to write big, we sometimes need to write small. A few telling details may be all the reader needs to understand the bigger picture. Sidman (2012) explains, "Why do I encourage children to write poetry? To watch them take a crisp, clean dive into the mysteries that confront them every day, find what tters beneath the surface, and emerge triumphant" (p. 34). Poetry, by its nature, asks us to think deeply about what we want to say and to write deeply when we decide what's important.

Poetry's time has come.

REFERENCES

Allington, R.L. (2001). *What really matters for struggling readers: Designing research-based programs.* New York, NY: Longman.

Blasingame, J. (2007). *Books that don't bore 'em: Young adult books that speak to this generation.* New York, NY: Scholastic.

Culham, R. (2014). *The writing thief: Using mentor texts to teach the craft of writing.* Newark, DE: International Reading Association.

Cullinan, B.E., Scala, M.C., & Schroder, V.C. (1995). *Three voices: An invitation to poetry across the curriculum.* York, ME: Stenhouse.

Deen, R., & Ponsot, M. (1985). *The common sense: What to write, how to write it, and why.* Upper Montclair, NJ: Boynton/Cook.

Fresch, M.J., & Harrison, D.L. (2013a). *Learning through poetry: Consonant blends and digraphs.* Huntington Beach, CA: Shell Education; Newark, DE: International Reading Association.

Fresch, M.J., & Harrison, D.L. (2013b). *Learning through poetry: Consonants.* Huntington Beach, CA: Shell Education; Newark, DE: International Reading Association.

Fresch, M.J., & Harrison, D.L. (2013c). *Learning through poetry: Long vowels.* Huntington Beach, CA: Shell Education; Newark, DE: International Reading Association.

Fresch, M.J., & Harrison, D.L. (2013d). *Learning through poetry: Rimes.* Huntington Beach, CA: Shell Education; Newark: DE: International Reading Association.

Fresch, M.J., & Harrison, D.L. (2013e). *Learning through poetry: Short vowels.* Huntington Beach, CA: Shell Education; Newark, DE: International Reading Association.

Fresch, M.J., & Wheaton, A. (2002). *Teaching and assessing spelling.* New York, NY: Scholastic.

Hansen, J. (2009). Young writers use mentor texts. In D.A. Wooten & B.E. Cullinan (Eds.), *Children's literature in the reading program: An invitation to read* (3rd ed., pp. 88–98). Newark, DE: International Reading Association. doi:10.1598/0699.09

Harrison, D.L., & Cullinan, B.E. (1999). *Easy poetry lessons that dazzle and delight.* New York, NY: Scholastic.

Harrison, D.L., & Edmondson, L. (2013). *Let's write this week with David Harrison* [Teacher's guide]. Honesdale, PA: Phoenix Learning Resources.

Harrison, D.L., & Fresch, M.J. (2014, May). *Turning early literacy learners into "recording stars": Interactive ways for children to have fun while developing phonemic awareness.* Paper presented at the 59th annual meeting of the International Reading Association, New Orleans, LA.

Harrison, D.L., & Holderith, K. (2003). *Using the power of poetry to teach language arts, social studies, math, and more: Engaging poetry lessons, model poems, and writing activities that help students learn important content.* New York, NY: Scholastic.

Juel, C., Griffith, P.L., & Gough, P.B. (1986). Acquisition of literacy: A longitudinal study of children in first and second grade. *Journal of Educational Psychology, 78*(4), 243–255. doi:10.1037/0022-0663.78.4.243

Ponsot, M., & Deen, R. (1982). *Beat not the poor desk: Writing: What to teach, how to teach it and why.* Montclair, NJ: Boynton/Cook.

Rasinski, T.V. (2003). *The fluent reader: Oral reading strategies for building word recognition, fluency, and comprehension.* New York, NY: Scholastic.

Rasinski, T.V., Harrison, D.L., & Fawcett, G. (2009). *Partner poems for building fluency, grades 4–6: 40 engaging poems for two voices with motivating activities that help students improve their fluency and comprehension.* New York, NY: Scholastic.

Rasinski, T., Rupley, W.H., & Nichols, W.D. (2008). Two essential ingredients: Phonics and fluency getting to know each other. Newark, DE. *The Reading Teacher, 62*(3), 257–260. doi:10.1598/RT.62.3.7

Robb, L. (2000). *Teaching reading in middle school: A strategic approach to teaching reading that improves comprehension and thinking.* New York, NY: Scholastic.

Sidman, J. (2012). Why I write poetry: A really good poem can reach kids in wondrous and unexpected ways. *School Library Journal, 58*(4), 32–35.

Terry, C.A. (1974). *Children's poetry preferences: A national survey of upper elementary grades.* Urbana, IL: National Council of Teachers of English.

Vardell, S.M. (2007). *Poetry people: A practical guide to children's poets.* Westport, CT: Libraries Unlimited.

Vardell, S.M. (2014). *Poetry aloud here 2: Sharing poetry with children.* Chicago, IL: ALA Editions.

CHILDREN'S LITERATURE CITED

Harrison, D.L. (2001). *When cows come home.* Honesdale, PA: Boyds Mills.

Prelutsky, J. (Ed.). (1983). *The Random House book of poetry for children.* New York, NY: Random House.

OTHER RECOMMENDED CHILDREN'S POETRY BOOKS

Dotlich, R.K. (2006). *What is science?* New York, NY: Henry Holt.

Driscoll, M. (2003). *A child's introduction to poetry.* New York, NY: Black Dog & Leventhal.

Fletcher, R. (2005). *A writing kind of day: Poems for young poets.* Honesdale, PA: Wordsong.

Franco, B. (2009). *Messing Around on the Monkey Bars and other school poems for two voices.* Somerville, MA: Candlewick.

Harrison, D.L. (2005). *Farmer's dog goes to the forest: Rhymes for two voices.* Honesdale, PA: Wordsong.

Harrison, D.L. (2006). *Sounds of rain: Poems of the Amazon.* Honesdale, PA: Wordsong.

Harrison, D.L. (2007). *Bugs: Poems about creeping things.* Honesdale, PA: Wordsong.

Harrison, D.L. (2008). *Pirates.* Honesdale, PA: Wordsong.

Harrison, D.L. (2012). *Cowboys: Voices in the western wind.* Honesdale, PA: Wordsong.

Heard, G. (1992). *Creatures of earth, sea, and sky.* Honesdale, PA: Wordsong.

Heard, G. (Ed.). (2009). *Falling down the page: A book of list poems.* New York, NY: Roaring Brook.

Lewis, J.P. (2012). *If you were a chocolate mustache.* Honesdale, PA: Wordsong.

Marsalis, W. (2005). *Jazz A-B-Z: An A to Z collection of jazz portraits.* Cambridge, MA: Candlewick.

Prelutsky, J. (2008). *Pizza, pigs, and poetry: How to write a poem.* New York, NY: Greenwillow.

Scheu, T. (2009). *I threw my brother out: A laughable lineup of sports poems.* Middlebury, VT: Young Poets'.

Sklansky, A.E. (2012). *Out of this world: Poems and facts about space.* New York, NY: Alfred A. Knopf.

Swinburne, S.R. (2010). *Ocean soup: Tide-pool poems.* Watertown, MA: Charlesbridge.

Tang, G. (2005). *Math potatoes: Mind-stretching brain food.* New York, NY: Scholastic.

Vardell, S., & Wong, J. (Eds.). (2013). *The poetry Friday anthology for middle school: Poems for the school year with connections to the Common Core.* Princeton, NJ: Pomelo.

Vardell, S., & Wong, J. (Eds.). (2014). *The poetry Friday anthology for science: Poems for the school year integrating science, reading, and language arts.* Princeton, NJ: Pomelo.

Yolen, J. (2007). *Shape me a rhyme: Nature's forms in poetry.* Honesdale, PA: Wordsong.

ABOUT THE AUTHOR

David L. Harrison has published 89 books of poetry, fiction, and nonfiction for young readers and educational books for teachers. He is poet laureate and also an adjunct faculty member of the School of Education and Child Development at Drury University, Springfield, Missouri, USA, and David Harrison Elementary School is named for him. His work has been anthologized in more than 120 books, translated into 12 languages, sandblasted in a library's sidewalk, painted on a bookmobile, and presented via television, radio, podcast, and video stream. *Let's Write This Week With David Harrison* (Phoenix Learning Resources, 2013), cocreated with Lauren Edmondson, is a 20-episode video program that brings writing tips into elementary classrooms and offers graduate college credit for teachers.

David has given keynote talks and college commencement addresses and been featured at hundreds of conferences, workshops, literature festivals, and schools across the United States. He holds degrees from Drury and Emory universities, and two universities have presented him with honorary doctorates of letters. His poetry collection, *Pirates* (Wordsong, 2008), represented Missouri at the 2013 National Book Fair in Washington, DC.

David can be contacted at davidlharrison1@att.net or through his website (davidlharrison.com) or blog (davidlharrison.wordpress.com).

CHAPTER 2

Teaching Nonfiction With Confidence

Learning to Love Inquiry

Marc Aronson, *Rutgers University*

Myra Zarnowski, *Queens College*

The two authors of this chapter come from different professional backgrounds and have different yet complementary perspectives on nonfiction. Marc is a children's and young adult nonfiction author, editor, and college instructor. Myra is a former classroom teacher (grades 3, 5, 6, and 7) and currently a college instructor in elementary and early childhood education. We both work a lot with teachers, librarians, and students, and we are both enthusiastic readers of nonfiction. In this chapter, we weigh in on what we think are two important questions for everyone teaching with nonfiction: What do we mean when we describe nonfiction as the "literature of inquiry," and how can we use this material in the classroom? What are some recommended nonfiction books to use in the elementary school classroom, and how can we find more titles like these?

What Is the Literature of Inquiry?

If we were to play word association with *nonfiction*, many of you would probably say true, factual, or reliable, although sadly some would really first think boring, dull, or textbook. Whether you answered what you guessed we wanted to hear or what you secretly thought, we would disagree. Nonfiction is not "true," nor is it limited to facts, nor is its highest value being reliable. All of those terms used as absolutes are the heritage of an era of scarcity—when a school had quite limited resources. As was often asked in those days, "What if this is the only book a student reads on X?" Thus, each book needed to cover its bases.

Today we live in an age of information glut. Our students are a keystroke away from contrary evidence, new approaches, and dissenting views. Our job, then, is to prepare them to inquire, to research, and to think.

Children's Literature in the Reading Program: Engaging Young Readers in the 21st Century (4th ed.), edited by Deborah A. Wooten & Bernice E. Cullinan. © 2015 by the International Literacy Association.

"Wait," we hear you say. "If I show my elementary school children two views on something, how am I to know which is right? What if they get it wrong?" Don't worry. Your job is not to make sure your students get it right; after all, experts are daily changing their views. Think of Pluto: You memorized a mnemonic to name nine planets, but now we aren't sure if there are 11, 13, or the latest count of 14. Your job is to teach your students the rules of evidence, argument, and comparing points of view.

If an author makes a claim, what is that claim based on? What evidence is there to be found—in the text or notes? If there is an opposing view, what evidence does it put forward? How does each author select and present the evidence? How can their views be tested and compared? That is what you are teaching—starting from preschool, where you might read/perform a traditional version of The Three Little Pigs, then read Jon Scieszka's (1989) *The True Story of the 3 Little Pigs!*, which needs to be in your reference section, and then ask your young detectives to compare the evidence and reach a conclusion.

"Wait, wait," we now hear you ask, "does this mean all arguments are equal? Are we to tell students that the Earth might be flat?" No, once we shift our focus from true, factual, and reliable to evidence and argument, we are in a position to judge authors. Do their books model the processes we need our students to learn? Or do their books say, "Trust me. I am an adult, so I know more than you do?" Books that invite the reader into the quest to know are what we call the "literature of inquiry." Such books aim to foster a classroom of detectives, doctors, historians, and engineers: problem solvers. A classroom abuzz with students pursuing evidence, comparing theories, and (respectfully) debating conclusions is nonfiction heaven.

By looking for nonfiction books that feature inquiry, you're giving your students the tools to think with whatever comes their way.

This leads us to the one term you should memorize: *Moore's law*. Gordon Moore was a computer scientist who became the head of Intel, the chip manufacturer. In 1965, he predicted that the processing power of computers (actually, the number of transistors that could be fit onto a microchip) would double every 18–24 months. He has been proven right. Thus, roughly every two years, the amount of data that computers can process doubles. We see that in products: tablets, smartphones, soon totally networked homes. But it also means that the amount of data we can gather—and the tools for analyzing that data—keeps doubling. A great deal of what seems reliable today will, inherently, be passé tomorrow.

Can you see why your classroom filled with explorers makes sense? By looking for nonfiction books that feature inquiry, you're giving your students the tools to think with whatever comes their way. You ground them in information, even as you continually expose them to exploration. If reading nonfiction as inquiry is challenging to you because it is not how you were taught to read nonfiction, well, that is the Moore's law moment that we are all in together. To teach, we need to learn differently ourselves, just as to learn, children need to be ready to make sense of new discoveries. We are all, as they say in hockey, changing on the fly.

Introducing the Literature of Inquiry in the Classroom

Why Read the Literature of Inquiry in the Elementary School Classroom?

Reading the literature of inquiry—seeing real people solve real problems—reveals problem solving in action. It shows how scientists and historians work by taking us to sites where people are actively researching and lets us see them and hear from them. In *The Elephant Scientist* by Caitlin O'Connnell and Donna Jackson (2011), we meet O'Connell, a scientist who is investigating how elephants communicate. In *Plastic Ahoy! Investigating the Great Pacific Garbage Patch* by Patricia Newman (2014), we meet Miriam Goldstein, Chelsea Rochman, and Darcy Taniguchi, scientists investigating the impact of large amounts of plastic dumped in the ocean. In *Searching for Sarah Rector: The Richest Black Girl in America*, author Tonya Bolden (2014) talks directly to us about her own inquiry into Sarah's life—how Bolden made sense of the evidence she uncovered. She tells us about gaps in the information, raises questions about Sarah that she wants to answer, speculates about some possible answers, and tells us about "facts" that she originally thought were true but later found out were not. Books like these show readers how knowledge is constructed.

> *Reading the literature of inquiry—seeing real people solve real problems—reveals problem solving in action.*

These books are excellent choices for classroom inquiries because students join researchers as they attempt to solve mysteries and understand the world better—its past and its present. It's easy, too, to connect these books to standards in science, mathematics, and social studies. That's because the literature of inquiry delivers both content and the process of discovering that content. It's a total package.

Reading for the Mystery: How to Do It

A number of science and history books can be read as mystery stories. In these books, scientists and historians are like detectives searching for answers to pressing questions like these: What causes yellow fever? How can it be treated? How can we learn what dinosaurs looked like? How can the world's strangest parrot, the kakapo, be saved? These books are often called medical mysteries or history mysteries, and they are page-turners. Readers want to see the case unfolding.

Using three science mysteries by Sandra Markle as an example, let's look at how to focus students' attention on reading for the mystery. The first book, *The*

Case of the Vanishing Golden Frogs: A Scientific Mystery (Markle, 2012), describes how scientists searched for clues about what was killing the Panamanian golden frogs, a national symbol of Panama. This book begins with a shocking discovery: A scientist visiting a forest reserve in Panama realizes that most of the frogs have vanished. The second book, *The Case of the Vanishing Honeybees: A Scientific Mystery* (Markle, 2014), describes scientists' ongoing search for what's killing the honeybees, essential partners in producing our food supply. Now known as colony collapse disorder, the problem of vanishing honeybees still puzzles scientists. The third book, *The Case of the Vanishing Little Brown Bats: A Scientific Mystery* (Markle, 2015), describes how researchers learned what was killing the little brown bats, animals that eat insects that destroy crops and spread disease. Once again, scientists were shocked to find them dying in large numbers. In each case, there is an animal in serious danger of extinction, and the cause is a mystery.

When reading these books and others like them, if you and your students complete a data chart, you'll see a number of similarities about the way scientists approach a problem. In Table 2.1, we've listed some sample answers for completing a data chart on these three books.

Reading only one of these books and answering the questions would be a worthwhile experience, but reading all three is even better. That way, certain consistencies emerge that you can emphasize:

- *The excitement of inquiry:* An author's note in each book points out the excitement of solving a mystery. Here's what the author says about honeybees: "No movie about tracking down killers could be more exciting than this true story" (Markle, 2014, p. 44). Check out the other author's notes. Look for evidence in each book that the scientists are also excited about inquiry.

- *Teamwork is required:* Scientists don't work alone in a lab. They consult one another and work together as teams. For example, biologist Karen Lips consulted pathologist Joyce Longore about sacs she saw on the skin of the golden frogs. Look for evidence of teamwork in each of the books.

- *Unanswered questions:* Sometimes the scientists don't discover a definitive answer to a mystery. Markle (2014) refers to the case of the honeybees as "case open" (p. 30). There are several possible causes of what is destroying the honeybees, all possibly working together.

- *Remaining questions:* Even when a case is solved, it usually raises other questions. In the case of both the golden frogs and the little brown bats, scientists still want answers. Can the viruses that are killing these animals be stopped? Can they survive long enough for this to happen?

The literature of inquiry is a great way to spark enthusiasm for nonfiction. Table 2.2 lists additional books that you can use with confidence.

Table 2.1. Science Mysteries

Question	The Case of the Vanishing Golden Frogs[a]	The Case of the Vanishing Honeybees[b]	The Case of the Vanishing Little Brown Bats[c]
What is the mystery that scientists want to solve?	What is killing the Panamanian golden frogs?	What is killing the honeybees?	What is killing the little brown bats?
What possible causes of the problem did scientists rule out?	Scientists ruled out these causes: (1) a change in habitat, (2) pollution, and (3) climate change.	Scientists ruled out these causes: (1) a change in habitat, (2) overwork, (3) mites, and (4) pesticides	Scientists ruled out these causes: (1) climate change, (2) pesticides, and (3) a virus.
What did scientists learn by gathering and interpreting evidence?	Scientists discovered that *Bd*, a type of fungus, was killing the frogs.	The case is still open. According to scientists, a lot of different things could be killing the honeybees. No one yet knows what combination of causes is killing them.	Scientists learned that a deadly new fungus called *Pd* was killing the little brown bats.
What questions do scientists still want to answer?	Could *Bd* be stopped from killing frogs? Could frogs survive long enough for this to happen?	What will the future be like for the honeybees? Will the killer be found?	Could *Pd* be stopped from killing the bats? Could the bats survive long enough for this to happen?

[a]Markle, S. (2012). *The case of the vanishing golden frogs: A scientific mystery.* Minneapolis, MN: Millbrook.
[b]Markle, S. (2014). *The case of the vanishing honeybees: A scientific mystery.* Minneapolis, MN: Millbrook.
[c]Markle, S. (2015). *The case of the vanishing little brown bats: A scientific mystery.* Minneapolis, MN: Millbrook.

Table 2.2. The Literature of Inquiry: Science Mysteries

Book	Annotation
Aronson, M. (with Parker Pearson, M., & the Riverside Project). (2010). *If stones could speak: Unlocking the secrets of Stonehenge.* Washington, DC: National Geographic Society.	Author Marc Aronson is on site with archaeologist Mike Parker Pearson and his project team to learn about their latest discoveries about Stonehenge.
Berger, L.R., & Aronson, M. (2012). *The skull in the rock: How a scientist, a boy, and Google Earth opened a new window on human origins.* Washington, DC: National Geographic Society.	When 9-year-old Matthew Berger, son of scientist Lee Berger, finds a fossil, it stimulates a rethinking of the path of human evolution.
Burns, L.G. (2010). *The hive detectives: Chronicle of a honey bee catastrophe.* Boston, MA: Houghton Mifflin Books for Children.	Scientists try to figure out what is causing honey bees to die—a phenomenon known as colony collapse disorder. This is an excellent book to use with Sandra Markle's *The Case of the Vanishing Honeybees.*[a]
Crump, M. (2013). *The mystery of Darwin's frog.* Honesdale, PA: Boyds Mills.	Join scientists as they continue to unravel the mystery of Darwin's frog, an animal discovered more than 175 years ago by Charles Darwin.
Kirkpatrick, K. (2011). *Mysterious bones: The story of Kennewick Man.* New York, NY: Holiday House.	A chance discovery of a human skull in the Columbia River in Kennewick, Washington, by two young college students sparks the beginning of a scientific investigation of what turns out to be one of the oldest and most complete skeletons ever found in the United States.
Montgomery, S. (2010). *Kakapo rescue: Saving the world's strangest parrot.* Boston, MA: Houghton Mifflin Books for Children.	Learn how the National Kakapo Recovery Team is working to save the world's largest and heaviest parrot from extinction. Join scientists, technicians, and volunteers who are working together as a team on site in New Zealand.
Thimmesh, C. (2009). *Lucy long ago: Uncovering the mystery of where we came from.* Boston, MA: Houghton Mifflin Books for Children.	While working in Ethiopia, paleoanthropologist Donald Johanson and his team discover a 3.2 million-year-old skeleton that provides clues to the origins of life on Earth. How they raise and answer questions based on this evidence is fascinating and instructive.
Thimmesh, C. (2013). *Scaly spotted feathered frilled: How do we know what dinosaurs really looked like?* Boston, MA: Houghton Mifflin Harcourt.	Because we have no photographs of dinosaurs to help us out, figuring out what dinosaurs looked like has become the work of paleoscientists and paleoartists. How they work together is detailed in this fascinating book.
Walker, S.M. (2002). *Fossil fish found alive: Discovering the coelacanth.* Minneapolis, MN: Carolrhoda.	When a coelacanth, a fish thought to have been extinct for 70 million years, is suddenly found to be alive, scientists, fishermen, and governments begin working together to protect it and learn more about it.

[a]Markle, S. (2014). *The case of the vanishing honeybees: A scientific mystery.* Minneapolis, MN: Millbrook.

Sharing nonfiction that includes the literature of inquiry can begin in the early grades. A list of recommended titles is included at the end of this chapter.

How to Shop in the Nonfiction Aisle: Keys to Picking and Sharing Great Books

Typically, nonfiction books are described by their subject: a biography of Jackie Robinson, a book about World War II or sharks or the *Titanic*. We consider that a mistake. After all, in talking about novels, you wouldn't say books about a girl, a dog, or a couple. You'd be able to define many different genres: romance, mystery, science fiction, young adult realism, fantasy, and so on. Does nonfiction have genres? Yes, indeed, it does.

Think of an event that took place yesterday and had a winner and a loser, such as a game, an election, or a court decision. In our view, there are seven ways a nonfiction text could describe what took place: data, expository, narrative, disciplinary thinking, inquiry, interpretation, or action. You could have who, what, where, and when as facts, and you could use those four plus why to write more broadly about a subject: You can use the event to show how a professional thinks and works. You can model the actual process of gathering and sharing information. You can proffer a compelling interpretation of the event. You can use the instance to stir the reader and inspire him or her to take action. A book need not be limited to one category; it could be, for example, an interpretive call to action or an inquiry that models disciplinary thinking. But once you look at nonfiction by what it does rather than merely what it's about, the world of nonfiction blooms.

None of these kinds of books is necessarily more "true" than another; rather, each uses a different mode of engaging with the event. Once we begin to recognize distinct styles or genres of nonfiction, we can match types of books with individual students and help students compare and contrast different approaches. At the same time, we want to look at quality—how well each book has fulfilled the task of seeking truth and engaging readers.

At the risk of being seen as pitchmen, we'll use three of Marc's books to highlight different nonfiction approaches and genres. The first book is an example of nonfiction as inquiry and disciplinary thinking.

Ain't Nothing but a Man: My Quest to Find the Real John Henry *by Scott Reynolds Nelson (2008)*

Nelson is a professional historian who teaches at the College of William and Mary. Marc used Nelson's effort to find out if there was a real John Henry of song and story to model what a historian does and to demonstrate, step by step, how Nelson examined evidence and solved the mystery. The book thus offers his interpretation of the legend.

Here are the six steps that Nelson followed, as the authors outlined in the book:

1. *He read carefully through previous interpretations.* This is similar to what we ask students to do when we tell them to use more than one source.

2. *He checked to see where those previous authors found their information—* much as we caution students who use Wikipedia to check all of the links in the article.

3. *Comparing and contrasting the accounts, he looked for gaps and disagreements—*just as a detective probes an alibi.

4. *With this clear map of what is already known, what is not known, and where there are contradictions, he sought out new evidence.* This is like asking students to look at a primary source or a museum exhibit only after they have background knowledge.

5. *When the trail of new evidence turned cold, he asked new questions and sought out new sources.* Marc's favorite moment in presenting this book to students comes when he asks, "Have you ever been stuck doing a homework assignment?" Many scream yes and add that they prayed, slept, bothered their sister, or tried harder. Marc then tells them what Nelson did, to their great relief.

6. *When he reached his own conclusions, he shared them with peers to get their insights.* This is what any good team does, from the youngest students to the most senior professionals.

In sharing a book like *Ain't Nothing but a Man* with students, you're offering them a model of how knowledge is constructed. The book is not there to end inquiry but to begin it.

The second book we'll share focuses on narrative and exposition.

Trapped: How the World Rescued 33 Miners From 2,000 Feet Below the Chilean Desert *by Marc Aronson (2011)*

This book presented a very different challenge from the one that Marc wrote with Nelson. In this case, Marc crafted the book on his own and so close in time to the rescue of the miners that there were no other books or authorities to consult. As he explained in an afterword, he was in the position of many students who rush onto the Internet to do their research. Marc had no choice: Understandably enough, the miners wanted to be paid for their stories, so he had to rely on whatever reports he could find. Rather than following one expert in his search for answers, Marc needed to find a format that would both engage readers and give them enough background to understand the events. This book, then, combined expository and narrative.

The key to the narration actually came from the research: Marc read through the day-by-day news reports that described the mine collapse and then the rescue as it happened. But, of course, these reports could only begin to tell the miners' perspective of the story after they were rescued. Marc was able to supplement the articles by interviewing many of the drillers and rescuers. Still, he had to map out the chronology as it unfolded aboveground first, then match those stages with what the men later reported they had experienced while they were underground. This dual approach gave Marc his structure: He would give background, then split chapters into "Above" and "Below," until the moment of contact, in Chapter 7, when the two worlds touched.

Some readers might assume that a data book, one made up of names, dates, "facts," and figures, is necessarily more true—more of an informational text than either interpretation or narrative. This isn't so. Stripping information down to bare bones may, in some cases, be more misleading if the author doesn't feel obliged to explain why he or she selected that version of that fact. For example, when cowriting *For Boys Only: The Biggest Baddest Book Ever* (Aronson & Newquist, 2007) with HP Newquist, Marc wanted to list the world's deadliest snake. The problem is that the designation can mean two opposite things: the snake whose venom is most deadly (the taipan, which is a solitary snake that almost never interacts with humans) or the snake responsible for the most deaths (the carpet viper, which lives around people). What began as a list turned into a discussion. Many "facts" are the same: The world's largest country? It depends on how you count. Baseball's greatest hitter? How do you measure Babe Ruth's astonishing accomplishments in his all-white era against modern athletes who play in an integrated league with stars from all over the globe?

All nonfiction is a conversation with sources and readers, and as teachers, we are inviting our students to participate in the discussion.

How do you select nonfiction? First, get to know it. Take a stack of books off the shelf and see if you can separate them by style or genre. Remember that nonfiction is not merely a stunted form of fiction: Sometimes and for some readers, pure data can be more satisfying than vivid narration. Look for authors you (and/or your students) like. There is as much variation in nonfiction writing as in fiction.

Finally, like Scott Reynolds Nelson, pay attention to the evidence the authors present, where the evidence comes from, and where there might be gaps or opposing views. All nonfiction is a conversation with sources and readers, and as teachers, we are inviting our students to participate in the discussion.

Becoming a Confident Reader of Nonfiction: Selecting Nonfiction for Your Classroom

Because we each took a different route into nonfiction, we'll begin here by discussing how Myra became a more confident reader of nonfiction. She thinks that much of what she learned will be helpful to you, too. Myra learned about nonfiction by reading large quantities of it. First, she served on the Notable Children's Trade Book Committee of the National Council for the Social Studies and then on the Orbis Pictus Award Committee of the National Council of Teachers of English. These are big jobs. Committee members read hundreds of books. In the process of working with others to select award-winning books, Myra faced these questions every single day: Is this book good? How do I know?

Here's what she learned about *good* nonfiction.

It's True or as Close to True as Possible

Sometimes what we assume is a fact we later find out is not true at all. Do you remember the story of Pluto, now no longer a planet? Or the idea that no life exists deep in the ocean, only to find out that it does? As one author put it, "Science doesn't always follow a clear-cut path. Sometimes discoveries happen that completely derail everything we thought we knew" (Hague, 2012, p. 10). The same is true for social studies. Thanks to newer research techniques, which you can read about in *The Many Faces of George Washington: Remaking a Presidential Icon* by Carla Killough McClafferty (2011), we now know more about what George Washington looked like than our parents or grandparents did when they were our age. Our understanding of the world is subject to change.

Despite this, we can be reasonably sure that much of what we read is correct, if we're provided with evidence of accuracy. That is, the author explicitly tells us how the facts were derived. In *Coral Reefs*, for example, author Jason Chin (2011) tells readers that he traveled to the Belize barrier reef as part of his research. He also lists books and websites that he used extensively. Look for information like this that can help you and your students build a case for accuracy. Did the author travel, consult with experts, and research extensively? If so, that can help you build your case.

Style Matters: Nonfiction Should Be Interesting to Read

We all know what it's like to read books that we refer to as dull, dry, and boring. Good nonfiction is exactly the opposite. It's surprising, interesting, and stimulating. Nonfiction authors can use the same techniques that fiction authors can use: interesting words and phrases, figurative language, descriptive words that appeal to the senses, varied types of sentences, and new and surprising information. The only thing they can't do is make up information.

Here's how Sarah Albee (2014) piques the reader's interest as she begins Chapter 1 of her book *Bugged: How Insects Changed History*:

> Nearly everyone has a strong opinion about insects. But whether you love them or loathe them, you know they're impossible to avoid. For every pound of us, there are three hundred pounds of insects. And while most insects keep a pretty low profile, there are some that have a huge impact on our lives. (p. 7)

Three hundred pounds of insects to every pound of us! That is one surprising fact. We want to know more, don't you?

Albee's headings and subheadings are also surprising, consisting of amusing puns. Here are a few examples: "Crawler ID," "Survival of the Flittest," and "East Meets Pest." This style is appealing. When you and your students are reading nonfiction, look for language that makes you pause and wonder or makes you stop and smile. Consider these questions: What makes this language so appealing? What makes me want to continue reading?

It's Organized

There are many formats for organizing a nonfiction book: chronological, cause and effect, comparison/contrast, problem and solution, descriptive, or enumerative. Of course, an author may use a mix of formats. The type of format used is less important than understanding that whatever organization the author selects, it should fit the content and help readers understand it.

A good example of a well-chosen organizational format is Brian Floca's (2013) *Locomotive*, the 2014 Caldecott Medal–winning book. *Locomotive* informs readers about train travel in 1869, right after the completion of the transcontinental railroad. To understand this trip, readers join members of a family traveling from Omaha, Nebraska, to San Francisco, California. Here's how the author invites us on the trip: "Here your trip begins, / at the depot, on the platform" (n.p.). A chronological organization enables the author to introduce the sights and sounds that this family experienced along the way. As the trip unfolds, we get a rich presentation of descriptive details through both text and illustrations.

When you and your students are discussing how a nonfiction book is organized, consider the following questions: How did the author organize the information? How does this organization fit the content? How does this organization help you understand the content?

The Pages Are Well Designed

Do you ever feel like you need a magnifying glass to read the small print? Is the text all squished together, filling the entire page, with no white space? Do you have to keep turning the pages to see the illustration being discussed? This isn't good! Instead, the pages should be appealing and varied. They should be interesting to look at.

The 2014 winner of the Robert F. Sibert Informational Book Medal, *Parrots Over Puerto Rico* by Susan Roth and Cindy Trumbore (2013), is beautifully designed. The first page of this book immediately transports you to the forest of Puerto Rico, where you are instructed to look up to find the parrots. Amid a collage of greens and browns, you can spot the parrots. The book is held lengthwise, so looking up really means looking up, up, up. There's a wonderful match between lush, inviting illustrations and descriptive text. Here's how the text directs the reader's gaze:

> Above the treetops of Puerto Rico flies a flock of parrots as green as their island home. If you look up from the forest, and you are very lucky, you might catch the bright blue flashes of their flight feathers and hear their harsh call. (n.p.)

As you discuss format with your students, consider the following questions: Is the book attractive and readable? Do illustrations complement and extend the text? Is the placement of the illustrations appropriate? Is the font appropriate?

It's Connected Somehow to the School Curriculum and to Other Nonfiction Books

As teachers, we're always looking for excellent nonfiction material to grab our students' interests and develop curricular topics. Table 2.3 lists and briefly describes a number of websites to consult for suggestions. Finding the right book enables you to develop thought-provoking inquiries and lessons.

As you select nonfiction material for teaching, ask yourself the following questions: Is information in this book true? Is the writing interesting to read? Are the pages well designed? Does this book support my curriculum? If so, you can select this material with confidence because you'll be using the criteria used by the Orbis Pictus Award Committee.

Respect for the Reader: Myra's Sibert Secret

As we explained above, the Sibert Medal is awarded by the American Library Association for excellence in informational books for readers through grade 8. Marc was thrilled when his book *Sir Walter Raleigh and the Quest for El Dorado* (Aronson, 2000) won the very first medal in 2001.

Table 2.3. Websites for Finding Outstanding Nonfiction

Website	Contents
NCTE Orbis Pictus Award for Outstanding Nonfiction for Children: www.ncte.org/awards/orbispictus	A yearly list of the award-winning title, up to five honor books, and several recommended titles going back to 2000
Notable Social Studies Trade Books for Young People: www.socialstudies.org/notable	A yearly list of recommended social studies titles from 2000 to the present
Outstanding Science Trade Books for Students K–12: www.nsta.org/publications/ostb	A yearly list of recommended science titles going back to 1996
Reading Rockets: www.readingrockets.org/books/awardwinners	Links to many children's literature awards lists and other best-of lists, including the Publishers Weekly's Best Children's Nonfiction list
Robert F. Sibert Informational Book Medal: www.ala.org/alsc/awardsgrants/bookmedia/sibertmedal	A list of winners and honor books from 2001 to the present

We writers are a competitive and envious lot, and Marc heard that some authors felt that he got the prize not for his writing but for his footnotes. Perhaps there's something to that—but in a way that he claims with pride. Part of Marc's respect for young readers is reflected in his conviction that we must always give them a way to discover where we found our information. We must show that every sentence, every date, every claim in our book is based on specific research. This obligation isn't because we need to prove that we've been diligent or haven't plagiarized. Rather, it's because when we show that everything we say comes from somewhere, we invite the reader to question, to check, to find other sources, to come up with other conclusions. Our books, then, don't lecture young people, browbeating them into submission because we're adults and have the say-so. Instead, our books include an Ariadne's thread—a trail of cookie crumbs—leading back to where and how we know what we know. That is the ultimate respect for the reader: (1) I respect you in sharing this knowledge, and (2) I respect you in showing how this knowledge was built—because you may want to inquire, question, or investigate further. You may be able to see what I have missed.

Final Thoughts

This chapter is your own personal invitation to the journey, the quest, that is nonfiction in the 21st century. We hope that as you explore some of the books we've mentioned, you'll experience the same thrill, the same sense of expectancy, that we do. We hope you and your students will open each nonfiction book not with the dread of the dull and dry but with a sense of a grand adventure about to start. That is what *every* good nonfiction book has to offer—one more step into the endless secrets, mysteries, and treasures of the universe.

CHILDREN'S LITERATURE CITED

Albee, S. (2014). *Bugged: How insects changed history*. New York, NY: Walker.

Aronson, M. (2000). *Sir Walter Raleigh and the quest for El Dorado*. New York, NY: Clarion.

Aronson, M. (with Parker Pearson, M., & the Riverside Project). (2010). *If stones could speak: Unlocking the secrets of Stonehenge*. Washington, DC: National Geographic Society.

Aronson, M. (2011). *Trapped: How the world rescued 33 miners from 2,000 feet below the Chilean desert*. New York, NY: Atheneum Books for Young Readers.

Aronson, M., & Newquist, H.P. (2007). *For boys only: The biggest, baddest book ever*. New York, NY: Feiwel and Friends.

Berger, L.R., & Aronson, M. (2012). *The skull in the rock: How a scientist, a boy, and Google Earth opened a new window on human origins*. Washington, DC: National Geographic Society.

Bolden, T. (2014). *Searching for Sarah Rector: The richest black girl in America*. New York, NY: Abrams Books for Young Readers.

Burns, L.G. (2010). *The hive detectives: Chronicle of a honey bee catastrophe*. Boston, MA: Houghton Mifflin Books for Children.

Chin, J. (2011). *Coral reefs*. New York, NY: Flash Point.

Crump, M. (2013). *The mystery of Darwin's frog*. Honesdale, PA: Boyds Mills.

Floca, B. (2013). *Locomotive*. New York, NY: Atheneum Books for Young Readers.

Hague, B. (2012). *Alien deep: Revealing the mysterious living world at the bottom of the ocean*. Washington, DC: National Geographic Society.

Kirkpatrick, K. (2011). *Mysterious bones: The story of Kennewick Man*. New York, NY: Holiday House.

Markle, S. (2012). *The case of the vanishing golden frogs: A scientific mystery*. Minneapolis, MN: Millbrook.

Markle, S. (2014). *The case of the vanishing honeybees: A scientific mystery*. Minneapolis, MN: Millbrook.

Markle, S. (2015). *The case of the vanishing little brown bats: A scientific mystery*. Minneapolis, MN: Millbrook.

McClafferty, C.K. (2011). *The many faces of George Washington: Remaking a presidential icon*. Minneapolis, MN: Carolrhoda.

Montgomery, S. (2010). *Kakapo rescue: Saving the world's strangest parrot*. Boston, MA: Houghton Mifflin Books for Children.

Nelson, S.R. (with Aronson, M.). (2008). *Ain't nothing but a man: My quest to find the real John Henry*. Washington, DC: National Geographic Society.

Newman, P. (2014). *Plastic ahoy! Investigating the great Pacific garbage patch*. Minneapolis, MN: Millbrook.

O'Connell, C., & Jackson, D.M. (2011). *The elephant scientist*. Boston, MA: Houghton Mifflin Books for Children.

Roth, S.L., & Trumbore, C. (2013). *Parrots over Puerto Rico*. New York, NY: Lee & Low.

Scieszka, J. (1989). *The true story of the 3 little pigs!* New York, N.Y: Puffin.

Thimmesh, C. (2009). *Lucy long ago: Uncovering the mystery of where we came from*. Boston, MA: Houghton Mifflin Books for Children.

Thimmesh, C. (2013). *Scaly spotted feathered frilled: How do we know what dinosaurs really looked like?* Boston, MA: Houghton Mifflin Harcourt.

Walker, S.M. (2002). *Fossil fish found alive: Discovering the coelacanth*. Minneapolis, MN: Carolrhoda.

OTHER RECOMMENDED NONFICTION CHILDREN'S BOOKS

Arndt, I. (2013). *Best foot forward: Exploring feet, flippers, and claws.* New York, NY: Holiday House.

Aronson, M. (with Mayor, A.). (2014). *The griffin and the dinosaur: How Adrienne Mayor discovered a fascinating link between myth and science.* Washington, DC: National Geographic Society.

Aronson, M., & Glenn, J.W. (2007). *The world made new: Why the Age of Exploration happened and how it changed the world.* Washington, DC: National Geographic Society.

Burns, L.G. (2012). *Citizen scientists: Be a part of scientific discovery from your own backyard.* New York, NY: Henry Holt.

Gandhi, A., & Hegedus, B. (2014). *Grandfather Gandhi.* New York, NY: Atheneum Books for Young Readers.

Heiligman, D. (2013). *The boy who loved math: The improbable life of Paul Erdös.* New York, NY: Roaring Brook.

Jenkins, S. (2009). *Actual size.* Boston, MA: Houghton Mifflin.

Jenkins, S. (2013). *The animal book: A collection of the fastest, fiercest, toughest, cleverest, shyest—and most surprising—animals on earth.* Boston, MA: Houghton Mifflin Harcourt.

Kamkwamba, W., & Mealer, B. (2009). *The boy who harnessed the wind: Creating currents of electricity and hope.* New York, NY: HarperLuxe.

Markel, M. (2013). *Brave girl: Clara and the Shirtwaist Makers' Strike of 1909.* New York, NY: Balzer + Bray.

Nivola, C.A. (2002). *Life in the ocean: The story of oceanographer Sylvia Earle.* New York, NY: Frances Foster.

Simon, S. (2013). *Seymour Simon's extreme oceans.* San Francisco, CA: Chronicle.

Stone, T.L. (2013). *Who says women can't be doctors? The story of Elizabeth Blackwell.* New York, NY: Henry Holt.

ABOUT THE AUTHORS

 Marc Aronson earned his doctorate in American history at New York University, focusing on the history of book publishing while he was beginning his career as an editor of books for children and teenagers. As first an editor and then an author, he aims to give young people the insights and discoveries being made by experts. He enjoys both writing his own books and collaborating with others. Marc now teaches full time in the Graduate School of Communication and Information at Rutgers University, training future librarians in how to select and share books with children and teenagers. He can be contacted at bookmarch@aol.com.

 Myra Zarnowski is a professor in the Department of Elementary and Early Childhood Education at Queens College, where she teaches courses in children's literature and social studies. A former classroom teacher in grades 3, 5, 6, and 7, she now enjoys working with teachers to include more nonfiction in their classrooms. Myra is the author of *Making Sense of History: Using High-Quality Literature and Hands-On Experiences to Build Content Knowledge* (Scholastic, 2006) and *History Makers: A Questioning Approach to Reading and Writing Biographies* (Heinemann, 2003), two books that deal with teaching history using nonfiction literature. She is also a frequent contributor to the blog The Uncommon Corps (nonfictionandthecommoncore.blogspot.com). Myra can be contacted at mzarnowski@verizon.net.

CHAPTER 3

What Do Biographies Tell Us?
A Journey Into Books and Lives
That Shape the Present

Deborah A. Wooten & Kimberly F. McCuiston, *University of Tennessee, Knoxville*

As Mark Twain (1980) noted, "There was never yet an uninteresting life. Such a thing is an impossibility. Inside of the dullest exterior there is a drama, a comedy, and a tragedy" (p. 317). A biographical picture book gives students a glimpse into the life of a person who has gone through the furnace of trials and reached his or her goals in the face of adversity. Most biographies are action packed with the ups and downs of life, helping students gain an appreciation and better understanding of people who have made an impact on history. Illustrations work in harmony with the text in making this journey more visually enjoyable.

Benefits of Using Biographical Picture Books

A biography tells an account of a person's life written in the third person in a narrative structure (Fountas & Pinnell, 2012). Biographies can be studied to learn about how people reacted to, shaped, and constructed opportunities during historical periods and the cultural contexts in which they lived (Eibling, Gilmartin, & Skehan, 1959; Hakim, 2003). They provide nonfiction information and communicate why a person's legacy is so important that it is documented. Reading biographies can help students reflect about how they should feel about historical people and events in terms of a dynamic process of continuity and change (Egan, 1979). Moreover, people in history are humanized by biographies that allow students to be drawn close to the past as they experience specific personalities and realities (Clabough & Turner, 2013). Through this, biographies offer students a richer context of history, providing more opportunities for engagement as they connect with the people as well as the events of the times.

Children's Literature in the Reading Program: Engaging Young Readers in the 21st Century (4th ed.), edited by Deborah A. Wooten & Bernice E. Cullinan. © 2015 by the International Literacy Association.

Studying people's lives offers numerous learning opportunities, and the illustrations in biographical picture books amplify the learning potential.

Studying people's lives offers numerous learning opportunities, and the illustrations in biographical picture books amplify the learning potential. Medina (2014), a developmental molecular biologist who has extensively studied how the brain organizes information, says his research indicates that vision trumps all other senses when learning. This finding emphasizes that illustrations provide visual entry points that guide students' imaginations to a better understanding of the story. "Visual literacy allows students to make meaning from images, and excellent illustrations have the potential to increase comprehension skills" (Chick, 2011, p. 70). In essence, biographies draw students to a better orientation with the text by helping them visually encounter characterization and expand on setting, while conveying mood, action, tone, and emotions (Sheridan, 2001). Because of the narrative style and illustrations, picture book biographies appeal to students on multiple learning levels.

This chapter presents five picture book biographies with complementary activities. The strategies are designed to help students grasp the big picture or themes in people's lives. Each activity builds on the previous one to prepare students for the complexities of higher order thinking skills.

Inferring Themes in a Legacy's Life With *Fifty Cents and a Dream*

Most biographies are about ordinary people who accomplish extraordinary feats. Many of these people's legacies provide positive role models for students in showing how life's challenges can be overcome (Lickteig, 2000). Picture book biographies allow teachers to highlight famous people's accomplishments on a more personal basis. There are numerous themes that could reflect successful people. Many books will have some or all of these characteristics because of the overlapping nature of the themes in the books, and some examples are listed here:

- Determination/persistence
- Civil rights
- Groundbreaking/innovation
- Risk taking

- Humanitarianism
- Creativity
- Vision
- Strong work ethic

Many, if not all, of these themes are evident in Booker T. Washington's life. *Fifty Cents and a Dream: Young Booker T. Washington* by Jabari Asim (2012) tells the story of Washington's (1856–1915) determination to learn to read after the emancipation of slaves in the United States. This led him on a 500-mile journey, mostly on foot, from his West Virginia home to Hampton Institute in Virginia. When Washington left home, he had only 50 cents and a fervent dream to achieve his goal. His dreams became reality as he broke new ground for African Americans and earned the degree that made possible his becoming a noteworthy author, a vocal advocate for African Americans, and the founder of the Tuskegee Institute in Alabama. Asim describes Washington's life in prose and includes carefully researched backmatter, such as a timeline, a bibliography, and an overview of Washington's enduring legacy.

Award-winning illustrator Bryan Collier expands and supports the narrative. If you take a closer look at Washington's portrait on the cover of the book, you'll see the words from the moving "Cast Down Your Bucket Where You Are": Booker T. Washington's Atlanta Compromise speech (Washington, 1895). Collier makes use of the endpapers to show pages from the first book that Washington used to learn to read, *The American Spelling Book* by Noah Webster (1795). The illustrations' deep earth tones help set the mood for students to visually sense the hardships of Washington's life before and after the Civil War.

Making Inferences With Booker T. Washington's Life

The goal of the activity is for students to infer the theme(s) reflective of Washington's life with the support of a graphic organizer. Start with discussing the themes that are listed above and how and why they are reflective in people's lives.

Below are steps for the graphic organizer that help students infer themes about Washington's life:

1. Have students write a brief description of Washington's life.
2. Write important supportive facts, such as time period, events, and setting.
3. Write his major obstacle(s).
4. List ways in which he overcame his obstacle(s), resulting in changing his life.
5. Infer a theme(s) about Washington's life based on the information from the graphic organizer and book.

This activity will prepare students for an insightful discussion and perhaps for writing a persuasive essay about the themes inferred during this process. Figure 3.1 is an example of a graphic organizer that will help students infer themes in Washington's life. (A blank reproducible is also provided at the end of this chapter.)

Figure 3.1. Inferring Themes in a Legacy's Life Graphic Organizer for *Fifty Cents and a Dream: Young Booker T. Washington*[a]

Inferring a Legacy's Theme(s)

Describe the life of Booker T. Washington in a couple of sentences and then list three important facts about his life. Next, write obstacles that Washington faced and how he overcame them. Then, list a theme or themes that you infer are evident in his life.

Write a description of Washington's life.		
He was a freed slave who worked hard and walked about 500 miles to get an education. After he went to college, he became famous.		

Fact 1:	Fact 2:	Fact 3:
Born 1856 and died in 1915	Home: Virginia	Became an author

What was the obstacle or obstacles that he faced?	How did he overcome the obstacle(s)?
He was poor and didn't have enough money to go to college.	He walked about 500 miles to go to college and had to work hard to pay his tuition and survive.

Infer a theme or themes that characterize Washington's life and list it or them below.

Note. The silhouette is reprinted by permission of Jason J. McCuiston.
[a]Asim, J. (2012). *Fifty cents and a dream: Young Booker T. Washington.* New York, NY: Little, Brown.

Engaging in Close Reading With *Monsieur Marceau*

In *Monsieur Marceau: Actor Without Words*, winner of the 2013 Orbis Pictus Award for Outstanding Nonfiction for Children, author Leda Schubert (2012) details the complex life of Marcel Marceau (1923–2007), née Marcel Mangel (Marcel Marceau, 2013), arguably the most renowned mime in the world. Marceau overcame many hardships as a French Jewish youth during World War II to become like his hero, Charlie Chaplin, such as joining the French underground movement to fight the Nazis. Schubert's articulate word choice parallels the difficulties and successes of Marceau's life. Lacing direct quotes from Marceau throughout the text, Schubert portrays the artist's poignancy and humor. The reader easily visualizes his dramatic movements as a mime through Schubert's words, which combine to form a staccato cadence. The author's extensive research provides the reader with both a look at Marceau's multifarious life and artistic information for those interested in pursuing mime.

Illustrator Gérard DuBois chooses colors as masterfully as Schubert chooses her words. He juxtaposes wartime hardships using rich yet dark colors of browns, golds, and blacks with Marceau's success as a mime, using bright whites and bold reds. White space is used expertly to display Marceau's dramatic movements when he chases butterflies without a net and becomes a fish. Each illustration is complex, a perfect symbol of the life of the bold and courageous mime.

Close Reading

Two purposes of close reading are to allow students to connect new information to their own experiences and prior knowledge and to practice the habits needed when reading complex texts (Fisher & Frey, 2012). Close readings require the deep and critical analysis of a quality text. Because reading necessitates a deep understanding of a text, teacher guidance, along with a compelling text (Dalton, 2013), is needed. Schubert and DuBois's portrayal of Marceau's life provides students with an interesting, quality, complex text.

First, the teacher reads the book to the students, asking them to think about the big idea and key details that make up the story. Students talk with a partner about what they believe the big idea and key details are in the text. Student responses, for instance, might include that Marceau demonstrates perseverance and determination through events such as hiding U.S. parachutists in a French monastery. Students document their big idea and key details in their notes (see Figure 3.2).

The next step is a second reading of the text. This time students need to look more closely at specific details. For *Monsieur Marceau*, students are divided into small groups, each of which is given one of two sections of the text for analysis: Marceau's time during the war and his time after the war has ended. The groups analyze their portion of the text for word choice, sentence construction, and color and figure placement in illustrations. Students write their analysis in their notes (see Figure 3.3).

Figure 3.2. Sample Student Notes About *Monsieur Marceau: Actor Without Words*[a]

Big Idea	Key Details
Marceau shows determination and persistence in fighting against the Nazis and in becoming a world-renowned mime.	1. Marceau fights the Nazis by joining the French underground movement. 2. He helps U.S. parachutists by hiding them in a French monastery until the war is over. 3. Marceau helps Jewish orphans escape to safety in Switzerland.

[a]Schubert, L. (2012). *Monsieur Marceau: Actor without words*. New York, NY: Roaring Brook.

Figure 3.3. Sample Student Analysis of *Monsieur Marceau: Actor Without Words*[a] During World War II and Postwar

Analysis of the Text (description of words used, sentence styles, etc.)	Analysis of the Illustrations (description of colors used, faces made, objects, etc.)
▪ During the War: Sentences are longer; words demonstrate less action, such as "led" and "pretended" ▪ Postwar: Sentences are more clipped, shorter; words are more active, such as "chases" and "walks against"	▪ During the War: Colors used are browns, yellows, and blacks; faces are looking down, frowns, thoughtful looks, closed mouths ▪ Postwar: Reds, blues, whites; faces are looking straight ahead or up, smiles, open mouths

[a]Schubert, L. (2012). *Monsieur Marceau: Actor without words*. New York, NY: Roaring Brook.

Students may, for example, write that the illustrations depicting Marceau's life during the war are made with browns, yellows, and greens or that sentences used to describe his life after the war are full of active words. When finished, groups share their analysis with the class. Together, the class writes a short paragraph of all of their analyses with teacher guidance.

The final step in the close reading is to integrate the new knowledge and ideas gained from another source with another text or media. An appropriate accompaniment for *Monsieur Marceau* is a short clip from Charlie Chaplin's (1918) film *Shoulder Arms*. In the clip, Chaplin plays a soldier away at war, waiting to receive letters from home. Many in his platoon receive packages and letters during mail call, but he doesn't. Chaplin's facial expressions portray a sad man, yet his antics, such as reading over a comrade's shoulder, keep the audience laughing. Reading *Monsieur Marceau* and viewing *Shoulder Arms* allows the reader to compare and contrast the mood of each piece. Students reflect on the mood that the author and illustrator create in their depiction of Marceau's life during the war with that in Chaplin's clip. Reflections are written on a graphic organizer (see Figure 3.4). Some students may find the mood in Chaplin's film closer to the one set in the second part of the book, dealing with Marceau's successes after the war.

This activity also lends itself to a discussion of the difference between the author's tone (the author's attitude toward the topic and audience) and the mood (the atmosphere or feeling of the piece) of a text. For instance, both the text and the video clip tackle, at least in part, a similar subject, war; however, the attitudes portrayed about the topic are quite different. The text documenting Marceau's life during the war has a somber tone, whereas the Chaplin clip portrays the soldier waiting for mail in a lighthearted manner. The mood of each piece is affected by the tone the author or director takes. The text's somber tone creates a depressing

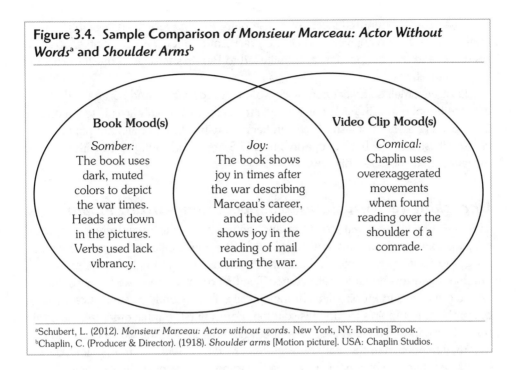

Figure 3.4. Sample Comparison of *Monsieur Marceau: Actor Without Words*[a] and *Shoulder Arms*[b]

Book Mood(s)

Somber:
The book uses dark, muted colors to depict the war times. Heads are down in the pictures. Verbs used lack vibrancy.

Joy:
The book shows joy in times after the war describing Marceau's career, and the video shows joy in the reading of mail during the war.

Video Clip Mood(s)

Comical:
Chaplin uses overexaggerated movements when found reading over the shoulder of a comrade.

[a]Schubert, L. (2012). *Monsieur Marceau: Actor without words*. New York, NY: Roaring Brook.
[b]Chaplin, C. (Producer & Director). (1918). *Shoulder arms* [Motion picture]. USA: Chaplin Studios.

environment, whereas the video clip provides a comical mood. A class reading of the text requires some time and structure for students to be able to read deeply and critically. The time and effort, however, allow students to experience the pieces more fully and to evaluate the text on a much deeper level.

Exploring Biographical Text Structures Through *A Splash of Red*

A Splash of Red: The Life and Art of Horace Pippin by Jen Bryant (2013) received the prestigious NCTE Orbis Pictus Award for Outstanding Nonfiction for Children and was named a Robert F. Sibert Informational Honor Book. Bryant has clearly conducted substantial research as she braids the narrative with tightly written events and humanizing quotes. Horace Pippin (1888–1946), an African American self-taught artist, overcame poverty and disability to rise as a nationally known artist. His passion for art started at an early age and never ebbed. Pippin still found time to draw while he was fighting in the trenches during World War I. During the war, he was shot in his right shoulder, resulting in paralysis in that arm. This tragedy prevented him from drawing until one day when he used his left hand to guide his right hand and was able to draw again. It took him nearly three years and a hundred layers of house paint to complete his first painting after his injury. One auspicious day, the president of a local artists' club spotted his work, and that connection eventually led to Pippin's fame as a master artist in the United States.

Illustrator Melissa Sweet combines watercolor, gouache, and collage with compositional bordering in a folk art style to celebrate Pippin's artistic technique. Each page renders "a splash of red," in keeping with Pippin's hallmark palette. She cleverly illustrates the back endpapers as a U.S. map, indicating cities with major museums that showcase his artwork.

Unpacking Text Structures to Support Summarizing Pippin's Life

This activity addresses text structures and the use of graphic organizers to prepare students to write a summary and connection. Students create and organize mental images to enhance their comprehension (Pressley, 2002) through the use of two graphic organizers about text structures. The first graphic organizer helps students record the events in Pippin's life chronologically. The second has students articulate the problem in Pippin's life and his solution. For the first graphic organizer, students trace their hand on a blank piece of paper and write important events in the order that they happened in the story on each finger, starting with the thumb. If students have more than five events, they can list the important events between their fingers. See Figure 3.5 for an example of this graphic organizer.

Next, the teacher distributes the second graphic organizer for students to complete. The major problem in the story arises when Pippin loses the use of his right arm, and the solution is when he figures out how to draw again. Figure 3.6 is an example of this kind of graphic organizer. It provides space for students to write a summary of Pippin's life, along with connections from his life to another famous person's.

Having students summarize has a positive impact on their comprehension (Calfee & Patrick, 1995; National Institute of Child Health and Human Development, 2000). Employing both of these graphic organizers helps students articulate and organize their thinking, and their summaries are more precisely written, with supportive evidence. Using these graphic organizers also guides students to analyze how and why events in Pippin's life developed throughout his life.

Template for Providing Connections

After students have completed their summaries, they can write about a connection of Pippin's life to another famous person's life, an event, or another book. A template for formatting a connection between these two is provided (if

Figure 3.5. Sample Student Sequencing Graphic Organizer About *A Splash of Red: The Life and Art of Horace Pippin*[a]

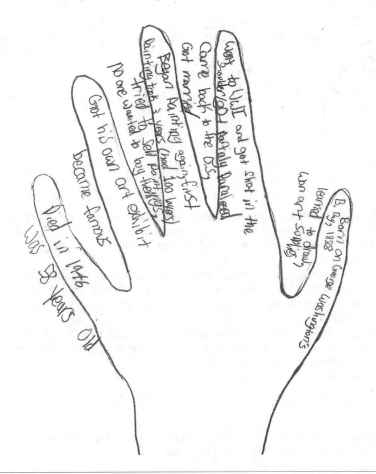

Horace Pippin

Birth and Death Years

1888   1946

Trace your open hand on the space below. List on each finger a major event in Horace Pippin's life. Write them in sequential order and let your thumb represent the first event in his life. You can add more events in between each finger on your hand.

B. Born on George Washington's
learned to draw
Won art supplies

Went to WWII and got shot in the
Came back to the U.S.
Got married

Began painting again first
painting took 3 years (had 100 wires)
tried to sell paintings
no one wanted to buy them?

Got his own art exhibit
became famous

Died in 1946
was 58 years old

[a]Bryant, J. (2013). *A splash of red: The life and art of Horace Pippin*. New York, NY: Alfred A. Knopf.

Figure 3.6. Sample Student Problem-and-Solution Graphic Organizer About *A Splash of Red: The Life and Art of Horace Pippin*[a]

Name: Sarah Winter

Topic: What was the major problem that Horace Pippin had to overcome after World War I to become a famous artist? What was his solution?

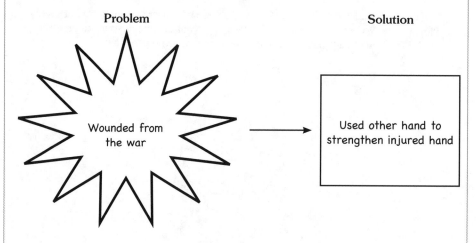

Use your story sequence graphic organizer and this problem-and-solution graphic organizer to write a summary about Pippin's life. Use evidence from the book to support the information that you have collected.

    Horace Pippin loved to draw and paint very much. He was born on the same day as George Washington in 1888. He learned to draw and then saw an add with a picture on it that said, "draw me and win a prize". He drew it and won his very first set of art supplies.

    He went to World War I and got shot in the shoulder and couldn't draw because it was his right arm. Then he came back to the U.S. and got married to Jenny Wade. After he learned how to grab his right arm with his left hand he learned to draw again.

    His first painting had one hundred layers of paint and took 3 years to finish. His paintings didn't sell. Then people came by and offered to give him an art exhibit and he took their offer. Then he became famous.

    He died in 1946.

Connect Horace Pippin's life to a famous person and explain how they relate to each other.

    This story reminds me of Monsieur Marceau because they both expressed their feelings in their work and they both did a type of art.

[a]Bryant, J. (2013). *A splash of red: The life and art of Horace Pippin*. New York, NY: Alfred A. Knopf.

needed) for students to write their connection to identify how and why the two connect:

This [story or person] reminds me of ____ because ____ just like ____.

The student sample in Figure 3.6 connects preexisting knowledge from *Monsieur Marceau* to Pippin's life. When a connection is created, learning is fortified because two pieces of information are united. Schema theory suggests that a student will remember and file the newly comprehended information more readily by associating it with information that's already in his or her mental filing cabinet, or knowledge base (Anderson, 1977; Rumelhart, 1980). In this case, the student remembers learning about Marceau and then connects him to Pippin because both artists expressed feelings through their work, albeit art of two different forms.

Making connections should be a consistent part of our thinking processes. Thus, having students write connections on a regular basis will enhance their comprehension (Wooten, 2000; Wooten & White, 2009).

Composing a Poem About Teddy Roosevelt's Life

Award-winning author Doreen Rappaport's (2013) picture book *To Dare Mighty Things: The Life of Theodore Roosevelt* weaves together Roosevelt's (1858–1919) biography with two strands: narrative prose and direct quotes. The book's prose describes Roosevelt's life, while each quote captures the heartbeat of selected pivotal events that culminated to make this man a national hero. For example, among his other noteworthy accomplishments, he was responsible for creating 18 national parks and 50 national forests and for saving and protecting 230 million acres of undeveloped land in the United States. The quotation that marks Roosevelt's position on conservation is "We are not building this country for a day. It is to last through the ages" (n.p.). The quote provides the big picture statement in the text by using Roosevelt's words to support what he achieved.

The cover of the book, a full-bleed pastel portrait of Roosevelt, depicts him with a jubilant smile so wide that it causes his eyes to almost shut. Illustrator C.F. Payne visually chronicles each layer of Roosevelt's life as he becomes one of America's strongest leaders. The final page is a portrait of him with the U.S. flag in the background, portraying him as a man whose determination and persistence helped make the country a better place for all.

Roosevelt Free Verse Poem Activity

This activity is designed to have students write a free verse poem using characteristics reflective of Roosevelt's life. Students will need to refer to their notes taken while the book was read aloud for this activity. Students can work in pairs to create a free verse or other style of poem depicting Roosevelt's life. The poem should end with big-picture words that encapsulate his legendary persona. Students will experience the autonomy of distilling information about Roosevelt's life in a free verse poetic format that is both challenging and doable. Here's an example of a free verse poem for this activity:

Teddy: The Visionary President

Teddy,
Wheezy
Pale and puny
Loved nature
Weak physique
Thick glasses
Climbed mountains
Studied long hours
Author
Our 26th president
Nobel Peace Prize
Conservationist
Rebel
Builder
Overcomer
Hero

Using poetry in the classroom has numerous benefits, including opening a new literary realm that helps students think differently about their surroundings (Galda, Cullinan, & Sipe, 2009). Using poetry to respond to biographies encourages students to explore valuable issues in content areas that reach beyond their lives. Just as important, poetry is enjoyable, amusing, and inspirational (Harrison, 2009). Although it's easy to neglect this genre, as teachers, we should capitalize on the wealth that poetry brings into our teaching practices.

Understanding Question–Answer Relationships With *Hoop Genius*

In *Hoop Genius: How a Desperate Teacher and a Rowdy Gym Class Invented Basketball*, author John Coy (2013) and illustrator Joe Morse document how James Naismith (1861–1939) invented the game of basketball. Naismith reluctantly becomes the teacher of a rowdy, all-male gym class and learns that the usual games are too combative for his rough-and-tumble students. The young men remind Naismith of himself and inspire him to create a game based on his past experiences. The game as he creates it values accuracy more than force. Naismith writes up the first rules to his new game of basketball and posts them in the school gym. He procures two peach baskets to use as hoops and introduces the game to his students. The students soon learn that the game requires them to play with more accuracy and to be less forceful to play successfully. Naismith's students teach their friends and family the game, and soon people in cities and towns are playing.

Just like in basketball, Coy and Morse use their talents together to portray a fascinating history of the game. Coy's use of illustrative prose describes Naismith's actions in a way that demonstrates his perseverance and imagination. Just as the students in Naismith's gym class were boisterous and active, so are Coy's use of action verbs. These words complement the rich images offered by Morse. Vibrant colors of maroon, blue, and brown are offset by lighter tones of cream and beige to depict the uniforms of the time. The dichotomy of events in Naismith's life is contrasted using less vibrant colors in scenes of low points or flashback events. Sharp angles of the players point the reader's eyes swiftly from left to right, giving the pictures the feeling of dynamic movement. Morse's positioning of the characters on the pages places the reader in the center of the action. The endpapers offer readers a glimpse at the original draft of the basketball rules penned by Naismith.

Question–Answer Relationship (QAR)

The QAR strategy for reading comprehension helps students understand the relationship between the questions posed about a text and the methods for retrieving the answers to those questions (Raphael & Pearson, 1985). In this strategy, there are two categories of questions used (Kinniburgh & Baxter, 2012), each with two subcategories, as shown in Table 3.1.

To teach the QAR strategy to students using *Hoop Genius*, the teacher first reads the book aloud to the class. Then, the teacher explains the types of questions in Table 3.1 to the students, providing examples of questions related

Table 3.1. Questioning Table

Category Question	Subcategory Question	Subcategory Question
In the book: Requires the student to answer questions by looking in the text	*Right there:* The answer is found directly in the text.	*Think and search:* The answer is collected from different sections of the text.
In my head: Requires the student to use background knowledge	*Author and you:* The answer requires background knowledge and information found in the text.	*On my own:* The answer is found using only background knowledge.

to the book. Next, students are taught how to find the answer to each type of question via teacher modeling. For instance, a question asking what was first used as a basketball hoop would be a "right there" question because the answer (two peach baskets) can be found directly in the text. An "author and you" question would be one that asks how the reader knows Naismith is excited about introducing his game to his students, as the reader must identify in the text that Naismith stays up late thinking about the game and relate it to his or her own experience with excitement. After modeling how to find the answers for each type of question, students practice finding answers to posed questions from the different QAR categories. Here are some sample questions (and answers) about *Hoop Genius*:

- *Right there:* When did basketball become an Olympic sport? (1936)
- *Think and search:* How can a reader tell when Naismith is reminiscing? (The colors in the illustrations are muted.)
- *Author and you:* Why was Naismith shocked by the women players protesting? (because they were protesting as loudly as men, which was unusual for the time)
- *On my own:* Have you ever created your own game? What were the rules? (Answers will vary.)

Next, students create their own questions from the text, identifying the type of relationship each question and answer has from the four subcategory question choices in Table 3.1. This can be done in small groups. By having students create their own questions, the teacher can assess students' comprehension of the text and their understanding of the four subcategories of questions using the QAR strategy. Students then share the questions they created with their classmates in a whole-class setting.

Finally, using the questions and answers, both the ones posed to the whole class by the small groups or individually and the questions they created, students each write an interview between themselves and Naismith. They synthesize the information garnered from using the QAR strategy with *Hoop Genius* to create a historically fictional piece of writing that demonstrates both their comprehension of the text and their understanding of the differing relationships between questions and answers.

Conclusion

There is a growing appetite to use more nonfiction text with students, and picture book biographies offer an attractive option because they unite facts and illustrations in a reader-friendly narrative. Teachers need to be particularly careful in selecting types of books that portray their subjects' lives accurately and authentically. Although there are several credible sources for picture book biographies, the Robert F. Sibert Informational Book Medal (www.ala.org/alsc/awardsgrants/bookmedia/sibertmedal) and NCTE Orbis Pictus Award (www.ncte.org/awards/orbispictus) nonfiction book winners and honor books have proven reliable. If we teachers are to strengthen students' literacy skills, we must select books that are written with integrity and have strong literary merit. At the end of this chapter is a list of current favorite picture book biographies endorsed by us and students.

REFERENCES

Anderson, R.C. (1977). The notion of schemata and the educational enterprise: General discussion of the conference. In R.C. Anderson, R.J. Spiro, & W.E. Montague (Eds.), *Schooling and the acquisition of knowledge* (pp. 415–431). Hillsdale, NJ: Erlbaum.

Calfee, R.C., & Patrick, C.L. (1995). *Teach our children well: Bringing K–12 education into the 21st century*. Stanford, CA: Stanford Alumni Association.

Chaplin, C. (Producer & Director). (1918). *Shoulder arms* [Motion picture]. USA: Chaplin Studios.

Chick, K.A. (2011). Picture book biographies: Fostering active student involvement in Women's History Month. *Social Studies Research and Practice*, 6(2), 69–84.

Clabough, J.C., & Turner, T.N. (2013). Revolutionary Renaissance men: Looking at colonial scientists through reading children's biographies. *Oregon Journal of the Social Studies*, 1(2), 64–73.

Dalton, B. (2013). Engaging children in close reading: Multimodal commentaries and illustration remix. *The Reading Teacher*, 66(8), 642–649. doi:10.1002/trtr.1172

Egan, K. (1979). What children know best. *Social Education*, 43(2), 130–134, 139.

Eibling, H.H., Gilmartin, J.G., & Skehan, A.M. (1959). *Great names in our country's story*. River Forest, IL: Laidlaw Bros.

Fisher, D., & Frey, N. (2012). Close reading in elementary schools. *The Reading Teacher*, 66(3), 179–188. doi:10.1002/TRTR.01117

Fountas, I.C., & Pinnell, G.S. (2012). *Genre study: Teaching with fiction and nonfiction books*. Portsmouth, NH: Heinemann.

Galda, L., Cullinan, B.E., & Sipe, L.R. (2009). *Literature and the child* (7th ed.). Belmont, CA: Wadsworth/Cengage Learning.

Hakim, J. (2003). *Freedom: A history of U.S.* New York, NY: Oxford University Press.

Harrison, D.L. (2009). Yes, poetry can! In D.A. Wooten & B.E. Cullinan (Eds.), *Children's literature in the reading program: An invitation to read* (3rd ed., pp. 45–56). Newark, DE: International Reading Association. doi:10.1598/0699.05

Kinniburgh, L.H., & Baxter, A. (2012). Using question answer relationships in science instruction to increase the reading achievement of struggling readers and students with reading disabilities. *Current Issues in Education*, 15(2). Retrieved from cie.asu.edu/ojs/index.php/cieatasu/article/viewFile/915/334

Lickteig, M.J. (2000). African American scientists, explorers, and innovators: Resources for elementary and secondary classrooms. *Journal of African American Studies*, 4(4), 37–48. doi:10.1007/s12111-000-1020-9

Marcel Marceau. (2013). In *Encylopædia Britannica*. Retrieved from www.britannica.com/EBchecked/topic/364094/Marcel-Marceau

Medina, J. (2014). *Brain rules: 12 principles for surviving and thriving at work, home, and school* (2nd ed.). Seattle, WA: Pear.

National Institute of Child Health and Human Development. (2000). *Report of the National Reading Panel. Teaching children to read: An evidence-based assessment of the scientific research literature on reading and its implications for reading instruction* (NIH Publication No. 00-4769). Washington, DC: U.S. Government Printing Office.

Pressley, M. (2002). Comprehension strategies instruction: A turn-of-the-century status report. In C.C. Block & M. Pressley (Eds.), *Comprehension instruction: Research-based best practices* (pp. 11–27). New York, NY: Guilford.

Raphael, T.E., & Pearson, P.D. (1985). Increasing students' awareness of sources of information for answering questions. *American Educational Research Journal, 22*(2), 217–235. doi:10.3102/00028312022002217

Rumelhart, D.E. (1980). Schemata: The building blocks of cognition. In R.J. Spiro, B.C. Bruce, & W.F. Brewer (Eds.), *Theoretical issues in reading comprehension: Perspectives from cognitive psychology, linguistics, artificial intelligence, and education* (pp. 33–58). Hillsdale, NJ: Erlbaum.

Sheridan, N. (2001). Using picture books in content area classes: Some applications for content area reading. *Focus on Elementary, 14*(1), 1–6.

Washington, B.T. (1895). *"Cast down your bucket where you are": Booker T. Washington's Atlanta Compromise speech.* Retrieved from historymatters.gmu.edu/d/88

Webster, N. (1795). *The American spelling book*. Hartford, CT: Hudson & Goodwin.

Wooten, D.A. (2000). *Valued voices: An interdisciplinary approach to teaching and learning*. Newark, DE: International Reading Association.

Wooten, D.A., & White, P.W. (2009). Inviting all students into the literacy arena through writing and sharing connections. In D.A. Wooten & B.E. Cullinan (Eds.), *Children's literature in the reading program: An invitation to read* (3rd ed., pp. 121–129). Newark, DE: International Reading Association. doi:10.1598/0699.12

LITERATURE CITED

Asim, J. (2012). *Fifty cents and a dream: Young Booker T. Washington*. New York, NY: Little, Brown.

Bryant, J. (2013). *A splash of red: The life and art of Horace Pippin*. New York, NY: Alfred A. Knopf.

Coy, J. (2013). *Hoop genius: How a desperate teacher and a rowdy gym class invented basketball*. Minneapolis, MN: Carolrhoda.

Rappaport, D. (2013). *To dare mighty things: The life of Theodore Roosevelt*. New York, NY: Disney-Hyperion.

Schubert, L. (2012). *Monsieur Marceau: Actor without words*. New York, NY: Roaring Brook.

Twain, M. (1980). The refuge of the derelicts. In J.S. Tuckey (Ed.), *The devil's race-track: Mark Twain's great dark writings* (pp. 282–368). Berkeley: University of California Press.

OTHER RECOMMENDED BIOGRAPHICAL PICTURE BOOKS FOR CHILDREN

Berne, J. (2013). *On a beam of light: A story of Albert Einstein*. San Francisco, CA: Chronicle.

Brown, D. (2013). *Henry and the cannons: An extraordinary true story of the American Revolution*. New York, NY: Roaring Brook.

Bryant, J. (2014). *The right word: Roget and his thesaurus*. Grand Rapids, MI: Eerdmans Books for Young Readers.

Cummins, J. (2013). *Flying solo: How Ruth Elder soared into America's heart*. New York, NY: Roaring Brook.

Ferris, J.C. (2012). *Noah Webster and his words*. Boston, MA: Houghton Mifflin Harcourt.

Malaspina, A. (2012). *Touch the sky: Alice Coachman, Olympic high jumper*. Chicago, IL: Albert Whitman.

Rappaport, D. (2012). *Helen's big world: The life of Helen Keller*. New York, NY: Disney·Hyperion.

Rosenstock, B. (2014). *The noisy paint box: The colors and sounds of Kandinsky's abstract art*. New York, NY: Alfred A. Knopf.

Rusch, E. (2013). *Electrical wizard: How Nikola Tesla lit up the world*. Somerville, MA: Candlewick.

Sís, P. (2014). *The pilot and the little prince: The life of Antoine de Saint-Exupéry*. New York, NY: Frances Foster.

ABOUT THE AUTHORS

 Deborah A. Wooten is an associate professor of reading in the Department of Theory and Practice in Teacher Education at the University of Tennessee, Knoxville, USA. Before joining the university faculty, she taught elementary school for 23 years. After earning her PhD from New York University, she continued to teach in the elementary classroom for 10 years to research practical new methods for using children's literature to foster connections across content areas while scaffolding students to think metacognitively.

Deborah has served on children's and young adult book award committees and is currently a board member for the Children's Literature Assembly. She is an author and editor of numerous books, chapters, and articles, including coediting and contributing to *The Continuum Encyclopedia of Young Adult Literature* (Continuum, 2005) and *Children's Literature in the Reading Program: An Invitation to Read* (third edition; International Reading Association, 2009). Deborah can be contacted at dwooten1@utk.edu.

 Kimberly F. McCuiston is a PhD candidate in the Department of Theory and Practice in Teacher Education at the University of Tennessee, Knoxville, USA. Prior to her return to school to earn her graduate degree, she taught reading and language arts in middle schools for 13 years. Kimberly's passion for utilizing high-interest texts in the classroom has resulted in coauthored publications on text complexity and her own publication on using online book reviews to garner interest in reading.

Kimberly and her husband, Jason, an aspiring writer, enjoy searching for first editions of their favorite books and playing with their two dogs, Grendel and Winky. Kimberly can be contacted at kmccuist@vols.utk.edu.

Inferring a Legacy's Theme(s)

Describe the life of _____ in a couple of sentences and then list three important facts about his/her life. Next, write obstacles that he/she faced and how he/she overcame them. Then, list a theme or themes that you infer that are evident in his/her life.

Write a description of the life of _____.		
Fact 1:	Fact 2:	Fact 3:
What was the obstacle or obstacles that he/she faced?		How did he/she overcome the obstacle(s)?

Infer a theme or themes that characterize the life of _____ and list it or them below.

CHAPTER 4

Series Books

For Seeking Reading Pleasure and Developing Reading Competence

Anne McGill-Franzen & Natalia Ward, *University of Tennessee, Knoxville*

For over a hundred years, serialized fiction has hooked readers and kept them reading. To wit, look at the explosive popularity of the contemporary George R.R. Martin (1996–2011) five-book fantasy series, collectively called A Song of Ice and Fire and produced for television as *Game of Thrones*. There are about 4.5 million copies in print, and each book of the series has enjoyed over a hundred weeks on *The New York Times* Best Seller List. Often considered anathema to teachers and librarians, or light reading at best, series books have been part of the literary landscape since the 1880s. Given the ubiquity of series books, it is surprising that few people have taken a serious look at what makes them attractive or their effects on readers. Ross (1995), a Canadian university professor in the library sciences and a scholar of readers' preferences, has written extensively on "what makes readers and keeps them reading" (p. 201).

A Brief History of Series Books

In a historical review of the emergence of reading for pleasure, Ross (1995) suggests that dime novels and other serialized materials democratized pleasure reading. Previously restricted to reading a few religious texts and the Bible, the masses obtained access to secular fiction materials because of the cheaper processes for printing and distribution during the latter part of the 19th century. Ross cites several historical accounts of how story papers, dime novels, and cheap libraries opened up reading for pleasure to those who had not read before. Dime novels were the predecessors of series books. Beadle & Adams, a famous dime novel publisher of the era, published a new novel every couple of weeks in a numbered series. Similar to the experiences of series authors today, dime

Children's Literature in the Reading Program: Engaging Young Readers in the 21st Century (4th ed.), edited by Deborah A. Wooten & Bernice E. Cullinan. © 2015 by the International Literacy Association.

novelists would be given a title, a plot, and other specifications by the publisher and asked to quickly compose a story.

This system was perfected by Edward Stratemeyer, whose Stratemeyer Syndicate extended the audience for serialized fiction to juveniles (Ross, 1995). He and anonymous writers created dozens of series for children, including the long-running and still available Nancy Drew and Hardy Boys books, and provided a model for today's series books—formulaic school stories, family stories, science fiction, detective stories, and mysteries. Although librarians and literature experts of the day disparaged the literary quality of series books, an early 20th-century American Library Association survey demonstrated that young readers, then as now, overwhelmingly preferred them (Soderbergh, as cited in Ross, 1995).

Reading for Pleasure

Ross herself had enjoyed reading series books as a child and wondered about the reading experiences of others. In an ethnography of reading published by Libraries Unlimited, Ross, McKechnie, and Rothbauer (2006) explored avid readers' perceptions of the reading experience and what may have influenced them to become readers. Ross (1995) conducted over 142 open-ended interviews over several years, and almost to a person, she found that series books led the interviewees into reading for pleasure. This reader's response was typical of what Ross called "committed readers" (p. 216)—those who identify reading for pleasure as a very important part of their lives:

> The first book that I distinctly remember reading would probably have to be *The Enchanted Forest* by Enid Blyton. It's about these kids that go into a forest and they go up this tree, and there's different worlds at the top of this tree....The next book would have been *The Magic Faraway Tree* which was a continuation of that story. My grandmother had a whole closet full of Enid Blyton books—the original hard cover, all dusty and yellow. (p. 218)

The story line of the Enid Blyton series evokes a familiar motif: Both The Chronicles of Narnia by C.S. Lewis (1950–1956) and the Magic Tree House series by Mary Pope Osborne (1992–2014; some with coauthors) share plot and setting elements with Blyton's work, and who knows, the earlier series may have inspired the contemporary series!

At any rate, Ross (1995) asked the adult readers in her study what made series books so pleasurable for them as children and adolescents. Two themes emerged from their responses. First was the reassurance of the familiar that supported novice readers, and the second was identification of the reader with not only the character but also other readers of the series. Ross pointed out that although we think of reading as a solitary activity, readers describe series book reading "as a social activity embedded in the social relations of childhood. Series books have the cachet of something precious, to be collected, hoarded, discussed, and...'traded like baseball cards'" (p. 226). As one reader put it, "I read them just because everybody else was," and another, "I read [all the books] I could get my hands on!" (p. 224).

> **"Series books have the cachet of something precious, to be collected, hoarded, discussed, and...'traded like baseball cards.'"**

Series Books Today—as Popular as Ever

R.L. Stine (1992–1997) and his wildly popular Goosebumps series of the 1990s did much to rekindle interest in and arguments about the worth of series books and whether schools and libraries should permit children to read them. The Goosebumps series, with equal portions of humor and horror, made Stine the biggest selling author in the United States for three years in a row, at one point selling over 4 million copies a month (Stelter, 2008).

The Maze of Bones by Rick Riordan (2008), the first book of a more recent series—39 Clues by a collaboration of authors (Riordan et al., 2008–2015)—was released in early September 2008 and immediately appeared on *The New York Times* Children's Book List for the next seven consecutive weeks! Indeed, even a cursory examination of contemporary best-selling children's books demonstrates the enduring popularity of series books. Osborne's Magic Tree House and Barbara Park's (1992–2014) Junie B. Jones series appeared in the top 10 best-selling children's books for close to 200 consecutive weeks. More recently, Riordan's (2005–2009) Percy Jackson & the Olympians series appeared in the top 10 list for 338 consecutive weeks and Jeff Kinney's (2007–2014) Diary of a Wimpy Kid series for 288 weeks. For a time, Stephenie Meyer's (2005–2008) Twilight Saga series became the most popular books among preadolescents, only to be usurped more recently by Suzanne Collins's (2008–2015) The Hunger Games. J.K. Rowling's (1997–2007) Harry Potter maintains a loyal following among both middle elementary and adolescent readers and has been a best seller for over 300 weeks. Even primary-grade children have favorite series, notably Pete the Cat, a madcap singing character created by Eric Litwin (2008–2014) and illustrator James Dean that has been on the top 10 picture books list for over 100 weeks (see Table 4.1).

Because of the success of series that originally targeted children in grades 3–5, authors and publishers have either extended these books to students in higher grade levels or, more frequently, developed related series that are accessible to younger or struggling readers. Dav Pilkey (1997–2015, 2000–2014), author of the Captain Underpants series, later developed the Ricky Ricotta's Mighty Robot

Table 4.1. *The New York Times* Best-Selling Children's Series Books as of August 2014

Series	Synopsis	Interest Level	Number of Weeks on the Top 10 Children's Book Lists
Collins, S. (2008–2015). The hunger games [Series]. New York, NY: Scholastic.	A girl fights for survival.	Ages 12+	204
Kinney, J. (2007–2014). Diary of a wimpy kid [Series]. New York, NY: Amulet.	Adolescence in cartoons	Ages 9–12	288
Litwin, E. (2008–2014). Pete the cat [Series]. New York, NY: HarperCollins.	Pete shows off his well-shod feet.	Ages 3–7	101
Meyer, S. (2005–2008). Twilight saga [Series]. New York, NY: Little, Brown.	Vampires and werewolves in high school	Ages 12+	219
Osborne, M.P. (& various coauthors). (1992–2014). Magic tree house [Series]. New York, NY: Random House Children's.	Children travel in time.	Ages 6–9	272
Park, B. (1992–2014). Junie B. Jones [Series]. New York, NY: Random House.	Antics in the classroom	Ages 4–8	180
Riordan, R. (2005–2009). Percy Jackson & the Olympians [Series]. New York, NY: Disney·Hyperion.	A boy battles mythological monsters.	Ages 9–12	338
Rowling, J.K. (1997–2007). Harry Potter [Series]. New York, NY: Scholastic.	A boy wizard fights evil.	Ages 10+	309

Note. Adapted from *The New York Times* Children's Book Lists online archive on August 10, 2014.

books, a similar series written at a lower readability level (see Table 4.2 for titles at a range of difficulty levels).

Similarly, Joanna Cole (1986–2010; Cole, Brimner, & West, 1998–1999) created the Liz books for students reading on the first- or second-grade level to capitalize on the interest generated by the more difficult The Magic School Bus

Table 4.2. Sampling of Series Books by Dav Pilkey

Book	Reading Level
Captain Underpants series (interest level: grades 3–5)	
Pilkey, D. (1997). *The adventures of Captain Underpants.* New York, NY: Scholastic.	3.5
Pilkey, D. (1999). *Captain Underpants and the attack of the talking toilets.* New York, NY: Scholastic.	4.2
Pilkey, D. (2003). *Captain Underpants and the big, bad battle of the Bionic Booger Boy, part 1: The night of the nasty nostril nuggets.* New York, NY: Scholastic.	3.9
Pilkey, D. (2006). *Captain Underpants and the preposterous plight of the purple potty people.* New York, NY: Scholastic.	5.2
Ricky Ricotta's Mighty Robot series (interest level: grades K–5)	
Pilkey, D. (2000). *Ricky Ricotta's Mighty Robot.* New York, NY: Scholastic.	1.8
Pilkey, D. (2000). *Ricky Ricotta's Mighty Robot vs. the Mutant Mosquitoes from Mercury.* New York, NY: Scholastic.	2.2
Pilkey, D. (2002). *Ricky Ricotta's Mighty Robot vs. the Jurassic Jackrabbits from Jupiter.* New York, NY: Scholastic.	2.4
Pilkey, D. (2005). *Ricky Ricotta's Mighty Robot vs. the Uranium Unicorns from Uranus.* New York, NY: Scholastic.	2.8

series (see Table 4.3 for a sample of titles at different difficulty levels). For the uninitiated, Liz is a lizard, the class pet in Ms. Frizzle's class. Like all lizards, Liz can live in many diverse environments—a recurring theme of The Magic School Bus series. Given the range of readability now available for many popular series, at least one or two books in a series should be accessible to most readers within a particular grade level, making author or series studies a realistic option for teachers.

Indeed, the adult committed readers in Ross's (1995) ethnography spoke of moving from one set of series books to another as they matured in both interest and reading skill. The early pleasure they experienced in reading series books sustained and motivated them to dip into less familiar and more complex literature, leading them ultimately to read classic literature. What was comforting and appealing to young, relatively novice readers may seem trite, redundant, and formulaic to more proficient readers. However, the very redundancy and formulaic patterns of series books provide support to novice readers at every stage of literacy development—those readers who are developing automaticity in word recognition, those who are building a robust vocabulary, and those who are developing understanding and interpretation of text.

Table 4.3. Sampling of The Magic School Bus Series Books by Joanna Cole and Others

Book	Reading Level
The Magic School Bus series (interest level: grades K–3)	
Cole, J. (1992). *The Magic School Bus on the ocean floor.* New York, NY: Scholastic.	3.5
Cole, J. (1996). *The Magic School Bus inside a beehive.* New York, NY: Scholastic.	3.7
Cole, J. (1998). *The Magic School Bus in the rain forest.* New York, NY: Scholastic.	2.6
Cole, J. (1999). *The Magic School Bus sees stars: A book about stars.* New York, NY: Scholastic.	2.9
The Magic School Bus Liz series (interest level: grades pre-K–2)	
Brimner, L.D. (1998). *Lightning Liz.* New York, NY: Scholastic.	1.5
West, T. (1998). *Liz sorts it out.* New York, NY: Scholastic.	2.1
West, T. (1999). *Liz finds a friend.* New York, NY: Scholastic.	1.9
West, T. (1999). *Liz on the move.* New York, NY: Scholastic.	1.7

Developing Fluency and Automatic Word Recognition From Language Redundancy

A surprising finding of the comprehensive fluency studies initiated at the University of Georgia (Kuhn et al., 2006) was that wide reading of a number of different books was as effective in developing fluency among second graders as repeated readings of exactly the same text. With the repetition of names (e.g., characters' names, the names of places) and other potentially troublesome vocabulary typical of series books, it is easy to see that reading all of the Ricky Ricotta's Mighty Robot books or The Magic Tree House books would provide ample support for fluent reading. For example, Chapter 2 of *Ricky Ricotta's Mighty Robot* (Pilkey, 2000a) is entitled "The Bullies." There are only 85 words in that chapter, but every 12th word or so is *bullies*, as in the following excerpt:

> This was because Ricky was very small, and sometimes bullies picked on him.
> "Where do you think you are going?" asked one of the bullies.
> Ricky did not answer. He turned and started to run.
> The bullies chased him. (pp. 9–12)

Experiencing Complex Language
and Challenging Vocabulary in Context

One of the most accepted ideas in educational research is that reading supports language development. Several decades ago, Chomsky (1972) demonstrated that experience with children's literature is the most powerful correlate of advanced language development in children 7–10 years old—even more so than age, IQ, family income, or mother's education. She was speaking of children's understanding of complex syntax (embedded ideas in sentences), and many studies since then have demonstrated the contribution of wide reading to vocabulary development as well. Although much has been made of the importance of oral language development and children's interactions with parents recently (see, e.g., Hart & Risley, 1995), it is through reading that children and adolescents are exposed to challenging vocabulary.

Rare words—that is, words with more specialized meanings that are not likely to be used frequently—appear as often in preschool books as in conversations among college graduates (Hayes & Ahrens, 1988). Rare words appear slightly more often in children's books than in transcripts of expert witness testimony, and comic books include more than twice as many rare words as expert testimony. Clearly, reading a lot will give children and adolescents many more opportunities to experience vocabulary in context and many more exposures to nuanced meanings of words.

As Stahl (2003) pointed out, it is through repeated encounters with a word that readers develop an idea of its meaning. He noted that prior studies found that four encounters with a word are not enough to learn it, but 12 encounters are. Each time readers see a word in context, they learn a bit more about it. Stahl called this incremental learning over multiple exposures. Students who engage in wide reading will have many more exposures to challenging words, so many more opportunities to add to their knowledge of vocabulary.

Even though series books have a reputation for being easy, there are innumerable challenging vocabulary words presented in very rich contexts. Take, for example, this description of an interaction between Ms. Ribble, a cranky old teacher, and the hapless principal, Mr. Krupp, taken from *Captain Underpants and the Wrath of the Wicked Wedgie Woman* by Dav Pilkey (2001):

> She opened the card and read the inside.
> "Will you marry me? Signed Mr. Krupp."
> "Eeeeeeeeeeeeeeeeeeeeeeeeeeeewww!" cried the children. The teachers gasped. Then the room grew silent. Ms. Ribble glared over at Mr. Krupp, who had turned bright red and began sweating profusely. (p. 46)

Similarly, Stephan Pastis (2013–2014), cartoonist and creator of Timmy Failure, a memo-writing school phobic turned "detective," imbues his character with not only misplaced confidence in his "greatness," often to laugh-out-loud comic effect, but also an unusually mature vocabulary for expressing his perceptions, albeit delusional, of his popularity among peers in school and his acumen in solving "crimes." The first book in the series, *Timmy Failure: Mistakes Were Made* (Pastis, 2013), looks a lot like the format of the wildly popular Diary of a Wimpy Kid series and includes a possibly imaginary pet polar bear, a riff on the popular comic strip *Calvin and Hobbes* by Bill Watterson. Timmy sometimes flat-out explains what particular words mean, as in this passage:

> I have to depend on my business partner, who I asked to do some reconnaissance in my absence. That means scoping out the scene of the crime and gathering information in a discreet way that does not draw attention. (p. 59)

However, more often than not, Timmy's cartoonlike drawings convey to the reader the meaning of challenging and likely unfamiliar words. In introducing the reader to "smart" kids in his class, for example, Timmy references "the girl whose face I've obscured" (p. 20) by drawing a little girl with a black box covering her entire head—completely redacting her face! Similarly, Pastis depicts "the rotund boy... Rollo Tookus" (p. 19) by drawing a very round boy and giving him the name Rollo.

Noticing the Conventions of Reading for Understanding and Interpretation

Literary critic Peter Rabinowitz (1987/1998) describes the rules of notice and signification that are automatic for proficient readers but must be learned by the novice. Although automatic and invisible, these rules enable understanding and interpretation of narratives. Because series books are formulaic and inherently highly patterned, many of the conventions of reading, such as challenging vocabulary, are made explicit to the novice, thereby easing the transition into longer and longer stretches of text.

Because series books are formulaic and inherently highly patterned, many of the conventions of reading, such as challenging vocabulary, are made explicit to the novice, thereby easing the transition into longer and longer stretches of text.

Chapter titles need to be noticed and support understanding, often serving as minisummaries. For example, in *Ricky Ricotta's Mighty Robot*, Chapter 11 is entitled "The Big Battle," Chapter 14 "Justice Prevails," and Chapter 15 "Back Home" (Pilkey, 2000a, pp. 65, 103, 105), providing a succinct summary of the plot. The names of characters, not subtle at all in most series books, provide clues about what to expect from them. In *Ricky Ricotta's Mighty Robot*, one of the characters is Dr. Stinky McNasty—clearly a villain.

Repetitions bear noticing as well. Ricky Ricotta is a lonely mouse, pining for a friend. His father tells him, "Someday something BIG will happen, and you will find a friend" (Pilkey, 2000a, p. 8). Later, at the end of Chapter 2 (beginning and final sentences in chapters are important, too), this idea is repeated: "And *every* day, Ricky wished that something BIG would happen" (p. 14); and again, at the beginning of Chapter 3, "Ricky did not know that something BIG was about to happen, but it was!" (p. 16). The big event was the arrival of the robot on Earth, a turning point in the story.

Typographical features such as italics, or all capital letters as in the previous examples, are also flags to pay attention. Sometimes italics signal a flashback or a change in point of view. In the Ricky Ricotta example, the word *big* in all capital letters is a play on words—something big, meaning important, was going to happen, but the new character, Mighty Robot, was literally monstrously huge.

In Geronimo Stilton, a series by Geronimo Stilton (2000–2015), the pseudonym of Elisabetta Dami, about a well-mannered mouse journalist of *The Rodent's Gazette* and a best-selling author who happens to find himself in a number of risky and peculiar ventures, words are not just capitalized and italicized, but they also take on a life of their own, supporting the novice reader. Take, for example, this passage from *The Stinky Cheese Vacation* (Stilton, 2014): "It was a dreary November evening. A cold wind blew, shaking the last dry leaves from the branches of the trees that swayed just outside my office window" (p. 1). The text itself illustrates the use of imagery to support word learning, making the words and the meanings more memorable. The letters in the word *cold* are blue topped with snow, and the word *shaking* literally appears to be shuddering on the page.

Occasionally, one of the characters in the series will come right out and tell the reader exactly what's significant to know to understand the story.

Occasionally, one of the characters in the series will come right out and tell the reader exactly what's significant to know to understand the story. Such is the case in the following excerpt from *Ramona the Pest* by Beverly Cleary (1968/1982), which Rabinowitz (1987/1998) uses to illustrate a rule of significance—that the writer does not need to tell the reader every detail about a particular character, only what is relevant to the story:

> Miss Binney stood in front of her class and began to read aloud from *Mike Mulligan and His Steam Shovel*....Ramona...listened quietly with the rest of the kindergarten to the story of Mike Mulligan's old-fashioned steam shovel, which proved its worth by digging the basement for the new town hall of Poppersville in a single day....
>
> "Miss Binney, I want to know—how did Mike Mulligan go to the bathroom when he was digging the basement of the town hall?"

Miss Binney's smile seemed to last longer than smiles usually last. Ramona glanced uneasily around and saw that others were waiting with interest for the answer....

"Well—" said Miss Binney at last. "I don't really know, Ramona. The book doesn't tell us....The reason the book does not tell us how Mike Mulligan went to the bathroom is that it is not an important part of the story. The story is about digging the basement of the town hall, and that is what the book tells us." (Cleary, 1968/1982, pp. 22–24)

As these examples suggest, the patterned structure of series books offers the novice explicit guidance, scaffolding the reader's comprehension of increasingly longer and more complex texts.

Providing Opportunities to Develop Inferences at a Deeper Level

Inference building is hard work for inexperienced readers in that it requires the reader to hold in mind events that take place early on and relate them to subsequent events to develop an understanding of the text as a coherent whole. Taking again the example of Timmy Failure, the character narrator of the story of mistakes that were made, the author (Pastis, 2013) places a firm hand on the reader's shoulder to guide him or her toward the realization that Timmy is not reliable. According to literary theorist Phelan (2005), characters who tell their own stories perform three functions: They report what they experience, they interpret that experience, and they evaluate it. "A character narrator is 'unreliable' when he or she offers an account of some event, person, thought, thing, or other object in the narrative world that deviates from the account the implied author would offer" (p. 49). When the reader realizes that the narrator's words cannot be trusted, the reader either rejects what the narrator says outright and constructs another view, or accepts the narrator's telling but "supplement[s] the account" (p. 51). In other words, the reader must hold in mind what he or she knows thus far in the story and develop an interpretation that differs from that of the narrator, referencing the text world to support the alternative interpretation. For example, in *Timmy Failure: Mistakes Were Made*, the author draws a sad scene in which Timmy is sitting by himself petting his imaginary pet polar bear through a chain link fence while the rest of his class plays kickball. Timmy tells the reader,

> When lunch is over, we have fifteen minutes to play whatever we want. Most kids play kickball. I sit by the fence and pet Total.
> ....What I will talk about is the fact that my sitting by the fence is hard on the other schoolchildren.
> Hard because I am popular and they want to spend time with me. (pp. 34–35)

Timmy goes on to say that he and the yard lady spend most recesses together: "But that's okay. It's all part of being popular" (p. 37).

Through drawings and text, the author makes explicit that Timmy's view is at odds with reality and that he is an unreliable narrator. Timmy's cluelessness provides the humor in the series but also invites the reader to think about the character on a different level—his relation to school, especially tests, and his home experiences and how those may influence his feelings about himself. Exposing readers to a broad range of texts beyond the canon of traditional children's literature— and certainly comic journals such as those of Pastis and Kinney—will make available a variety of interpretive strategies.

Exposing readers to a broad range of texts beyond the canon of traditional children's literature— and certainly comic journals such as those of Pastis and Kinney— will make available a variety of interpretive strategies.

Building and Affirming Identity: Embracing Diversity

Besides the embedded scaffolds that are supportive of novice readers, reading series books can help build and affirm a reading identity. It is important not to overlook how finding the "just right" series can become a life-changing event in a child's reading career. Being able to connect to familiar cultural narratives and main characters who represent that culture is critical for children in today's diverse classrooms.

For the longest time, series books have depicted and embraced a kaleidoscope of main characters that all manner of young readers could identify with. In 1945, Pippi Longstocking, a mighty, kind, and quirky heroine created by Swedish author Astrid Lindgren (1950–2001), started her journey of taking over the hearts and bookshelves of children around the world. Pippi, not a typical child of her time, paved the way for many girls to discover that they too could be tough and adventurous. The Tía Lola series, which Julia Alvarez (2001–2011) initially wrote for her nephew, tells the story of an aunt (kind of a Hispanic Mary Poppins) who flies to Vermont from the Dominican Republic to take care of Miguel and his sister after their parents' divorce, and as the title of the first book in the series suggests—*How Tía Lola Came to ~~Visit~~ Stay* (Alvarez, 2001)—Tía Lola stayed. With humorous and entertaining plots, these books grapple with complex issues of our time, such as dealing with divorce, finding one's cultural and linguistic identity, and learning to fit in.

Most recently, author and librarian Jacqueline Jules (2010–2014) introduced Freddie Ramos, a typical boy living in an apartment building by the train tracks who one day finds a pair of extraordinary shoes that give him Zapato Power! Similar to Timmy Failure, Freddie is raised by a single mother who works hard to make ends meet. With Spanish interspersed throughout the book and home experiences that young readers can relate to, Zapato Power books connect children's worlds to a literary text.

When cultural and linguistic heritage is affirmed and validated through reading materials offered for self-selected reading, students have greater motivation to engage in literacy practices in and out of school. In her work with poor, working-class, preteen girls, Hicks (2004) argues that "particular forms of language invoke certain identities and address specific reading audiences" (p. 65). With purposeful introduction of diverse texts that value all languages and identities, teachers open spaces where students' lived experiences are treasured, identities are negotiated, and the concepts of self are reimagined. And because schools are active institutions in identity construction, including reading identity, the nature and the number of texts made available to students matter a whole lot!

Reading a Lot Makes People Smarter

In studies of out-of-school reading by fifth graders, researchers (Anderson, Wilson, & Fielding, 1988) have found great variability in the time these upper elementary students spend reading (see Table 4.4). Those who read the most read an average of 90 minutes each day, whereas those who read the least read less than one minute a day! Students who read a lot (i.e., those at the 90th percentile) read as many minutes in a few days as students at the 10th percentile read in a whole year. The authors of *Becoming a Nation of Readers: The Report of the Commission on Reading* (Anderson, Hiebert, Scott, & Wilkinson, 1985) extrapolate stunning implications from these studies—namely, that increasing out-of-school reading time by just a few minutes each day will increase standardized test scores by up to 10 percentile points.

Other compelling evidence that wide reading supports achievement comes from studies of summer reading loss. Close examination of achievement test scores before and after summer break led researchers to notice that students from middle class homes appeared to gain a month or so in their reading level each summer but that children from low-income families appeared to lose two or more months each summer. Digging deeper into the data, researchers discovered that the

Table 4.4. Total Minutes of Reading Each Day

Readers' Percentile Rank	Minutes
98	90.7
90	40.4
80	31.1
70	21.7
60	18.1
50	12.9
40	8.6
30	5.8
20	3.1
10	1.6
2	0.2

Note. Data from "Growth in Reading and How Children Spend Their Time Outside of School," by R.C. Anderson, P.T. Wilson, and L.G. Fielding, 1988, *Reading Research Quarterly, 23*(3), p. 292. Copyright 1988 by the International Reading Association.

summer activity that made the difference was reading, an activity available to advantaged youths but, unfortunately, not to those without easy access to books or libraries.

As these studies demonstrate, differences in time spent reading likely will translate into significant disparities in reading achievement over the course of a school year or many school years. Close reading, or as Rabinowitz (1987/1998) notes, "deep reading can complement wide reading, but it cannot replace it" (p. 231). Clearly, teachers and parents must do everything in their power to make books accessible, to encourage reading, to develop engagement, to nurture reading for pleasure, and most importantly, to honor children's and adolescents' preferences for books. Through the ages—or at least the past 100 years—series books have made readers and kept them reading.

Including Book Series Discussions in Professional Learning Communities

Time is a precious commodity in schools today, but dedicating a portion of collaborative time to selecting series books that can promote literacy and engagement in classrooms seems warranted. Choosing to focus a portion of the professional learning community time on researching series books and their integration within daily instruction can be a lot of fun and an opportunity for drawing on the expertise of the school librarian. From research, we know that students are more likely to pick up books that were previously read and discussed by their teacher. Thus, introducing series books through interactive read-alouds or engaging book trailers can be a successful pathway to get students hooked on reading.

However, prior to the class read-aloud, it is necessary that teachers familiarize themselves with the book content through careful, in-depth reading. We recommend that the book be read at least twice: the first time as a proficient reader, a teacher, looking for opportunities to address specific standards and skills, and the second time as a struggling reader, noticing and noting possible roadblocks in vocabulary, plot, or ideas presented in the text.

Highlighting and jotting down what a particular series offers in terms of overarching literacy goals is critical for ensuring instructional cohesion and pedagogical purpose. For instance, books in the Timmy Failure or Geronimo Stilton series offer a number of built-in strategies for making complex vocabulary accessible. Emphasizing the use of illustrations and typographical features to assist with vocabulary comprehension can help students become strategic in reading literature and, possibly, other contexts across content areas. Reading as a novice reader, thinking deeply about parts of the text that might startle or confuse students, helps teachers purposefully select stopping points in the book where think-alouds and class discussions will be most beneficial.

REFERENCES

Anderson, R.C., Hiebert, E.H., Scott, J.A., & Wilkinson, I.A.G. (1985). *Becoming a nation of readers: The report of the Commission on Reading.* Washington, DC: National Institute of Education, U.S. Department of Education.

Anderson, R.C., Wilson, P.T., & Fielding, L.G. (1988). Growth in reading and how children spend their time outside of school. *Reading Research Quarterly, 23*(3), 285–303. doi:10.1598/RRQ.23.3.2

Chomsky, C. (1972). Stages in language development and reading exposure. *Harvard Educational Review, 42*(1), 1–33.

Hart, B., & Risley, T.R. (1995). *Meaningful differences in the everyday experience of young American children.* Baltimore, MD: Paul H. Brookes.

Hayes, D.P., & Ahrens, M.G. (1988). Vocabulary simplification for children: A special case of 'motherese'? *Journal of Child Language, 15*(2), 395–410. doi:10.1017/S0305000900012411

Hicks, D. (2004). Back to Oz? Rethinking the literary in a critical study of reading. *Research in the Teaching of English, 39*(1), 63–84.

Kuhn, M.R., Schwanenflugel, P.J., Morris, R.D., Morrow, L.M., Woo, D.G., Meisinger, E.B., ... Stahl, S.A. (2006). Teaching children to become fluent and automatic readers. *Journal of Literacy Research, 38*(4), 357–387. doi:10.1207/s15548430jlr3804_1

Phelan, J. (2005). *Living to tell about it: A rhetoric and ethics of character narration.* Ithaca, NY: Cornell University Press.

Rabinowitz, P.J. (1998). *Before reading: Narrative conventions and the politics of interpretation.* Columbus: Ohio State University Press. (Original work published 1987)

Ross, C.S. (1995). "If they read Nancy Drew, so what?": Series book readers talk back. *Library & Information Science Research, 17*(3), 201–236. doi:10.1016/0740-8188(95)90046-2

Ross, C.S., McKechnie, L., & Rothbauer, P.M. (2006). *Reading matters: What the research reveals about reading, libraries, and community.* Westport, CT: Libraries Unlimited.

Stahl, S.A. (2003). How words are learned incrementally over multiple exposures. *American Educator, 27*(1), 18–19, 44.

Stelter, B. (2008, March 25). 'Goosebumps' rises from the literary grave. *The New York Times.* Retrieved from www.nytimes.com/2008/03/25/books/25stin.html

LITERATURE CITED

Alvarez, J. (2001). *How Tía Lola came to visit stay.* New York, NY: Knopf Books for Young Readers.

Alvarez, J. (2001–2011). Tía Lola [Series]. New York, NY: Knopf Books for Young Readers.

Brimner, L.D. (1998). *Lightning Liz.* New York, NY: Scholastic.

Cleary, B. (1982). *Ramona the pest.* New York, NY: Dell. (Original work published 1968)

Cole, J. (1986–2010). The Magic School Bus [Series]. New York, NY: Scholastic.

Cole, J. (1992). *The Magic School Bus on the ocean floor.* New York, NY: Scholastic.

Cole, J. (1996). *The Magic School Bus inside a beehive.* New York, NY: Scholastic.

Cole, J. (1998). *The Magic School Bus in the rain forest.* New York, NY: Scholastic.

Cole, J. (1999). *The Magic School Bus sees stars: A book about stars.* New York, NY: Scholastic.

Cole, J., Brimner, L.D., & West, T. (1998–1999). Liz [Series]. New York, NY: Scholastic.

Collins, S. (2008–2015). The hunger games [Series]. New York, NY: Scholastic.

Jules, J. (2010–2014). Zapato Power [Series]. Chicago, IL: Albert Whitman.

Kinney, J. (2007–2014). Diary of a wimpy kid [Series]. New York, NY: Amulet.

Lewis, C.S. (1950–1956). The chronicles of Narnia [Series]. New York, NY: HarperCollins.

Lindgren, A. (1950–2001). Pippi Longstocking [Series]. New York, NY: Viking.

Litwin, E. (2008–2014). Pete the cat [Series]. New York, NY: HarperCollins.

Martin, G.R.R. (1996–2011). A song of ice and fire [Series]. New York, NY: Bantam.

Meyer, S. (2005–2008). Twilight saga [Series]. New York, NY: Little, Brown.

Osborne, M.P. (& various coauthors). (1992–2014). Magic tree house [Series]. New York, NY: Random House Children's.

Park, B. (1992–2014). Junie B. Jones [Series]. New York, NY: Random House.

Pastis, S. (2013). *Timmy Failure: Mistakes were made.* Somerville, MA: Candlewick.

Pastis, S. (2013–2014). Timmy Failure [Series]. Somerville, MA: Candlewick.

Pilkey, D. (1997). *The adventures of Captain Underpants.* New York, NY: Scholastic.

Pilkey, D. (1997–2015). Captain Underpants [Series]. New York, NY: Blue Sky.

Pilkey, D. (1999). *Captain Underpants and the attack of the talking toilets.* New York, NY: Scholastic.

Pilkey, D. (2000a). *Ricky Ricotta's Mighty Robot.* New York, NY: Scholastic.

Pilkey, D. (2000b). *Ricky Ricotta's Mighty Robot vs. the Mutant Mosquitoes from Mercury.* New York, NY: Scholastic.

Pilkey, D. (2000–2014). Ricky Ricotta's Mighty Robot [Series]. New York, NY: Blue Sky.

Pilkey, D. (2001). *Captain Underpants and the wrath of the wicked Wedgie Woman.* New York, NY: Scholastic.

Pilkey, D. (2002). *Ricky Ricotta's Mighty Robot vs. the Jurassic Jackrabbits from Jupiter.* New York, NY: Scholastic.

Pilkey, D. (2003). *Captain Underpants and the big, bad battle of the Bionic Booger Boy, part 1: The night of the nasty nostril nuggets.* New York, NY: Scholastic.

Pilkey, D. (2005). *Ricky Ricotta's Mighty Robot vs. the Uranium Unicorns from Uranus.* New York, NY: Scholastic.

Pilkey, D. (2006). *Captain Underpants and the preposterous plight of the purple potty people.* New York, NY: Scholastic.

Riordan, R. (2005–2009). Percy Jackson & the Olympians [Series]. New York, NY: Disney·Hyperion.

Riordan, R. (2008). *The maze of bones.* New York, NY: Scholastic.

Riordan, R., Korman, G., Lerangis, P., Watson, J., Carman, P., Park, L.S., … Standiford, N. (2008–2015). 39 clues [Series]. New York, NY: Scholastic.

Rowling, J.K. (1997–2007). Harry Potter [Series]. New York, NY: Scholastic.

Stilton, G. (Elisabetta Dami). (2000–2015). Geronimo Stilton [Series]. New York, NY: Scholastic.

Stilton, G. (Elisabetta Dami). (2014). *The stinky cheese vacation* (J. Heim, Trans.). New York, NY: Scholastic.

Stine, R.L. (1992–1997). Goosebumps [Series]. New York, NY: Scholastic.

West, T. (1998). *Liz sorts it out.* New York, NY: Scholastic.

West, T. (1999a). *Liz finds a friend.* New York, NY: Scholastic.

West, T. (1999b). *Liz on the move.* New York, NY: Scholastic.

OTHER RECOMMENDED CHILDREN'S SERIES

Adler, D.A. (1980–2014).Cam Jansen [Series]. New York, NY: Viking.

Bridwell, N. (1963–2014). Clifford [Series]. New York, NY: Scholastic.

Brown, M. (1976–2011). Arthur [Series]. Boston, MA: Little, Brown.

Capucilli, A.S. (1996–2015). Biscuit [Series]. New York, NY: HarperCollins.

Danziger, P., Coville, B., & Levy, E. (1994–2014). Amber Brown [Series]. New York, NY: Scholastic.

Hunter, E., (Kate Cary, Cherith Baldry, & Tui Sutherland). (2003–2015). Warriors [Series]. New York, NY: HarperCollins.

McDonald, M. (2000–2014). Judy Moody [Series]. Cambridge, MA: Candlewick.

Rylant, C. (1987–2010). Henry and Mudge [Series]. New York, NY: Aladdin.

Schachner, J. (2003–2014). Skippyjon Jones [Series]. New York, NY: Grosset & Dunlap.

Smith, J. (1991–2004). Bone [Series]. Columbus, OH: Cartoon.

Stilton, T. (Elisabetta Dami). (2009–2014). Thea Stilton [Series]. New York, NY: Scholastic.

RECOMMENDED SERIES BOOKS WEBSITES

The Berenstain Bears (Stan, Jan, & Mike Berenstain): www.berenstainbears.com

Dork Diaries (Rachel Renée Russell): dorkdiaries.com

Junie B. Jones (Barbara Park): www.juniebjones.com

Magic Tree House (Mary Pope Osborne): www.magictreehouse.com

Percy Jackson and the Olympians (Rick Riordan): www.rickriordan.com/ my-books/percy-jackson/percy-jackson-olympians.aspx

Skippyjon Jones' Closet (Judy Schachner): www.skippyjonjones.com

Warriors (Erin Hunter: Kate Cary, Cherith Baldry, & Tui Sutherland): www.warriorcats.com

Wimpy Kid (Jeff Kinney): www.wimpykid.com

ABOUT THE AUTHORS

Anne McGill-Franzen is a professor of education in the Department of Theory and Practice in Teacher Education and the director of the Reading Center at the University of Tennessee, Knoxville, USA. Formerly a reading specialist and classroom teacher, she has written extensively on early literacy as well as reading disabilities and instructional interventions to mitigate the problems faced by struggling readers and their classroom teachers. Anne is a coeditor of *Summer Reading: Closing the Rich/Poor Reading Achievement Gap* (Teachers College Press & International Reading Association, 2013) and *Handbook of Reading Disability Research* (Routledge, 2011), a coauthor of *No More Summer-Reading Loss* (Heinemann, 2013), and the author of *Kindergarten Literacy: Matching Assessment and Instruction in Kindergarten* (Scholastic, 2006). She can be contacted at amcgillf@utk.edu.

Natalia Ward is currently a PhD student and a graduate teaching associate in the Department of Theory and Practice in Teacher Education at the University of Tennessee, Knoxville, USA. She assists with teacher education courses on topics of diagnosing and remediation of reading difficulties and emergent literacy. Previously, Natalia taught English as a second language in K–12 public school settings in the United States and Russia. In 2013, she was named the East Tennessee ESL Educator of the Year by Tennessee Teachers of Speakers of Other Languages. Natalia can be contacted at nward2@utk.edu.

PART II

Investigating Texts and Images

CHAPTER 5

Illustrations in Picture Books

The Art of Reading Images

Cyndi Giorgis, *University of Texas at El Paso*

> *The most difficult part for me is that stage between writing/thinking/*
> *sketching and beginning the final art. I am always fearful that I won't be*
> *able to execute the idea to its full potential. Because the art style is, for me,*
> *determined by the text, I am often experimenting with a new style designed*
> *specifically for each book. This is at once exciting and frightening!*
>
> —Seeger (as quoted in Danielson, 2012, para. 33)

Picture books appeal to readers of all ages because they offer a compelling interplay between text and illustrations. Wolfenbarger and Sipe (2007) state, "In a picturebook, words and pictures never tell exactly the same story. It is this dissonance that catches the reader's attention" (p. 274). Scholars agree that reading pictures is indeed a multifaceted act (Pantaleo, 2005). In addition, children often look at illustrations more closely and see details in the pictures (Kiefer, 1995) that are missed by "skipping and scanning" adults (Meek, 1988, p. 19). Therefore, children are generally more proficient and skilled at reading images, such as those in picture books, as they attend to the illustrations to interpret the perceived meaning of the story.

A picture book has been defined as an aesthetic object, an art form (Bader, 1976). It is one in which text and illustration work in concert to create meaning (Serafini & Giorgis, 2003). How this meaning is generated is dependent on the relationship of the illustrations to the text. This relationship has been viewed by scholars in five unique ways (Agosto, 1999; Nikolajeva & Scott, 2000):

1. *Symmetry:* The illustrations closely correlate with the text rather than adding varied interpretations or nuances. Robert McCloskey's (1941,

Children's Literature in the Reading Program: Engaging Young Readers in the 21st Century (4th ed.), edited by Deborah A. Wooten & Bernice E. Cullinan. © 2015 by the International Literacy Association.

1948) books, such as *Make Way for Ducklings* and *Blueberries for Sal*, demonstrate this category in that the illustrations reflect what has been stated in the text.

2. *Complementary:* Words and illustrations provide different but complementary information. *Oh, No!* by Candace Fleming (2012) provides a bouncy rhyme coupled with Eric Rohmann's relief prints that follow the plight of various animals as they fall into a hole (Oh, no!) while a salivating tiger lurks nearby.

3. *Enhancement:* The illustrations enhance or extend the text while providing opportunities for multiple interpretations. Mo Willems's (2003, 2008) pigeon books, *Don't Let the Pigeon Drive the Bus!* and *The Pigeon Wants a Puppy!*, depict a hilarious and unflinching character who pleads, wheedles, and begs in an attempt to get what he thinks he wants, but is sometimes surprised by the outcome.

4. *Counterpoint:* Words and illustrations tell different stories. In *Wolves* by Emily Gravett (2006), Rabbit borrows *Wolves* (by E Grrrabbit!) from the West Bucks Public Burrowing Library and is totally unaware that the information he is reading becomes a suspenseful tale for the reader. Gravett (2009, 2010) also uses this device in many of her other books, such as *Spells* and *The Rabbit Problem*.

5. *Contradiction:* Illustrations seem to be contrary to the text. In *Dear Mrs. LaRue: Letters From Obedience School*, Mark Teague (2002) employs a split spread to illustrate Ike's imaginative letter writing contrasted to the reality of his obedience school experience. Mem Fox's (1994) classic *Tough Boris* tells of the tough, scary, and greedy pirate, but the illustrations convey a much different character who is kind and compassionate.

In discussing picture books, children may not know the terms indicated in this list, but they often demonstrate their understanding of the relationship between text and illustrations by the comments and connections that they share through oral or written means.

In discussing picture books, children may not know the terms indicated in this list, but they often demonstrate their understanding of the relationship between text and illustrations by the comments and connections that they share through oral or written means. Students who live in states adopting the Common Core State Standards are being asked to explain how specific aspects of a text's illustrations contribute to what is conveyed by the words in a story, particularly in relation to mood, character, and setting (National Governors Association Center for Best Practices & Council of Chief State School Officers, 2010).

Picture books that teachers and parents might share with students are those receiving a Caldecott Medal or Honor Book award. Each year, the Caldecott Award Selection Committee is charged with the task of reading, analyzing, and discussing the illustrations in picture books that have been published during the preceding year. The committee members consider the visual elements while also deliberating over the physical aspects, such as the book cover, dust jacket, endpapers, title page, and front matter, that might contain storytelling components. Although not consciously tasked with discussing the categories highlighted in the previous list, given that the award is to be given "to the artist of the most distinguished American picture book for children" (Association for Library Service to Children, 2008, para. 1), the members delve into reflecting and pondering the relationship between text and illustration. They recognize that unless it is a wordless picture book, there needs to be interplay between the two given that *every* aspect of the book is meaningful.

According to Sipe (2008b), "the literary understanding of picturebooks includes learning to read the visual text of the illustrational sequence" (p. 18). Picture books provide a source for readers to develop their visual aesthetic understanding (Sipe, 2008a) and an appreciation for the role of visual images in a book's narrative, the art elements, and the principles of design. Each aspect of a picture book is carefully choreographed to create a unified whole.

Elements of Picture Book Design

To assist readers with recognizing how the various aspects of a picture book work together to create meaning, it is beneficial to provide them with an understanding of the elements of book design. The layout and design of a picture book involve a very conscious decision-making process engaged in by the illustrator, art designer, and often the editor. The book's features become an integral part of the total reading experience. It is important to view a picture book as a whole, which begins and ends with the cover of the book, while the endpapers and typography also contribute to the potential for enabling readers to build and interpret story meaning.

Book Covers

The cover of a picture book sets the tone and mood for the story contained inside. It also serves as an invitation to readers, so it's important that the initial illustration displayed on the cover be eye-catching. A removable dust jacket often encases the outside of a book and offers a summary, along with author and illustrator information. An illustration on the dust jacket is often identical to that found on the cover, but sometimes there is a treasure on the hardcover of a book that's discovered after the dust jacket is removed. This treasure may be a different illustration, an embossed image, or a single color. In addition, the illustration found on the cover and/or the dust jacket may or may not be replicated within the book. Decisions about the book cover and dust jacket are often the last to be made and may be influenced by the input of the marketing staff at the publishing company.

Overall, the cover and dust jacket provide the first look for readers who may base their decision on selecting a book merely on this one component.

The cover art of *Grandpa Green* by Lane Smith (2011) presents a fanciful, giant, green elephant topiary and supplies a glimpse into this touching story of family history and the sense of legacy. This attention-grabbing illustration also complements the engaging story inside. Jerry Pinkney's (2009) Caldecott Medal–winning book, *The Lion & the Mouse*, is a wordless adaptation of the classic Aesop fable. The dust jacket features the king of the jungle with a sideways glance that compels the reader to turn the book over, only to discover the mouse gazing back. The book cover underneath the jacket shows two panels—one of the lion and the other of the mouse—while the back cover displays the various animals of the African Serengeti, where the story is set. *All the World* by Liz Garton Scanlon (2009), a story that presents a celebration of the world and humankind, displays a charming watercolor illustration on the cover of the two main characters. However, this particular illustration is not found within the story itself. When readers remove the dust jacket from *The Pilot and the Little Prince: The Life of Antoine de Saint-Exupéry* by Peter Sís (2014), they discover a textured, deep blue cover with the image of a small plane embossed on the front.

Endpapers

When a hardcover picture book is opened, the endpapers are the first and last pages that the reader views. Endpapers serve a practical purpose of holding the pages to the cover, but they also represent a conscious design decision. Endpapers may display a solitary color, a decorative pattern or design, or the beginning of the story. The front endpapers may differ from those at the conclusion of the story and may depict a change that occurs within the book.

In the delightful wordless picture book *Daisy Gets Lost* by Chris Raschka (2013), Daisy the dog loses her way after merrily chasing a squirrel into the woods. The dark, forest green endpapers provide a sense of how Daisy felt surrounded by vegetation while unable to find her owner. The endpapers of Giles Andreae's (1999) *Giraffes Can't Dance* contain three horizontal rows of eight pictures showing gangly giraffe Gerald engaged in a variety of poses. When readers move their eyes across each row, they will insist that Gerald is indeed dancing. Paul Zelinsky's (1997) *Rapunzel* is a stunning interpretation of the classic tale that mimics the masters of the Italian Renaissance. The front endpapers show a villager with his donkey facing to the right, inviting the reader to turn the page and enter the story. On the back endpapers, the reversed image of the Italian Renaissance–style painting depicts the villager looking left, toward the final pages. The front endpapers of *The Zoo* by Suzy Lee (2007) show a gorilla escaping through a break in his cage on the far left side of the spread, while on the far right side, readers will spy a small monkey looking at the gorilla along with the trunk of an elephant peeking out. On the back endpapers, the far right side now has the monkey pictured with his hands on the gorilla's behind as he pushes him back through the break in the cage. The scene on the endpapers of *The Zoo* isn't contained within the pages of the book, as none of the animals are actually depicted inside cages or fences.

Typography

The typography, also referred to as the font or typeface, plays a significant role in the overall design of a picture book. The size and style of the typeface may match the content of the text or the stylistic features of the illustrations. The typeface should complement the illustrations while being readable for the intended audience. The font also offers clues as to how the word or phrase should be read given its size, shape, or color.

Polar Bear Night by Lauren Thompson (2004) contains bold black type that complements the feel of Stephen Savage's linoleum block illustrations. The art director for this retro-style book wanted the type to feel definite and confident, the same way the bear cub feels as she ventures out to explore the world (Marcus, 2012). David Macaulay's (1990) Caldecott Medal winner, *Black and White*, employs four different fonts—one for each seemingly unrelated story about a boy sitting on a train, parents acting silly, a convict's escape, and a tardy commuter train. The font becomes a storytelling device along with the nonlinear plots. Another Caldecott Medal winner, *The House in the Night* by Susan Marie Swanson (2008), imparts a cumulative story featuring a golden key and contains spectacular scratchboard illustrations by Beth Krommes that are splashed with gold. The striking gold color is also used for the font on pages with a black background. Hand-lettered text provides a playful mood in *A Couple of Boys Have the Best Week Ever* by Marla Frazee (2008). Eamon's grandparents plan a week of nature camp for him and his friend, James, but the two boys seem to prefer watching television, eating snacks, and avoiding the great outdoors. However, even the most reluctant of campers can discover something exciting when the adventure is shown onscreen.

Borders and Frames

Borders and frames can envelop text or illustration and be composed of a simple line or contain intricate details. At times, borders are used to add to the overall tone and mood of a picture book. Other times, there are no borders or frames at all, and the illustrations extend beyond the boundaries of the page. Illustrators may also imply the illusion of a border by surrounding the image(s) with white space, which gives the impression of a framed picture.

Allen Say (1993) is known for his portrait-like illustrations in books such as *Grandfather's Journey*, which exhibits large, formally composed paintings in sepia tones to convey Say's family history. Each exquisite watercolor painting is framed with a thin, black line that sets it apart from the text by the use of white space. A bear experiences his first autumn in *Leaves* by David Ezra Stein (2007). The joyously colored illustrations framed in a thin, uneven, black line hang on the pages like paintings, while other times Stein uses white space to convey the expansiveness and excitement of frolicking in the leaves. In *Swamp Angel*, Anne Isaacs's (1994) witty tall tale about Angelica Longrider, who became the greatest woodswoman of Tennessee, the feisty (and gigantic) protagonist breaks the frame in several illustrations, as if she's too large to fit inside the book. Mélanie Watt (2006–2013) uses borders and frames extensively in her series of books about Scaredy Squirrel. Watt's boxes and borders are used to visually separate the illustrations that appear somewhat as a list divided into a grid of nine boxes, all of which illustrate the squirrel's preparedness for potential danger.

Examining the Art Elements in Books by Laura Vaccaro Seeger

In addition to exploring the components of picture book design, it's also advantageous to inform readers about how elements of art are used by illustrators. A way to do this effectively would be to examine the work of one illustrator, such as Laura Vaccaro Seeger. Her picture books are colorful, imaginative, and innovative. *First the Egg* (Seeger, 2007b) and *Green* (Seeger, 2012) have both received a Caldecott Honor Award, and her many other titles have been lauded for various state and organization awards as well. An initial glimpse at Seeger's (2003, 2004, 2008b) *The Hidden Alphabet*, *Lemons Are Not Red*, or *One Boy* might warrant the idea that these are concept books. However, on closer examination, readers will discover that most of her titles contain a narrative storyline along with an ingenious use of artistic and design elements. In addition, the relationships of text and illustration exhibit many of the categories, such as complementary, enhancement, and counterpoint, that were described earlier in the chapter.

> *In addition to exploring the components of picture book design, it's also advantageous to inform readers about how elements of art are used by illustrators.*

Use of Color

Illustrators such as Seeger use color to portray characters, convey mood or emotion, or present a concept. Color is one of the most expressive elements and can range from a full spectrum to black and white. Conscious color choices are made regarding hue, tone, and saturation. Subdued colors can suggest boredom or serenity, whereas intense colors may evoke a sense of excitement or energy.

Lemons Are Not Red presents 12 colors and images by telling what they are not in this interactive book. The reader gains a multidimensional definition and view of each object changing colors, such as on the opening pages: "Lemons are not RED. Lemons are YELLOW. Apples are RED" (n.p.). Seeger cleverly uses a die-cut that initially shows the lemon as red, but then it changes to yellow once the page is turned. In Green, various shades of the color are presented through lush acrylic paintings and skillfully positioned die-cuts. This stunning picture book doesn't focus only on the hues of green but also presents the notion of appreciating nature and the environment.

Use of Line

Line is the most commonly found element of design in picture books (Kiefer, 1995). Each mark on a page begins with a dot that grows into a line that may be slow and rolling, sleek and fast, or quiet and steady. Artists create lines to prompt the reader's eye to move in a particular direction. The use of thin lines creates an elegant or fragile quality, whereas thick or bold lines show strength or provide emphasis.

A stuffed bear and an ebullient dachshund, the best of friends, are featured in a beginning reader series by this author-illustrator. In Dog and Bear: Two Friends, Three Stories, Dog and Bear: Two's Company, and Dog and Bear: Three to Get Ready, Seeger (2007a, 2008a, 2009) uses bold, black lines to outline Dog and Bear, which allows them to stand out against the white background. Lines show movement and are also used to express emotions as the two interact and sometimes disagree. Even the font encompasses lines that appear to be childlike writing.

Use of Perspective

Perspective is an element that artists use to provide another layer of meaning or interpretation of a story. Readers might be given a bird's-eye view by looking down on a scene or a worm's-eye view that gazes up. Illustrators also use the placement of objects or characters on a page to provide perspective. The bottom third of a page is considered the foreground, and items placed in that location draw more attention. The center portion of the page is the middle ground and prompts the reader's eyes to move up or down to view the illustration. Items pictured in the background are smaller in size because they're farther away.

Seeger (2010) uses perspective as both an art element and a storytelling device in *What If?*:

> WHAT IF a boy found a beach ball and kicked it into the ocean?
> WHAT IF two seals found it and began to play?
> WHAT IF a third seal appeared on the beach looking for a friend? (front flap)

Seeger uses the same story with three different outcomes. The two seals are often pictured in the foreground, while the woeful-looking third seal is in the background. Perspective is created through the illustrations as well as the story possibilities that are generated by readers.

Use of Texture

Texture is an element that is found in many of Seeger's picture books. Texture tenders the illusion that an object feels hard or soft, smooth or rough. Readers often have the urge to touch the illustration in an attempt to feel the diversity of textures.

First the Egg contemplates the age-old question, Which came first, the chicken or the egg? Each full-color illustration invites readers to feel the texture of the brushstrokes as well as the well-positioned die-cuts. *Green* also offers texture, from the raised title on the book jacket to the various hues and shades of green on the double-page spreads.

Perusing **Bully**

To understand how the various art elements and design features create an effective picture book, it is beneficial to take a "walk" through Seeger's (2013) *Bully*. In this deceptively simple-looking story, Bully the bull doesn't have anything nice to say to any of his friends. When the other animals ask him to play, he responds in the way he's been taught: "Chicken!" "Slow poke!" or, "You stink!" (n.p.). Seeger's bold, graphic artwork and spare, powerful words provide a tender and thoughtful story.

The dust jacket and book cover display an eye-catching, stop-sign red background that emphasizes the brown bull's surly, if not angry, expression as he stands atop the large title. The title itself is featured in a textured, light brown color. Both the bull and the title are outlined with thick, black lines that provide emphasis against the solid red background. Inside, the endpapers exhibit the same texture as the book title and have a handmade paper quality with a barnyard hay–like appearance. This same paper provides the background on each page throughout *Bully*. Turning to the page after the front endpapers, Seeger provides a context for the story prior to the title page. On this page, she has illustrated a large and very angry, gray bull who roars, "GO AWAY!" to the story's protagonist, making him appear to look small and expressing a look of dejection.

This utterance also sets the story in motion before the title page and launches the angry, little bull on his tirade.

Seeger uses a palette of crisp, flat colors that includes red, brown, gray, pink, yellow, green, and white. Except for the title, which is featured in a bold, red font on the title page, the remaining text consists primarily of insults that are hurled by the little bull to his animal friends. These words are written in black font contained within speech bubbles with a white background.

The space on the pages is uncluttered and focuses on the text and the characters. When the bull shouts, "CHICKEN!" "BUZZ OFF!" or "BUTT OUT!" the font is in large, uppercase letters. As the bull utters each unkind remark, he appears more aggressive and powerful; both his body and the text get larger and larger. But when the feisty goat calls it like it is—"Bully!"—it sends the bull into a physical tailspin and represents his emotional upheaval. The now-deflated bull utters one small word, "Sorry," as a tear rolls down his cheek. His next words to the animals are "Wanna play?"

The final spread of *Bully* shows an opening in the fence, which was previously an unbroken fence line crossing every double-page spread that served as a measure of size, both actual and emotional, as well as a barrier to friendship. This fence opening is more than a casual design element, as it is the gate through which the bull and his newfound friends walk into an altered reality. The 18 words (22 if you count words uttered more than once) present a complicated topic through utter simplicity. The book design of *Bully* is key to the interplay of text and illustration.

What's significant about *Bully* is that the little bull is a sympathetic character throughout the story. Having shown us the reason for his anger, Seeger offers readers a way to root for him. She also provides a way out for the emotionally charged creature. Goat demonstrates that he doesn't need to act like a victim, and the other animals give the bull another chance.

The Art of Reading Images

Creating an awareness of the art and design elements of picture books allows readers to linger longer over illustrations and to appreciate and interpret stories on a deeper level. These elements are all a part of the storytelling process in creating meaning for the reader. Also, if children are to attend to both illustration and text as they make meaning, it is imperative for an adult to model awareness by stopping to discuss how line or color is used or to point out features such as the book cover or endpapers. To further generate understanding, students can be asked the following questions:

- How does the illustrator use line/color/texture/perspective?
- What's depicted on the dust jacket? Is the same illustration on the book cover? Is the illustration(s) found in the story?

- Who do you see in the illustration(s)? Describe them.
- What medium do you think the illustrator used to create the picture?
- What type of font is used? Are words or phrases emphasized using a different font?
- What feelings are evoked by the use of inventive font, type size, color, and word spacing?
- Did the illustrations display exactly what was in the text? If not, how did they differ?
- How have the text and illustration worked together to create meaning?

Art and text together create a relationship that allows them to reflect and expand on each other and hence create greater meaning than either can convey independently.

An illustrator study also provides an opportunity to view an individual's books, such as Seeger's, in further depth and detail. Invite students to select a favorite illustrator and read multiple books illustrated by that individual, taking time to linger over the book covers, endpapers, title pages, and illustrations. Share information with students about the illustrator, the medium that he or she uses, and the individual's process for creating art. Next, start a discussion, with examples drawn from individual books, about how elements of the books' design enhance the mood or theme of the stories. Have students create a visual response to the illustrator's work, using the same medium, if possible.

It's important for readers to recognize and understand the ways in which text and illustration work together. Art and text together create a relationship that allows them to reflect and expand on each other and hence create greater meaning than either can convey independently.

REFERENCES

Agosto, D.E. (1999). One and inseparable: Interdependent storytelling in picture storybooks. *Children's Literature in Education, 30*(4), 267–280. doi:10.1023/A:1022471922077

Association for Library Service to Children. (2008). *Caldecott Medal—terms and criteria* (Rev. ed.). Retrieved from www.ala.org/alsc/awardsgrants/bookmedia/caldecottmedal/caldecottterms/caldecottterms

Bader, B. (1976). *American picturebooks from* Noah's Ark *to* The Beast Within. New York, NY: Macmillan.

Danielson, J. (2012, April 17). Seven questions over breakfast with Laura Vaccaro Seeger [Web log post]. Retrieved from blaine.org/sevenimpossiblethings/?p=2331

Kiefer, B.Z. (1995). *The potential of picturebooks: From visual literacy to aesthetic understanding.* Englewood Cliffs, NJ: Merrill.

Marcus, L.S. (2012). Give 'em Helvetica: Typeface as an integral part of picture book design. *Horn Book Magazine, 88*(5), 40–46.

Meek, M. (1988). *How texts teach what readers learn.* Stroud, UK: Thimble.

National Governors Association Center for Best Practices & Council of Chief State School Officers. (2010). *Common Core State Standards for English language* arts and literacy in history/social studies, science, and technical subjects. Washington, DC: Authors.

Nikolajeva, M., & Scott, C. (2000). The dynamics of picturebook communication. *Children's Literature in Education, 31*(4), 225–239.

Pantaleo, S. (2005). "Reading" young children's visual texts. *Early Childhood Research & Practice, 7*(1). Retrieved from ecrp.uiuc.edu/v7n1/pantaleo.html

Serafini, F., & Giorgis, C. (2003). *Reading aloud and beyond: Fostering the intellectual life with older readers.* Portsmouth, NH: Heinemann.

Sipe, L.R. (2008a). Learning from illustrations in picturebooks. In N. Frey & D. Fisher (Eds.), *Teaching visual literacy: Using comic books, graphic novels, anime, cartoons, and more to develop comprehension and thinking skills* (pp. 131–148). Thousand Oaks, CA: Corwin.

Sipe, L.R. (2008b). *Storytime: Young children's literary understanding in the classroom.* New York, NY: Teachers College Press.

Wolfenbarger, C.D., & Sipe, L.R. (2007). A unique visual and literary art form: Recent research on picturebooks. *Language Arts, 84*(3), 273–280.

CHILDREN'S LITERATURE CITED

Andreae, G. (1999). *Giraffes can't dance.* New York, NY: Orchard.

Fleming, C. (2012). *Oh, no!* New York, NY: Schwartz & Wade.

Fox, M. (1994). *Tough Boris.* San Diego, CA: Harcourt Brace.

Frazee, M. (2008). *A couple of boys have the best week ever.* New York, NY: Harcourt.

Gravett, E. (2006). *Wolves.* New York, NY: Simon & Schuster Books for Young Readers.

Gravett, E. (2009). *Spells.* New York, NY: Simon & Schuster Books for Young Readers.

Gravett, E. (2010). *The rabbit problem.* New York, NY: Simon & Schuster Books for Young Readers.

Isaacs, A. (1994). *Swamp angel.* New York, NY: Dutton Children's.

Lee, S. (2007). *The zoo.* La Jolla, CA: Kane/Miller.

Macaulay, D. (1990). *Black and white.* Boston, MA: Houghton Mifflin.

McCloskey, R. (1941). *Make way for ducklings.* New York, NY: Viking.

McCloskey, R. (1948). *Blueberries for Sal.* New York, NY: Viking.

Pinkney, J. (2009). *The lion & the mouse.* Boston, MA: Little, Brown Books for Young Readers.

Raschka, C. (2013). *Daisy gets lost.* New York, NY: Schwartz & Wade.

Say, A. (1993). *Grandfather's journey.* Boston, MA: Houghton Mifflin.

Scanlon, L.G. (2009). *All the world.* New York, NY: Beach Lane.

Seeger, L.V. (2003). *The hidden alphabet.* New York, NY: Roaring Brook.

Seeger, L.V. (2004). *Lemons are not red.* New York, NY: Roaring Brook.

Seeger, L.V. (2007a). *Dog and Bear: Two friends, three stories.* New York, NY: Roaring Brook.

Seeger, L.V. (2007b). *First the egg.* New York, NY: Roaring Brook.

Seeger, L.V. (2008a). *Dog and Bear: Two's company.* New York, NY: Roaring Brook.

Seeger, L.V. (2008b). *One boy.* New York, NY: Roaring Brook.

Seeger, L.V. (2009). *Dog and Bear: Three to get ready.* New York, NY: Roaring Brook.

Seeger, L.V. (2010). *What if?* New York, NY: Roaring Brook.

Seeger, L.V. (2012). *Green.* New York, NY: Roaring Brook.

Seeger, L.V. (2013). *Bully.* New York, NY: Roaring Brook.

Sís, P. (2014). *The pilot and the little prince: The life of Antoine de Saint-Exupéry.* New York, NY: Frances Foster.

Smith, L. (2011). *Grandpa Green.* New York, NY: Roaring Brook.

Stein, D.E. (2007). *Leaves.* New York, NY: G.P. Putnam's Sons.

Swanson, S.M. (2008). *The house in the night.* New York, NY: Houghton Mifflin.

Teague, M. (2002). *Dear Mrs. LaRue: Letters from obedience school*. New York, NY: Scholastic.

Thompson, L. (2004). *Polar bear night*. New York, NY: Scholastic.

Watt, M. (2006–2013). Scaredy Squirrel [Series]. Toronto, ON, Canada: Kids Can.

Willems, M. (2003). *Don't let the pigeon drive the bus!* New York, NY: Hyperion Books for Children.

Willems, M. (2008). *The pigeon wants a puppy!* New York, NY: Hyperion Books for Children.

Zelinsky, P.O. (1997). *Rapunzel*. New York, NY: Dutton Children's.

OTHER RECOMMENDED CHILDREN'S BOOKS

Bryant, J. (2013). *A splash of red: The life and art of Horace Pippin*. New York, NY: Alfred A. Knopf.

Ehlert, L. (2014). *The scraps book: Notes from a colorful life*. New York, NY: Beach Lane.

Idle, M. (2013). *Flora and the flamingo*. San Francisco, CA: Chronicle.

Klassen, J. (2012). *This is not my hat*. Somerville, MA: Candlewick.

Polacco, P. (2012). *The art of Miss Chew*. New York, NY: G.P. Putnam's Sons.

Stead, P.C. (2010). *A sick day for Amos McGee*. New York, NY: Roaring Brook.

Tullet, H. (2011). *Press here*. San Francisco, CA: Chronicle.

Winter, J. (2013). *Henri's scissors*. New York, NY: Beach Lane.

RECOMMENDED WEBSITES FOR ADDITIONAL INFORMATION

Caldecott Medal (www.ala.org/alsc/awardsgrants/bookmedia/caldecottmedal/caldecottmedal): The Association for Library Service to Children provides information about the current and previous winners, as well as information about and descriptions of the illustrations that received this prestigious award.

Laura Vaccaro Seeger (www.studiolvs.com): In-depth information is provided about her books, along with interviews and links to book trailers.

Picturing Books (www.picturingbooks.com): This website provides information about illustration techniques and media used, as well as links to other websites containing additional resources about picture book illustration and design.

Society of Children's Book Writers and Illustrators (www.scbwi.org): The website contains information about the authors and illustrators who belong to the organization and provides links to their websites and blogs.

ABOUT THE AUTHOR

 Cyndi Giorgis is a professor of children's and young adult literature and the dean of the College of Education at the University of Texas at El Paso, USA. She has served on the American Library Association's Caldecott Medal, Newbery Medal, and Geisel Award committees and is now serving as the chair of the NCTE Orbis Pictus Award for Outstanding Nonfiction for Children Committee. Cyndi has published extensively in journals such as *The Reading Teacher, Language Arts*, and the *Journal of Children's Literature* and is a regular contributor to *Book Links* magazine. She has also created numerous curriculum guides for picture books and novels for use by teachers. Her presentations at the state, national, and international levels focus on the authentic sharing of children's literature in ways that evoke meaningful responses from readers. Cyndi can be contacted at cagiorgis@utep.edu.

CHAPTER 6

Reading Text and Image
Building Skills for Deep Understanding

Lauren Aimonette Liang, *University of Utah*

Lee Galda, *University of Minnesota*

Word-processing programs do not like the word *picturebook*. At every instance, they suggest a mistake, a misspelling, and clamor to break it into two separate words. But the complexity of this unique genre is in fact implied by the structure of its name: picturebook. Picturebooks are not illustrated books. They are built on the idea of synergy; the words of a picturebook tell us things that are not in the pictures, and the pictures tell us what the words do not (Galda, Sipe, Liang, & Cullinan, 2014; Sipe, 1998). To understand the story captured in a picturebook, readers must read both the words and the text. The compelling details, the humor, and the essence of the story are captured in the unique interaction of the words and the pictures.

Children who encounter outstanding picturebooks learn how to read the interaction and thus begin to notice and discuss the craft of the author and illustrator, to recognize and discuss theme, and to understand and discuss other complex literary concepts, such as foreshadowing, mood, and subplot. Helping students to better comprehend and discuss how picturebooks work prepares them for doing this in the future with text-only reading. To understand, and explain what is understood, requires close reading of the word–picture interaction and the use of textual evidence, both skills essential to deep comprehension (National Governors Association Center for Best Practices & Council of Chief State School Officers, 2010). Thus, teaching students to understand picturebook format and giving them the words with which to discuss it can be an early important step in the development of complex literary understanding.

In this chapter, we discuss what it means to teach elementary students about picturebooks as a format and what that might look like in your classroom. We begin with ways to help students notice and discuss illustrative details and styles, and then focus on deepening students' discussions of picturebook synergy (the interaction of text and pictures). We encourage teaching these concepts for

Children's Literature in the Reading Program: Engaging Young Readers in the 21st Century (4th ed.), edited by Deborah A. Wooten & Bernice E. Cullinan. © 2015 by the International Literacy Association.

multiple reasons. As seen in the classroom examples that we share in this chapter, students gain deeper understanding of both the picturebook at hand and how picturebooks work through discussions that focus on synergy, format and design, and illustrative style and technique (Arizpe & Styles, 2003; Kiefer, 1995; Pantaleo, 2008, 2014; Sipe, 2008). In these discussions, vocabulary increases, as does understanding of craft. Close reading, using textual evidence, and learning about literary elements through discussion of picturebook interaction is an essential and joyful part of picturebook discussion.

Teaching Picturebook Format

Teaching students to understand and interpret picturebook format involves two basic parts: (1) noticing and discussing illustrations and (2) examining and discussing the interaction of text and pictures. These steps help students understand how the synergy, or the interaction, creates meaning, deepens understanding, and highlights genre.

Noticing and Discussing Illustrations: Visual Elements and Beyond

A great way to begin helping students notice how picturebooks work is to discuss the visual elements in a picturebook's illustrations. Learning just a little about how illustrators use elements such as line (a mark on paper, used by illustrators to both pull the eye of the reader in a certain direction and to express particular meanings through its angle, width, and length), shape (the area or forms used to suggest feelings and ideas, direct the eye, and contribute to three-dimensional quality), texture (used to convey a sense of reality), and color (used most often to signify and intensify mood and emotion) helps students learn to pay attention to craft and leads them also to thinking more deeply about mood and main ideas. This is a particularly good starting place for discussions with preschool and early primary-grade students. At this age, they're already very attuned to visual elements and are mainly listening to teachers read picturebooks aloud. These young children are often closely attending to the illustrations while listening to the words. Knowing a little about these elements of art begins to get them paying attention to craft and leads them also to looking at mood. Talking about these elements also helps students acquire the vocabulary they need to discuss how picturebooks work. See Table 6.1 for a list of common elements of art and their definitions.

Deepening Awareness of Visual Elements: Classroom Examples

For example, after Ms. Lopez[1] shared *Bone Dog* by Eric Rohmann (2011) with her kindergarten class, she discussed the dark, strong, thick lines that outline each

Table 6.1. Common Picturebook Terminology

Term	Definition
Balance	The equal weight of lines, shapes, textures, and colors in an illustration or picture
Cross-hatching	Fine parallel lines, usually black, that are crossed with another set of parallel lines to produce the effect of shading
Dust jacket	The thick paper wrapper around the outside of a book, folded inside at the front and back to keep it in place
Endpages or *endpapers*	The inside of the front and back cover, consisting of two parts: a pastedown (affixed to the inside of the front and back covers) and the flyleaf (the part of the endpage that is not pasted down)
Flap	The part of the dust jacket that is folded inside the front and back covers (the case) of a book: Often, the front flap has a summary of the story, and the back flap has short biographies of the author and/or illustrator.
Gutter	When the book is opened, the middle of the spread where the pages are bound
Line	A mark on paper or a place where different colors meet
Medium	The material used to produce an illustration: The plural form is *media*.
Repetition and *variety*	Repetition in art is used to achieve visual harmony and balance. Variety creates a paradox or progression to lead the reader's eyes from one point to another.
Shape	An area or form with a definite outline
Technique	The method artists use to create art within the chosen medium
Texture	In an illustration, the appearance of having a smooth or rough surface
Trim size	The overall size and proportion of a book

Note. From *Literature and the Child* (8th ed., pp. 95–96), by Lee Galda, Lawrence R. Sipe, Lauren A. Liang, and Bernice E. Cullinan, 2014, Belmont, CA: Wadsworth/Cengage. Copyright 2014 by Wadsworth/Cengage. Adapted with permission. See *Literature and the Child* for a more in-depth discussion of these terms and many more.

character. She explained to the students that these lines were a deliberate choice by Rohmann. Several students noticed that the dark outlines made the characters "look like cartoons." Ms. Lopez commented that even though the scenes in *Bone Dog* are a little scary, they're also rather funny. When students gave examples of the times they were laughing, she pointed to the heavily outlined characters and explained that illustrators often use dark outlines to exaggerate situations and help evoke humor in an absurd situation. Sharing *Wolves* by Emily Gravett (2006) with her class at a later date, Ms. Lopez found that her students kept reaching out to pet the pages, commenting that the fur on the wolf looked real. Again she taught her students a bit about craft, explaining that the hatched pencil lines created texture and that a strong sense of texture makes things seem real even in a fantasy world.

With just a few simple conversations around read-alouds, Ms. Lopez's students already are building appreciation for the decisions that authors/illustrators make and understanding that these choices are deliberate. The students are also learning the vocabulary that allows them to discuss these decisions with authority and sophistication.

Considering Illustration Color and Mood: Classroom Examples

Children, and adults, also pay close attention to the visual element of color, instinctively reacting to colors when determining the mood of a book. "These are the happy books!" exclaimed one young preschooler with a pile of Lois Ehlert's books on her lap. The intensely hued, brightly colored illustrations clearly indicated to the nonreader that the mood of these books would be joyful. Similarly, without even reading a phrase, a seventh grader glancing through a stack of adolescent picturebooks quickly pushed away an opened copy of *Woolvs in the Sitee* by Margaret Wild and Anne Spudvilas (2007). Obviously reacting to the dark and foreboding blacks and sick yellows, the girl said, "Oh, no—look at that. That is much too creepy for me." Mood, a concept that's often challenging for students, is frequently easier to understand in a picturebook. Illustrators are well aware of color associations and carefully select their palettes for each book to help send subtle messages about mood. Discussing colors in a picturebook is often one of the easiest ways to begin children's understanding of mood and the deliberate choices that picturebook creators make.

Mr. Peterson, for example, noticed one of his third-grade students kindly putting an arm around her kindergarten reading buddy during a shared reading session. When he asked if everything was OK, the student explained that she was reassuring the younger child that everything would turn out fine for the two dogs in the book she was reading, *Boot & Shoe* by Marla Frazee (2012). Knowing that she hadn't read the book previously, Mr. Peterson asked how she knew this. "Because even though the dogs are crying, the colors *were* very dark, but *now* there is a little pink and yellow, and the background is all white again here. So, things are starting to feel more cheerful." An accomplished picturebook reader, the older student knew that a return of warmer, brighter colors usually meant a turn to a happier mood.

Discussing the Effect of Media and Technique: Classroom Examples

Discussing the choice of media and technique used in a picturebook furthers young readers' understanding of craft by highlighting how an illustrator's choice of artistic style for a book matches the mood and often the theme as well. Ms. Ford, for example, noticed a group of her second graders closely examining the woodblock prints with muted color pencil overlays in *A Sick Day for Amos McGee* by Philip Stead (2010). She explained to the children the careful, time-consuming process of woodblock prints and added that the choice of this illustrative style seemed to match the time-intensive, intricate friendships between Amos and his zoo friends. The children, used to these types of comments, noted that the soft colors matched "the quiet feel" of the book as well. Sharing Stian Hole's (2006) *Garmann's Summer* with a group of fourth-grade students, Ms. Ozburn highlighted Hole's ability to capture the literal understandings of a young boy by using the mixed media of real photographs and illustrations. As students exclaimed over an image of a superimposed X-ray on the pencil sketch of a small boy, she pointed out how Hole uses his craft to make a small instance in the story— Garmann hearing the phrase *butterflies in your stomach*—help the reader better understand the character's frequently confused point of view and the overarching mood of the book.

One simple way to help students better understand how the choice of illustrative style matches and extends the mood of a book is to use folklore. In her third-grade classroom, Ms. Garrett used multiple versions of Goldilocks and the Three Bears to highlight this. After first having the students work together to retell a basic outline of the well-known tale, she asked them to close their eyes and imagine what the story would look like if it was illustrated with photographs of real bears and real people. Ms. Garrett asked the students if the mood of this version would be happy, scary, sad, or some other emotion. She then had them close their eyes again to imagine a version illustrated with cartoon bears and people. Again, she led them in a simple discussion of the mood that these types of illustrations might create. With that, Ms. Garret passed around multiple versions of Goldilocks and the Three Bears, including Jan Brett's (1987) version, with intricate details and borders; James Marshall's (1988), with his strong colors and shapes; and the more unusual use of mixed media in Lauren Child's (2008) version. After exploration of the books and discussions with peers, Ms. Garrett led her class in seeing how each version uses its illustrations, as well as certain textual effects, to create a slightly different tone and offer slightly different interpretations of the well-known tale.

Noticing Illustrations: Attention to the Small Details

In recent years, the creation of a picturebook has spread beyond the story pages (do Rozario, 2012). The dust jacket (the thick, folded paper wrapped around the hard cover), endpages (the paper adhered to the inside of the front and back covers), inner flaps (the folded inner parts of the dust jacket that typically provide a brief description of the book and information about the author and illustrator), title page (the page containing the title, author, publisher, and sometimes the date published), and more are now decisions made by authors and illustrators, not just editors. These elements often contain additional illustrations and text, or colors and designs that hint at the mood or plot of the book, all of which may even extend the story. Books like Emily Gravett's (2013) *Again!*, for example, are only fully understood when the entire book is examined—including removing the dust jacket! Young readers are often better observers of these important details than adults (Kiefer, 1995; Meek, 1988) and can also handily discuss effects of choices in font, layouts across the gutter (the middle of the spread between two pages where the pages are bound), trim size (the overall size and proportion of a book), and other elements. The teacher's role here is to present and explain the correct vocabulary terms for these phenomena and encourage discussions about them. Conversations about these points help students understand the importance and benefits of attending to small details, another skill essential to later comprehension of text-only books.

Understanding Visual Elements as Textual Evidence

Classroom conversations about these visual elements of illustrations, such as the many discussed previously, not only begin the teaching of craft but also introduce the use of textual evidence. Young students reading picturebooks frequently make predictions about what will happen next in the story, using the illustrations as the basis for their educated guesses. Primary-grade teachers can build on this by asking students to identify what in the pictures made them think X was going to happen. Sophisticated ideas, such as deliberate use of composition and design, are easily introduced when students are already noticing it in a well-crafted picturebook. Following up on students' predictions by asking questions such as "How did you know that ___ was going to happen? What were the clues?" begins to get students paying attention to foreshadowing and the use of textual and illustrative evidence. Adding brief explanations of commonly used techniques, such as balance (the equal weight of lines, shapes, textures, and colors in a picture) or repetition (used to achieve visual harmony) and variety (creates a paradox or progression to lead the reader's eyes from point to point), alerts students to look for these techniques in other picturebooks, reminds them of their deliberate use by authors/illustrators, and prepares them in the future to better understand common, deliberately used writing techniques.

> *Classroom conversations about these visual elements of illustrations...not only begin the teaching of craft but also introduce the use of textual evidence.*

Visual Element Choices and Prediction: Classroom Examples

For example, when Ms. Chen read aloud *Lilly's Purple Plastic Purse* by Kevin Henkes (1996) to her first-grade class, she pointed out his wonderful use of repetition and variety to help the reader's eyes move from point to point. Calling children up to the front of room, she asked them to use a pointer to trace where their eyes went when they were viewing the page. Students commented on the similarity of the paths on so many pages and noticed how some very important pages changed from a series of three pictures to one very large one, particularly when young Lilly the mouse snuck her mean drawing into her teacher's bag. Together with Ms. Chen, the students discussed how Henkes "must have done that because it is such an important part! He wants us to really know that!" They noticed how pictures of Lilly in the bottom right corners of pages led them to want to turn the page to see what happened next. One student announced to Ms. Chen that the text of the story was also an example of repetition, explaining that there were often three reasons, three statements, or three details in three sentences, "just like there are three small pictures on so many pages." Classroom discussions like these help students better understand both the complex craft of picturebooks and the story itself.

Examining and Discussing the Interaction of Text and Pictures

Although discussing illustrations inherently means considering the way the text and pictures work together, explicit teaching about the type of synergy in any picturebook can be useful for helping students recognize how the pictures influence the reader's interpretation of the text and how the text influences the reader's interpretation of the pictures. Synergy exists in many forms in picturebooks, and academics describe these forms with several terms, such as *parallel* and *interdependent storytelling* (Agosto, 1999), *congruency, amplification, extension* (Doonan, 1993; Schwarcz, 1982), and *interdependence of word and image* (Lewis, 2001). In this section, we introduce three of the common ways that picture–text interaction works in picturebooks using the terms *complementary, contradictory,* and *stories within a story*. Understanding these common synergic relationships promotes students' growth of important complex literary skills, such as understanding point of view and reliable (and unreliable) narration. See Table 6.2 for a concise summary of some common picture–text interactions.

Discussing Complementary Picturebooks in the Classroom

Complementary, or enhancing, picturebooks represent perhaps the most common type of relationship between words and pictures. In these picturebooks, the words and pictures support each other and work together to both extend the emotional impact and deepen understanding. Sometimes this enhancement is subtle, but it can also be quite extensive. Most frequently, the visual narrative tells the same story as the verbal narrative but adds significant details. These details can, for example, heighten the mood of the book or add deeper characterization to the protagonist.

Table 6.2. Common Types of Interactions of Text and Pictures in Picturebooks

Term	Definition
Synergy	Reference to the fact that the illustrations and the verbal text of a picturebook combine to produce an effect that is greater than the sum of either part
▪ *Complementary*	An interaction of text and pictures where the illustrations enhance the story told in the text, providing rich details, context, and/or emotional impact
▪ *Contradictory*	An interaction of text and pictures where the story told in the illustrations contradicts or subverts the story told in the text, often providing much humor
▪ *Story within a story*	An interaction of text and pictures where the illustrations reflect and extend the main story but also offer one or more side stories

Reading aloud Kevin Henkes's (2007) *A Good Day* to her kindergartners, Ms. Dewing stopped on a two-page spread after reading the text "Little orange fox turned around, and there was his mother" (n.p.). She asked her students how the little fox was feeling. One student exclaimed, "He's so happy and not worried anymore, and his mom is happy, too, and telling him it is OK!" Ms. Dewing asked the student if it said this in the text that she had just read. When the student said no, Mrs. Dewing reread the exact text and then discussed with the class how Henkes's illustration of the very happy fox and his reassuring mother adds the feeling to that part of the book. She then took one of the class's favorite picturebooks, *Sylvester and the Magic Pebble* by William Steig (1969), off the shelf and said that this book does something similar to Henkes's *A Good Day*. Ms. Dewing turned to the page where Sylvester's parents speak to the police and read the text: "They went to the police. The police could not find their child" (n.p.). She pointed to the illustration and told the students that although the text doesn't say it, the illustration shows us that the police are very sad that they can't find Sylvester; the interaction of the text and pictures adds the emotion, or feeling, to the story. Prepping her students for future writing and reading, she explained that in chapter books, authors sometimes try to show how a character feels by describing his or her actions "like a picture" instead of just telling the reader how he feels.

Thinking About Contradictory Picturebooks in the Classroom

Unlike complementary picturebooks, in contradictory ones, the words and pictures work against each other and send contradictory messages. This is often called the counterpoint. These books, or pages within an otherwise complementary picturebook, often offer a good deal of fun and excitement for the reader. Students must grasp the contradictions in the two narratives to decide what's really happening in the story. Frequently, the humor of a picturebook is captured in this contradiction between what the text says about a character or incident and the corresponding image portrayed.

Discussing the humor of a picturebook is a natural way to help students better understand the concept of contradictory synergy. Ms. Dewing, for example, stopped her read-aloud of *Knuffle Bunny: A Cautionary Tale* by Mo Willems (2004) when her class erupted with laughter after the two-page spread showing young protagonist Trixie running around with a pair of jeans on her head and a sock and underwear on her hands. The text reads, "Trixie helped her daddy put the laundry into the machine" (n.p.). When Ms. Dewing asked the class what was so funny about this page, the students quickly explained that Trixie wasn't helping at all! Ms. Dewing praised the students for being so attentive to detail and then reminded her students about this example before several subsequent read-alouds, asking them to notice the relationship of the pictures to the text.

> *Students must grasp the contradictions in the two narratives to decide what's really happening in the story.*

Considering Multiple Stories Within a Story With Your Class

A third type of picturebook offers one or more additional stories within a story. The pictures enhance the story told in the text, much like a complementary picturebook, but also offer side stories. Readers are often tempted to revisit the book multiple times to follow the subplots offered. Liz Garton Scanlon's (2009) *All the World* is an excellent example where many individual stories can be found throughout the book; these stories even intersect to add greater meaning to the ending. Watching her class share books, Ms. Johnson noticed three children huddled around *All the World*, flipping pages quickly back and forth. As she walked closer, she could hear the students:

MAYA: Look, now look. See, here's the kids again in the back corner! And that's the same car as this page!

ALEXA: They're all together here at the end, see! They are all part of a big family. That's why it says, "Nanas and papas."

The students were following the various characters who appear from time to time on double-page spreads and noting how they come together in the last pages to illustrate the connectedness of the world. Clearly, these students had grasped the theme of the book by following the synergy of a story within the story.

Using Synergy Discussions to Highlight Specific Literary Elements

Once students begin to notice and comment on the different ways that the text and pictures interact, it is an easy step to discussing how these interactions help develop specific literary elements. How does the interaction develop the setting, the characters, the plot, and the mood? Students attuned to the interactions of text and pictures already understand this fundamentally, but adding the language of literary elements prepares them well for future discussions of literature. For example, in many picturebooks, students will recognize that the text is only telling them the what of the story and that it takes the pictures to explain the how. Discussing this with students as plot development helps plant seeds about the importance of rich details in writing a plot.

Character details also appear in illustrations; whereas the text might state one or two more obvious facts about the protagonist, the illustrations often add a much more complex picture through the tilt of the head, the small details of clothing, facial expressions, and so on. For example, popular children's character David, the star of *No, David!*, *David Goes to School*, and more by David Shannon (1998, 1999), is never described, nor do we read about his feelings in the text. Young readers follow his emotional journeys through the careful details found in each picture and understand that although he is very active, he is generally kindhearted and wants to please. Ms. Hower laughed when one of her preschool students walked straight from a little time in the cooldown area to bring her a book to read from the book nook. When he asked her to read *David Goes to School* (a very popular book in her pre-K classroom) again, she asked him why. "I like it. David is funny, and he doesn't mean to be bad sometimes. See, his teachers really like him, and he gets to make up for everything in the end." Ms. Hower's young student had clearly understood the text–pictures interaction that characterizes David and, perhaps, recognized David as a kindred spirit!

> *Students attuned to the interactions of text and pictures already understand this fundamentally, but adding the language of literary elements prepares them well for future discussions of literature.*

Conversations about text–picture interactions quickly build students' understanding of both craft and literary elements, strengthen their practice of close reading, and highlight the importance of using textual and pictorial evidence.

Conclusion

Why is this so important? School is much more than a place to learn an unrelated assortment of facts and skills. When we teachers do our jobs well, we help our students learn how to think, develop skills that they can apply to other situations, and build knowledge that allows them access to increasingly challenging content. Helping them notice and learn to articulate their understandings about how picturebooks work is not only relevant and necessary to their early literary education but also a relevant and rich source of knowledge and skills to rely on as they increasingly encounter text-only literature. Knowing, for example, that a character's intention can be implied in pictures, as in the David books, forms a foundation for understanding that character intention can be

Seeking to understand why a book is the way it is, rather than criticizing it for not being otherwise, is foundational for literary appreciation.

and is often implied. In picturebooks, it's frequently shown in the illustrations, but in chapter books and novels, it's through words. Understanding that authors and illustrators make intentional choices in picturebooks allows students to think about both how and why authors do the same in chapter books and novels. Seeking to understand why a book is the way it is, rather than criticizing it for not being otherwise, is foundational for literary appreciation. Finally, teaching children the vocabulary of the picturebook format allows them to explore and discuss books in increasingly insightful ways, coming to progressively more sophisticated literary understandings with their peers and, in our experience, often offering wonderful insights to the adults fortunate enough to be reading picturebooks with them.

NOTE

[1]All names are pseudonyms. Classroom examples are fictional, based on teacher-reported classroom conversations from 2004–2014.

REFERENCES

Agosto, D.E. (1999). One and inseparable: Interdependent storytelling in picture storybooks. *Children's Literature in Education, 30*(4), 267–280. doi:10.1023/A:1022471922077

Arizpe, E., & Styles, M. (2003). *Children reading pictures: Interpreting visual texts.* New York, NY: RoutledgeFalmer.

Doonan, J. (1993). *Looking at pictures in picture books.* Stroud, UK: Thimble.

do Rozario, R.-A.C. (2012). Consuming books: Synergies of materiality and narrative in picturebooks. *Children's Literature, 40,* 151–166. doi:10.1353/chl.2012.0013

Galda, L., Sipe, L.R., Liang, L.A., & Cullinan, B.E. (2014). *Literature and the child* (8th ed.). Belmont, CA: Wadsworth/Cengage.

Kiefer, B.Z. (1995). *The potential of picturebooks: From visual literacy to aesthetic understanding.* Englewood Cliffs, NJ: Merrill.

Lewis, D. (2001). *Reading contemporary picturebooks: Picturing text.* New York, NY: RoutledgeFalmer.

Meek, M. (1988). *How texts teach what readers learn.* Stroud, UK: Thimble.

National Governors Association Center for Best Practices & Council of Chief State School Officers. (2010). *Common Core State Standards for English language arts and literacy in history/social studies,* science, and technical subjects: Appendix A: Research supporting key elements of the standards and glossary of key terms. Washington, DC: Authors. Retrieved from www.corestandards.org/assets/Appendix_A.pdf

Pantaleo, S. (2008). *Exploring student response to contemporary picturebooks.* Toronto, ON, Canada: University of Toronto Press.

Pantaleo, S. (2014). Exploring the artwork in picturebooks with middle years students. *Journal of Children's Literature, 40*(1), 15–26.

Schwarcz, J.H. (1982). *Ways of the illustrator: Visual communication in children's literature.* Chicago, IL: American Library Association.

Sipe, L.R. (1998). Individual literary response styles of first and second graders. In T. Shanahan & F.V. Rodriguez-Brown (Eds.), *47th yearbook of the National Reading Conference* (pp. 76–89). Chicago, IL: National Reading Conference.

Sipe, L.R. (2008). *Storytime: Young children's literary understanding in the classroom.* New York, NY: Teachers College Press.

CHILDREN'S LITERATURE CITED

Brett, J. (1987). *Goldilocks and the three bears.* New York, NY: G.P. Putnam's Sons.

Child, L. (2008). *Goldilocks and the three bears.* New York, NY: Puffin.

Frazee, M. (2012). *Boot & Shoe.* New York, NY: Beach Lane.

Gravett, E. (2006). *Wolves.* New York, NY: Simon & Schuster Books for Young Readers.

Gravett, E. (2013). *Again!* New York, NY: Simon & Schuster Books for Young Readers.

Henkes, K. (1996). *Lilly's purple plastic purse.* New York, NY: Greenwillow.

Henkes, K. (2007). *A good day.* New York, NY: Greenwillow.

Hole, S. (2006). *Garmann's summer* (D. Bartlett, Trans.). Grand Rapids, MI: Eerdmans Books for Young Readers.

Marshall, J. (1988). *Goldilocks and the three bears.* New York, NY: Dial Books for Young Readers.

Rohmann, E. (2011). *Bone dog.* New York, NY: Roaring Brook.

Scanlon, L.G. (2009). *All the world.* New York, NY: Beach Lane.

Shannon, D. (1998). *No, David!* New York, NY: Blue Sky.

Shannon, D. (1999). *David goes to school.* New York, NY: Blue Sky.

Stead, P.C. (2010). *A sick day for Amos McGee.* New York, NY: Roaring Brook.

Steig, W. (1969). *Sylvester and the magic pebble.* New York, NY: Windmill.

Wild, M., & Spudvilas, A. (2007). *Woolvs in the sitee.* Asheville, NC: Front Street.

Willems, M. (2004). *Knuffle Bunny: A cautionary tale.* New York, NY: Hyperion Books for Children.

OTHER RECOMMENDED CHILDREN'S PICTUREBOOKS

Katz, K. (1999). *The colors of us.* New York, NY: Henry Holt.

Keats, E.J. (1962). *The snowy day.* New York, NY: Viking.

Klassen, J. (2012). *This is not my hat.* Somerville, MA: Candlewick.

Peters, L.W. (2003). *Our family tree: An evolution story.* San Diego, CA: Harcourt.

Raschka, C. (2011). *A ball for Daisy.* New York, NY: Schwartz & Wade.

Sidman, J. (2011). *Swirl by swirl: Spirals in nature.* Boston, MA: Houghton Mifflin Harcourt Books for Children.

Wiesner, D. (1991). *Tuesday.* New York, NY: Clarion.

RECOMMENDED WEBSITES FOR FINDING WONDERFUL PICTUREBOOKS

Association for Library Service to Children's Children's Notable Lists: www.ala.org/alsc/awardsgrants/notalists
Caldecott Medal: www.ala.org/alsc/awardsgrants/bookmedia/caldecottmedal/caldecottmedal

Coretta Scott King Book Awards: www.ala.org/emiert/cskbookawards
ILA Children's and Young Adults' Book Awards: www.reading.org/resources/AwardsandGrants/childrens_ira.aspx
USBBY Outstanding International Books List: www.usbby.org/list_oibl.html

ABOUT THE AUTHORS

Lauren Aimonette Liang is an associate professor of educational psychology at the University of Utah, Salt Lake City, USA. Her research and teaching focus on children's and adolescent literature. Lauren's work has been published in journals such as *Reading Research Quarterly*, the *Journal of Children's Literature*, and *Reading Psychology*, as well as in both professional and practitioner books. She is also a coauthor of the widely used children's literature textbook *Literature and the Child* (8th ed., Wadsworth/Cengage, 2014). Lauren serves on editorial boards for several journals and committees for the International Literacy Association (ILA), National Council of Teachers of English, American Library Association, Literacy Research Association, and United States Board on Books for Youg People. She was a long-time reviewer for *The Horn Book Guide* and other review publications and served as chair of ILA's Children's and Young Adults' Book Awards Committee for 2012–2015. Lauren can be contacted at lauren.liang@utah.edu.

Lee Galda was the first Marguerite Henry Professor of Children's and Young Adult Literature at the University of Minnesota, Minneapolis, USA, where she taught courses in transactional theory and various aspects of children's and adolescent literature after moving from the University of Georgia in 1998. She has received several awards for teaching from both institutions. Her research focused on response to literature, effective practice in the teaching of literature, and the nature of contemporary children's literature. Lee has published many refereed articles, book chapters, and books, as well as many invited articles and book reviews, and was the children's books editor for *The Reading Teacher*. Her research was funded by several grants and honored by several research awards. Lee received her PhD from New York University in 1980 and retired from the University of Minnesota in 2013. She can be contacted at galda001@umn.edu.

CHAPTER 7

Graphic Novels in Education

Comics, Comprehension, and the Content Areas

Stergios Botzakis, *University of Tennessee, Knoxville*

Historically, comic books have been taboo in classrooms, hidden between the pages of a textbook and read when the teacher wasn't paying attention. More recently, these types of texts have been expanded and called graphic novels. They've lost some of the stigma of being contraband, and some have come to be merited. Art Spiegelman's (1986) *Maus: A Survivor's Tale I: My Father Bleeds History* began this trend when it won the Pulitzer Prize Special Award in 1992, and it was continued when Gene Luen Yang's (2006) *American Born Chinese* was a finalist for the 2006 National Book Award in the category of young people's literature. Librarians have been advocating for the inclusion of graphic novels in school libraries (National Coalition Against Censorship, American Library Association, & Comic Book Legal Defense Fund, 2006; Weiner, 2003), and some researchers are finding that they are effective texts in reinforcing comprehension and memory (Short, Randolph-Seng, & McKenny, 2013). No longer relegated to the trash heap, graphic texts have come to prominence in educational settings.

Graphic novels have also come into more prominence in bookstores and in the buying habits of young readers. Manga, Japanese comics translated into English, have become particularly popular with young readers, especially girls (Glazer, 2005). As might be noticed by their prominence in bookstores, the sales numbers for graphic novels in general and manga in particular have been steadily growing in the United States (Goodnow, 2007). Past research has shown that students' reading preferences are typically not included in the curriculum (Worthy, Moorman, & Turner, 1999), and other research (Alvermann, Moon, & Hagood, 1999; Norton, 2003) suggests that students could become more motivated and successful when their interests are included in instruction.

Because graphic novels have become a popular reading choice of many young readers, it makes sense to look at how they might fit into an educational setting. With this growing attention to graphic novels, the point of this chapter is to report information about what they can do in general, to demonstrate some uses of

Children's Literature in the Reading Program: Engaging Young Readers in the 21st Century (4th ed.), edited by Deborah A. Wooten & Bernice E. Cullinan. © 2015 by the International Literacy Association.

particular examples, and also to provide information about where appropriate and appealing graphic novels might be found for students.

Why Should You Use Graphic Novels in the Classroom?

Popularity alone is not reason enough to include graphic novels in a curriculum, but there are a number of features unique to the medium that lend themselves well to instruction. Three of these text features are transitions, contextual information, and visual permanence, and I describe each in this section.

Reading graphic novels, like reading comics in general, requires the reader to make connections between images set apart by panels and gutters (the empty spaces between panels; McCloud, 1994). Such reading requires constant inference making, as readers have to assume that actions are occurring between the panels. When students assume action takes place in the time it takes them to move from one panel to another, they're engaged in higher level thinking skills, often without even knowing it, which is why comics are sometimes called "the invisible art" (Heath & Bhagat, 1997, p. 586). Making inferences from images is typically easier for students, and that skill can be introduced and taught using graphic novels (Frey & Fisher, 2004) and later revisited for more traditional text reading. What can be difficult for students to do with simple text can be more easily accomplished via reading more visually oriented materials.

Popularity alone is not reason enough to include graphic novels in a curriculum, but there are a number of features unique to the medium that lend themselves well to instruction.

Along with transitions that foster inference making, the illustrations in graphic novels also provide contextual information that can assist or enhance readers' ability to engage with text. This contextual information has been used successfully to engage with second-language learners (Cary, 2004) and struggling readers (Yang, 2008) because the use of images along with words provides clues for comprehension. Such learning need not be limited to concrete facts but can also be applied to more abstract learning. For example, the images in graphic novels can be used much in the same way that more print-based text features are discussed in language arts classes. Examining how an author draws a particular scene or character can extend the discussion to symbolism that authors create in poems and prose. The way Art Spiegelman uses imagery to convey character traits in *Maus* offers an avenue for teachers to speak about how Herman Melville (1851/2003) does the same thing in *Moby-Dick* or any of his other works. Exploring the interactions between text and image can open doors to further academic discussions.

One other feature of graphic novels that makes them useful to readers of varying ability is their "visual permanence" (Yang, 2008, p. 188). The words and pictures contained in graphic novels don't move and are fixed on a page, allowing the reader to choose how fast or slow to read it and also the degree to which to attend to the words and pictures. Graphic novels give the illusion of time passing, but they leave the rate of change up to the reader. Yang likens this feature of the graphic novels to being able to rewind and revisit information (or conversely, to keep on going), which is not unrelated to the rereading that students can do with more traditional print-based texts. The major difference lies in the presence of images, which can be more attention getting and unthreatening to more visually oriented youths. In short, he argues that graphic novels make it easier for students to read at a rate appropriate to them.

A note of caution: Just as putting a student in front of a computer doesn't guarantee that learning is taking place, having students read graphic novels doesn't necessarily mean that they are reading and understanding them. The ease associated with reading graphic novels and comic strips can be deceiving. Just because graphic novels are popular doesn't mean that students know how to read, produce, or even talk about them. Also not guaranteed is that all students will automatically love them. Taste and preference can be malleable, mercurial things, but the payoffs in discovering texts that students connect with and enjoy are many.

> **The ease associated with reading graphic novels and comic strips can be deceiving.**

Reading graphic novels for some, however, may lead to a passion in reading that leads to wide reading and increased reading volume, both associated with many positive learning outcomes, including increased reading fluency and more developed vocabulary awareness (Schwanenflugel, Hamilton, Kuhn, Wisenbaker, & Stahl, 2004). So, it's in students' best interests to include many potential types of interesting texts, including graphic novels, in the course of schooling. In the next section, I describe four different graphic novels and ways teachers can use them with their elementary-grade students.

Poseidon: Earth Shaker

Author/illustrator George O'Connor's (2013) *Poseidon: Earth Shaker* is the fifth in an ongoing series of books about the Greek Olympians (see O'Connor, 2014). He retells myths and legends in interesting ways by focusing on individual deities and tales associated with them. Here he details Poseidon and his complex personality as a father, brother, ally, and potentially destructive force of nature. This book is as much about relationships as it is about the main character. In the course of the book, many myths relating to Poseidon are recounted, including Odysseus's ordeal with the Cyclops, Theseus, and the Minotaur and the contest between Athena and Poseidon to be the patron god of Athens. This book is a clever retelling of all of these tales, which are exciting in their own right but also useful later in school when analyzing literature and recognizing classical symbols. What's more, the artwork is reminiscent of U.S. superhero comics, so this book is attractive and awe inspiring, as well as informative and educational.

Close Reading

One area that's being emphasized more with the adoption of the Common Core State Standards (National Governors Association Center for Best Practices & Council of Chief State School Officers, 2010) is the activity of close reading. This type of reading requires students to pay more attention to parsing texts, analyzing language in various formats to see symbolism, allusions, and other features. The ability to examine authors' words and find various meanings can be a difficult proposition for some students, but graphic novels use the sequential format, a combination of words and pictures. Sequential art lends itself to a more immediate kind of inference and meaning making that can be used as an analog for the kinds of close reading done with text that's solely composed of words. Put differently, graphic novels provide opportunities to read and interpret that accomplished readers do more intuitively. Being able to read and speak about how artists use images to convey meaning can be a springboard to how authors use words to convey meaning with the tools at their disposal.

Of course, being able to do such analyses requires using a text that has adequate quality and nuance to warrant them. After all, there are some traditional texts that are more prone to such academic work used in schools as a matter of course. O'Connor's book is populated with mindful and rich imagery that can be used to analyze how the words and pictures combine to convey meaning.

For example, on page 13 of this graphic novel, O'Connor uses cinematic techniques, beginning with a long shot of the ocean in the first panel. He begins to tighten up on the vague object in the second, and the reader can see it's a human. The third panel brings the figure into sharper focus, combined with the narrative boxes, which contain Poseidon's words and context for what the reader is viewing. The fourth panel differs from the other three vastly, with a series of figures battling in front of a red background that sharply contrasts with the deep aqua of the ocean. Not only can the teacher and students speak about the author's choice of words and how they relate to the images on the page, one type of analysis, but there's also the opportunity to simply look at the images and see how a story is told without the words.

Mythology

Along with the story, this book would be an excellent addition to a unit on mythology or heroes because it touches on many classical stories. It could be used as a companion to a great number of other texts that students read, a source of many stories that become the background knowledge needed to make textual analyses where allusion becomes important. Additionally, this book appears to be more a collection of adventure or action tales, but it subtly contains much information about a number of historical figures, civilizations, and religions. Such a book makes many cross-curricular connections possible.

Character Maps/Webs

Ostensibly about Poseidon, this book provides an excellent opportunity for character mapping in a number of senses. First, this story is about a Greek god of the oceans, and like those waters, he is of many moods and dispositions. He can be calm, violent, welcoming, or vengeful, depending on the context and his relation to a character. Reading this book creates an opportunity for teachers to teach about character mapping with a figure with complex emotions. Looking at Poseidon would be a great way to look at motivations and relationships to speak about a character who exhibits many characteristics. Teachers can use different graphic organizers to organize how he relates to various characters and what those relationships say about him. One such manner is shown in Figure 7.1.

Another way that characters could be mapped is displayed in the book's inside cover, which features a family tree of the Olympians. This book is full of many

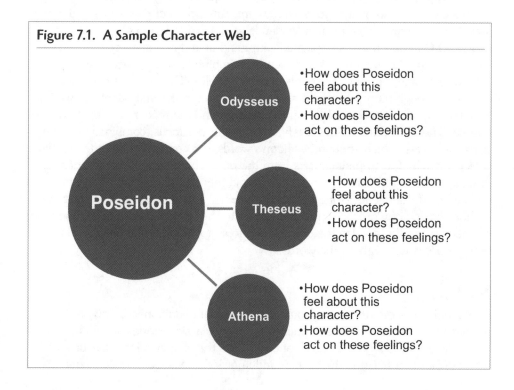

Figure 7.1. A Sample Character Web

Odysseus
- How does Poseidon feel about this character?
- How does Poseidon act on these feelings?

Poseidon — Theseus
- How does Poseidon feel about this character?
- How does Poseidon act on these feelings?

Athena
- How does Poseidon feel about this character?
- How does Poseidon act on these feelings?

characters who are related, and mapping out their family relations is another way to organize information and also analyze these stories. What does it mean that Poseidon has sons that include Theseus and the Cyclops? How is Athena related to Poseidon, and how does that relationship color their contest? These are some of the many questions that can arise from reading, thinking about, and discussing these tales, and answering them provides a chance to explore multiple useful ways of displaying and sorting information.

Amelia Earhart: This Broad Ocean

Sarah Stewart Taylor and Ben Towle's (2010) *Amelia Earhart: This Broad Ocean* tells two parallel stories, one fictional and one historical. The former follows Grace Goodland, a young woman who lives in Newfoundland and writes a town newspaper. The latter focuses on Amelia Earhart, the aviator who's there planning the first solo transatlantic airplane crossing by a woman. Both stories allow for a variety of viewpoints, from the mundane happenings of the day and typical details of the 1930s to the historic and monumental achievements of early aviators and their attempts to push the boundaries of human possibility using new technology and devices. The book is very human in its characters and situations, and with its combination of black, white, and blue colors throughout, it brings the past to life. Certainly, it is a book that has much merit for its truths and fictions.

Historical Connections

Probably the most apparent positive feature of this book is how it depicts the past with an eye to detail, scope, and facts. It shows what daily life was like in the 1930s, when telegrams were still commonly sent, news services were local and run by male reporters, women were relegated to more service-oriented careers, and flying in airplanes was a dangerous and volatile undertaking. But this book is also well researched and full of other information that situates it in history and opens a space for inquiry and curiosity.

For example, the story references the various other women who attempted the same feats as Earhart. She may be the only name mentioned today when discussing female aviation pioneers in schools, but there were others who challenged and came before her. Putting her actions in historical context doesn't detract from her actions, but it gives much more information about the setting and conditions for her exploits. This book provides just enough information to portray this environment but also spark curiosity about others' roles in the early days of air travel as well. There are many secondary figures who might be interesting for ancillary research projects for students.

Additionally, Earhart's travels took her many places, providing opportunities to insert some additional social studies content into the elementary curriculum.

Certainly, teachers and students could use maps and geography to chart her travels, explore the places she visited, and even conjecture about what her final fate might have been.

News Writing

Grace's occupation of reporter models activity that can lead to writing opportunities. Her broadsheets are posted at the local meeting places and post office, and students could replicate this activity with their own news of the day that could be obtained by interviewing teachers, family members, community figures, or classmates. Such authentic publication activities provide a touch of relevance and real-world application to the practice of student writing. Having a definite audience and a format that allows for easy sharing would be very motivational for students and may even get reluctant writers to participate.

Problem Solving

Another aspect that this book touches on is one of increasing focus in elementary schools, the STEM (science, technology, engineering, and mathematics) fields. One of the primary problems in the book that delays Earhart is calculating how much fuel is needed to make the journey in relation to how heavy the airplane and its contents are. This concern leads to much hand-wringing and anxiety about whether she would be successful. Another very real concern was having adequate supplies of food, water, and fuel while also making sure that the airplane wasn't weighted down so much as to make it inefficient or incapable of crossing that long distance.

Reading Amelia Earhart: This Broad Ocean opens up more opportunities for many cross-curricular projects and thinking.

Teachers could use this scenario as an opportunity to craft engineering problems for students to solve either on paper or in doing their own experiments with toy planes or other simulations. With such an emphasis on literacy and mathematics in today's classrooms, the curriculum often becomes narrow (Meier & Wood, 2004), and students don't get chances to do science or think in ways that will become more the focus of later schooling. Reading *Amelia Earhart: This Broad Ocean* opens up more opportunities for many cross-curricular projects and thinking.

Understanding Photosynthesis With Max Axiom, Super Scientist

Science is an area often given short shrift in the elementary school classroom, but there are a growing number of excellent science resources available for younger readers, and one of them is the Max Axiom, Super Scientist series by Liam O'Donnell and various other authors (2007–2015). The 24 books in this series follow the super scientist Max Axiom on his exploration of the universe and everything in it. His books cover a wide array of scientific fields, including physics, biology, chemistry, the scientific method, and ecology. Axiom possesses amazing abilities to shrink and grow as well as devices that allow him to travel through time and space. His stories are not so narratively driven, but he acts like the superhero curator of a Magic School Bus–like ride who isn't quite so silly.

These books are a great entryway into reading nonfiction texts, a particular focus of the Common Core. This book in particular explores photosynthesis in a number of capacities. It explores the biology of plants and plant cells, the chemistry involved in creating glucose, and the ecological concerns of plants in the water cycle and maintaining the environment. *Understanding Photosynthesis With Max Axiom, Super Scientist* by O'Donnell (2007) covers much ground in short order, but the graphic novel format allows such coverage in a direct and readable manner.

Charts and Content Area Textbooks

Of particular usefulness in these books is their format. The sequential art features break the text up into small chunks of dialogue that students can read, but these books go a step beyond and also combine text with images in ways that tell stories and also convey information in the same ways that textbooks do. For instance, multiple images show close-ups of the inside of plant cells, detailing the cell parts and also their functions. These illustrations prefigure the diagrams that will be in secondary school textbooks, providing a nonthreatening but informative introduction to such informational text features.

These illustrations prefigure the diagrams that will be in secondary school textbooks, providing a nonthreatening but informative introduction to such informational text features.

Drawing Diagrams

Max Axiom is able to shrink and grow to examine plants at various levels, and his actions provide an excellent model for an activity in which students could research and depict other life forms or objects in a similar manner. Students could research various types of animals, either large or microscopic, and then draw them at various scales. They could label such drawings and show how they work on the cellular level as well in their environments. This project would touch on many aspects of biology and ecology, providing rich opportunities for students to engage their curiosity about the natural world. Students would also have opportunities to practice academic skills in researching, recording, and displaying their knowledge in visual and written manners. These graphic novels provide excellent models for scientific inquiry and also effective communication.

The Secret Ghost: A Mystery With Distance and Measurement

Probably the content area least well represented in graphic novels is mathematics. Most of the ones that I am aware of deal with more complex thinkers such as Richard Feynman in areas such as calculus and physics. However, there's a series by Melinda Thielbar (2010–2011) called Manga Math Mysteries that is of interest for elementary school readers, and in particular the third entry in the series, *The Secret Ghost: A Mystery With Distance and Measurement* (Thielbar, 2010), is exceptional. This book, like the others in the series, follows the lives of several students. Here the main characters are Michelle and her older brother, Sam. The siblings have moved into a new house, and there's a strange noise coming from the walls in Michelle's room. Instead of attributing it to superstition, she and her friends figure out a way to get to the source of the issue, and they end up using geometry to determine the solution.

This book is not simply a dry account of mathematical problem solving, though. It contains bright and energetic illustrations and also portrays realistic relationships between friends, sibling rivals, and estranged parents who are dealing with the fallout of divorce. The characters and situations are fleshed out and well realized, making this more than a simple exercise in making a narrative of mathematical reasoning, although the way such reasoning is depicted makes this book well suited for academic use.

Mathematical Reasoning

Perhaps the most complicated and contentious aspect of the Common Core's adoption is in the area of explaining the thought processes behind mathematical solutions (e.g., Garelick, 2012). This book portrays the process not once but twice. The first time deals with the instructor at a karate school who needs to calculate the perimeter of a room to put in shelving. This type of mundane problem solving is demonstrated, and calculations are even provided to show the complete process.

Later on in the book, the siblings once again use simple geometry to measure the perimeter of Michelle's bedroom to determine its dimensions. They use this information to figure out that her room is short and that there's a space not accounted for behind her wall. The graphic novel format is used to good effect in detailing the thought process and steps in solving this problem. The explanation here is longer than the typical written response expected of students, but it can still serve as a clear and effective model for other explanations of mathematical reasoning. The dialogue and reasoning could also be broken down into steps that can contribute to a formula of sorts for expressing mathematical thinking.

Developing Problems

Mathematical writing need not simply be explanatory but can also be creative in its own right. *The Secret Ghost* is inventive in depicting a problem that can be solved using mathematics, and its narrative could also be used as a template for creative writing in mathematics. Students can come up with their own problems or scenarios in which mathematics would be used to come up with a solution. So much time and energy is put into reading and deciphering word problems, but it seems that having students write their own would demonstrate as much, if not more, understanding of mathematical concepts and mechanics. In the end, students could swap their writing, work on the problems, and check the work of their classmates. They could even draw pictures, diagrams, or a comic narrative to go along with the problem. This book opens up a number of possibilities for thinking about and depicting mathematics work that can be more inviting and attractive to students.

Concluding Thoughts and Further Resources

There is much about graphic novels that makes them appealing to both students and teachers. Both groups may be surprised to find that the characters they enjoy reading about in the stories also provide them with content information that ties in with what they learn/ teach in their classes. Teachers might be surprised to find material that can be used to drive, bolster, or supplement their instruction. Many graphic novel authors have taken time and care to include many accuracies and details in their work through historical or scientific research. From the small sample of books here, it should be apparent that graphic novels can be used to make many cross-curricular connections (Brozo, Moorman, & Meyer, 2014), as there's often much more to a graphic novel than comical scenes and one-liners.

There's often much more to a graphic novel than comical scenes and one-liners.

In recent years, the increased attention on graphic novels from both consumers and producers is leading to a surge in titles, series, and the amount of remarkable literature becoming available. The amount of graphic novels, however great, should also lend one pause. Although there's much that graphic novels offer in terms of attractiveness and academic usefulness, I'm not advocating here that every graphic novel is a treasure trove or should be used in school. Just as not every novel or textbook is appropriate for every class, so it is with graphic novels. Teachers should be informed about the content of graphic novels and also about where to find further information that may help them find appropriate resources. To that end, I have here included a few titles that can give a small start to a teacher interested in the possibilities of graphic novels. But there are also more elaborate resources, starting with Stephen Weiner's (2005) *The 101 Best Graphic Novels: A Guide to This Exciting New Medium* and also these websites that contain many links for an inquisitive teacher or student:

- My own blog, *Graphic Novel Resources*, where I review graphic novels that cover many different content areas and age groups: graphicnovelresources .blogspot.com
- Comics in the Classroom: comicsintheclassroom.net
- The University of Wisconsin–Madison's Cooperative Children's Book Center: www.education.wisc.edu/ccbc/books/graphicnovels.asp

Graphic novels offer students and teachers an invitation to engaging, educational reading.

REFERENCES

Alvermann, D.E., Moon, J.S., & Hagood, M.C. (1999). *Popular culture in the classroom: Teaching and researching critical media literacy.* Newark, DE: International Reading Association; Chicago, IL: National Reading Conference.

Brozo, W.G., Moorman, G., & Meyer, C.K. (2014). *Wham! Teaching with graphic novels across the curriculum.* New York, NY: Teachers College Press.

Cary, S. (2004). *Going graphic: Comics at work in the multilingual classroom.* Portsmouth, NH: Heinemann.

Frey, N., & Fisher, D. (2004). Using graphic novels, anime, and the Internet in an urban high school. *The English Journal, 93*(3), 19–25. doi:10.2307/4128804

Garelick, B. (2012, November 20). A new kind of problem: The Common Core Math Standards. *The Atlantic.* Retrieved from www.theatlantic.com/ national/archive/2012/11/a-new-kind-of-problem-the-common-core-math-standards/265444

Glazer, S. (2005, September 18). Manga for girls. *The New York Times.* Retrieved from www.nytimes.com/2005/09/18/books/ review/18glazer.html?pagewanted=all&_r=0

Goodnow, C. (2007, March 7). Teens buying books at fastest rate in decades. *Seattle Post-Intelligencer.* Retrieved from seattlepi.nwsource.com/books/306531_ teenlit08.html

Heath, S.B., & Bhagat, V. (1997). Reading comics, the invisible art. In J. Flood, S.B. Heath, & D. Lapp (Eds.), *Handbook of research on teaching literacy through the communicative and visual arts* (pp. 586–591). New York, NY: Macmillan Library Reference USA.

McCloud, S. (1994). *Understanding comics: The invisible art.* New York, NY: HarperPerennial.

Meier, D., & Wood, G. (Eds.). (2004). *Many children left behind: How the No Child Left Behind Act is damaging our children and our schools.* Boston, MA: Beacon.

National Coalition Against Censorship, American Library Association, & Comic Book Legal Defense Fund. (2006). *Graphic novels: Suggestions for librarians.* Retrieved from www.ala.org/offices/sites/ ala.org.offices/files/content/oif/ifissues/ graphicnovels_1.pdf

National Governors Association Center for Best Practices & Council of Chief State School Officers. (2010). *Common Core State Standards for English language arts and literacy in history/social studies, science, and technical subjects.* Washington, DC: Authors.

Norton, B. (2003). The motivating power of comic books: Insights from Archie comic readers. *The Reading Teacher, 57*(2), 140–147.

Schwanenflugel, P.J., Hamilton, A.M., Kuhn, M.R., Wisenbaker, J.M., & Stahl, S.A. (2004). Becoming a fluent reader: Reading skill and prosodic features in the oral reading of young readers. *Journal of Educational Psychology, 96*(1), 119–129. doi:10.1037/0022-0663.96.1.119

Short, J.C., Randolph-Seng, B., & McKenny, A.F. (2013). Graphic presentation: An empirical examination of the graphic novel approach to communicate business concepts. *Business and Professional Communication Quarterly, 76*(3), 273–303. doi:10.1177/1080569913482574

Weiner, S. (2003). *Faster than a speeding bullet: The rise of the graphic novel.* New York, NY: Nantier Beall Minoustchine.

Weiner, S. (2005). *The 101 best graphic novels: A guide to this exciting new medium* (2nd ed.). New York, NY: Nantier Beall Minoustchine.

Worthy, J., Moorman, M., & Turner, M. (1999). What Johnny likes to read is hard to find in school. *Reading Research Quarterly, 34*(1), 12–27. doi:10.1598/ RRQ.34.1.2

Yang, G. (2008). Graphic novels in the classroom. *Language Arts, 85*(3), 185–192.

LITERATURE CITED

Melville, H. (2003). *Moby-Dick.* New York, NY: Dover. (Original work published 1851)

O'Connor, G. (2013). *Poseidon: Earth shaker.* New York, NY: First Second.

O'Connor, G. (2014). Olympians [Boxed set]. New York, NY: First Second.

O'Donnell, L. (2007). *Understanding photosynthesis with Max Axiom, super scientist.* North Mankato, MN: Capstone.

O'Donnell, L., Biskup, A., Sohn, E., Lemke, D.B., Krohn, K.E., Harbo, C.L., … Gianopoulos, A. (2007–2015). Max Axiom, super scientist [Series]. North Mankato, MN: Capstone.

Spiegelman, A. (1986). *Maus: A survivor's tale I: My father bleeds history.* New York, NY: Pantheon.

Taylor, S.S., & Towle, B. (2010). *Amelia Earhart: This broad ocean.* New York, NY: Disney·Hyperion.

Thielbar, M. (2010). *The secret ghost: A mystery with distance and measurement.* Minneapolis, MN: Graphic Universe.

Thielbar, M. (2010–2011). Manga math mysteries [Series]. Minneapolis, MN: Graphic Universe.

Yang, G.L. (2006). *American born Chinese.* New York, NY: First Second.

OTHER RECOMMENDED GRAPHIC NOVELS FOR ELEMENTARY STUDENTS

Davis, E. (2009). *The Secret Science Alliance and the copycat crook.* New York, NY: Bloomsbury USA Childrens.

Duffy, C. (Ed.). (2013). *Fairy tale comics: Classic tales told by extraordinary cartoonists.* New York, NY: First Second.

Goh, C., & Woo, Y.Y. (2013). *Enter the dumpling.* Flushing, NY: Yumcha Studios.

Hale, N. (2012). *One dead spy.* New York, NY: Amulet.

Hatke, B. (2010). *Zita the spacegirl.* New York, NY: First Second.

Krosoczka, J.J. (2009). *Lunch Lady and the cyborg substitute.* New York, NY: Alfred A. Knopf.

Roman, D. (2011). *Astronaut Academy: Zero gravity.* New York, NY: First Second.

Spires, A. (2009). *Binky the space cat.* Tonawanda, NY: Kids Can.

Weiser, J. (2013). *Mermin: Book one: Out of water.* Portland, OR: Oni.

ABOUT THE AUTHOR

 Stergios Botzakis is an associate professor in the Department of Theory and Practice in Teacher Education at the University of Tennessee, Knoxville, USA. He received his doctorate from the University of Georgia in 2006, and prior to that, he spent five years teaching middle school reading, English, and study skills in Baltimore and the Boston area. He was an editorial assistant for *Reading Research Quarterly* and also one of the founding editors of the *Journal of Language & Literacy Education*, an open-access, online-only journal.

Currently, Stergios teaches classes on content area reading, middle school education, working with struggling adolescent readers, and new literacies. His research interests include middle and secondary education, adolescent literacies, popular culture, and media literacy. His work has been published in the *Journal of Adolescent & Adult Literacy, English Journal, Language Arts, The ALAN Review,* and *Teacher Education Quarterly.* Stergios can be contacted at sbotzaki@utk.edu.

PART III

Motivating All Students

CHAPTER 8

Reading Multiculturally, Globally, Critically

Incorporating Literature of Diversity in Literacy Education

Barbara A. Lehman, *The Ohio State University, Mansfield Campus*

C hildren's books are messengers, according to French critic Paul Hazard (1944), from the "universal republic of childhood" (p. 146). Jella Lepman (1969/2002), founder of the International Board on Books for Young People (IBBY), viewed children's books as bridges to understanding, and noted scholar and teacher educator Rudine Sims Bishop (1994) deemed literature as potential windows into the lives of other people. As mixed as these similes may be, they all convey the ideas of reaching out, viewing lives beyond our own, and making connections. These attributes are at the heart of multicultural and global literature for children, the focus of this chapter.

In the decades since Hazard's (1944) assertion, the need for cross-cultural messengers is more urgent than ever. Not only is the world shrinking as humans increasingly impact one another's lives both near and far, but also the United States itself is growing rapidly more multicultural. Latest national census figures show the white population proportion dropping, while percentages of persons of color are rising, especially for Hispanics/Latinos. Moreover, much of the increase in diversity is due to immigration, with an estimated 13% of U.S. residents being foreign born—a nearly 2% increase in a decade (U.S. Census Bureau, 2010). A majority of new immigrants today are from Latin America, and unsurprisingly, Spanish is by far the second most widely spoken home language in the United States after English. Many, if not most, teachers see these demographics reflected in their own classrooms and recognize the need for literature that reflects and capitalizes on this diversity. Humans need to know one another to understand and appreciate one another. The remarkable ability of literature to generate empathy and insight toward others—to know each other better—makes it a valuable resource for crossing cultural boundaries and building a "universal republic of childhood."

Children's Literature in the Reading Program: Engaging Young Readers in the 21st Century (4th ed.), edited by Deborah A. Wooten & Bernice E. Cullinan. © 2015 by the International Literacy Association.

Multicultural and Global Children's Literature

Luckily, there is a rich and growing body of literature that accurately and honestly portrays our diversity while also showing our common humanity. (Note: The Cooperative Children's Book Center publishes annual statistics about the number of children's books by and about people of color published in the United States. To view current and past figures since 1985, visit their website at ccbc.education.wisc.edu.) In addition to books published in the United States, there also are many imports, which expand perspectives beyond national boundaries to include the whole world. This global literature represents the places from where both current and past immigrants have come—that is, nearly all Americans (or their ancestors) with the exception of Native peoples. The United States is truly an immigrant nation—with all the richness, complexity, and tension that engenders—a fact that we should always remember and celebrate.

The United States is truly an immigrant nation—with all the richness, complexity, and tension that engenders—a fact that we should always remember and celebrate.

As readers, we all need literature that reflects and affirms our own lives and experiences. In this way, literature serves as a mirror (Bishop, 1994). Only being exposed to this kind of literature, however, can distort and restrict our view of the wider world. In particular, Bishop notes that reading only about others like ourselves teaches us "that [our] culture and way of life is the norm, and that people and cultures different from [us and our culture] are quaint and exotic at best, and deviant and inferior at worst" (p. xiv). Thus, all readers, especially those from a society's dominant culture, also need literature that opens windows onto realities that are different from their own. This is the role and value of multicultural and global literature.

Multicultural literature is named and defined in various ways, according to Botelho and Rudman (2009). They note that many scholars characterize it "as literary works that focus on African Americans, Native Americans, Latino Americans, and Asian Americans" (p. 77). These cultural designations, however, are race and ethnicity driven, and some definitions have been expanded to include religious minorities, sexual orientation, gender, class, age, region, and people with disabilities. Still other terms, such as *literature from parallel cultures, culturally diverse literature,* or *cross-cultural literature,* are favored by critics. Kiefer (2010) ascribes to "literature of diversity" (p. 85) as a more inclusive term. Regardless, all of these names signify such common elements as marginal status, historical underrepresentation, and exclusion from literary canons.

Cai and Bishop (1994) also offer a classification within multicultural literature of "world literature" (p. 62), which broadens the focus to literary works from outside the United States. Some scholars (e.g., Tomlinson, 1998) call this "international literature" and define it as "that body of books originally published for children in a country other than the United States" (p. 4). However, Freeman and Lehman (2001) prefer "global literature," which can include

> books written and published first in countries other than the United States..., books written by immigrants...about their home countries and published in the United States, books written by authors from countries other than the United States but originally published in the United States, and books written by American authors...with settings in other countries. (p. 10)

I use the term *global literature* in this chapter and distinguish it from *multicultural literature*, which, although closely related, portrays cultures within the United States.

Finally, although definitions are important and can be helpful, we also must be wary of their limitations, which can include divisiveness (creating a kind of literary apartheid) and essentializing, or reducing the complexity of all human beings to single attributes. At their best, these terms and definitions enable us to not only clarify our thinking but also broaden our awareness of the rich diversity of literature for and about all children.

Perhaps one of the best ways to grasp this diversity in literature is to see it demonstrated, and luckily there are numerous quality examples, a few of which I highlight here. Excellent multicultural books include Rita Williams-Garcia's (2010) *One Crazy Summer*, a story set in 1968 about three African American sisters who are sent to spend the summer with their artist mother in Oakland, California, during the rise of the Black Panthers there. An introduction to more radical thinking expands the girls' experience with the Civil Rights Movement. This title was both a Coretta Scott King Book Award winner and a National Book Award finalist. The picture book biography *Sacagawea* marks a fine collaboration by Ojibway writer Lise Erdrich (2003) and Ponca artist Julie Buffalohead that won a Carter G. Woodson Book Award. *Sacagawea* clearly distinguishes the known facts about this young Shoshone woman who was so crucial to the success of the Lewis and Clark Expedition while avoiding romanticizing her life and role. Yin's (2001) *Coolies* recounts the travails and triumphs of Chinese immigrant laborers who helped construct the transcontinental railroad in the 1860s. Chris Soentpiet's illustrations bring this historical period to life and were recognized as an honorable mention for the Asian/Pacific American Award for Literature. *Esperanza Rising* by Pam Muñoz Ryan (2000) combines multicultural and global literature with its beginning in Mexico in the 1930s, where Esperanza is the daughter of a wealthy landowner. Her life of privilege abruptly changes when she and her mother flee to California and become farm laborers during the Great Depression. This Pura Belpré Award winner portrays the immigrant experience that many workers still encounter today. Finally, Niki Daly's (1999–2009) series of picture book stories about the escapades of Jamela, a spunky young girl, is beloved internationally and allows readers everywhere to identify with her life in contemporary South Africa. Among other honors, Daly is a Hans Christian Andersen Award nominee.

As noted, these titles or their authors have been named to major awards and lists of recommended books. The American Library Association sponsors some of the most prominent prizes beyond the Newbery and Caldecott Medals. The Coretta Scott King Book Awards, established in 1970, recognize African American authors and illustrators whose work is published in the United States. Since 1996, the Pura Belpré Award honors Latino/a writers and illustrators for outstanding portrayals of the Latino cultural experience. The Stonewall Book Award has been presented since 2010 to meritorious books that represent the gay, lesbian, bisexual, and transgender experience. Finally, the Mildred L. Batchelder Award, founded in 1966, acknowledges translation and publication of quality literature first published in other countries.

Other organizations also sponsor noteworthy prizes. The Association of Jewish Libraries has sponsored the Sydney Taylor Book Award since 1968 for outstanding children's books that authentically portray the Jewish experience. The Carter G. Woodson Book Award has been presented annually since 1974 by the National Council for the Social Studies to distinguished children's books that depict ethnic and racial minorities. Likewise, through the Jane Addams Children's Book Award, the Jane Addams Peace Association has been recognizing since 1953 works that promote peace, social justice, equality, and world community. As identified in the description of this award, a global focus is part of its scope. Two other noteworthy prizes specifically recognize international children's literature. The IBBY has been presenting the Hans Christian Andersen Awards biennially since 1956 to authors and illustrators whose work has made a lasting contribution to world literature for children. Since 2003, the Astrid Lindgren Memorial Award, bequeathed by the Swedish government, recognizes international children's literature authors, illustrators, storytellers, and reading promoters. Two Americans, Maurice Sendak and Katherine Paterson, have been recipients so far. Finally, the United States Board on Books for Young People (the U.S. national section of IBBY) selects an annual list of outstanding international books to honor the best children's literature from other countries. (See Table 8.1 for the websites of all of the awards mentioned.)

All of these awards have their own criteria for evaluation and selection of the honorees, but common important elements for judging multicultural and global children's books include the following:

- *Literary merit:* These titles should reflect high literary quality in terms of a well-constructed plot, worthwhile themes, believable characters, an engaging style, an appropriate point of view, well-executed illustrations, and excellent design.
- *Authenticity and accuracy:* Especially important in contributing to this are the author's background relative to the culture being depicted; his or her other qualifications, such as expertise on the topic; and his or her attitude toward the book's topic. Additional considerations include accuracy of the material presented and culture portrayed; avoidance of stereotypes in characterization, relationships among characters, values and practices,

Table 8.1. Multicultural and Global Children's Literature Awards

Sponsoring Organization	Award	URL
American Library Association	Coretta Scott King Book Awards	www.ala.org/awardsgrants/coretta-scott-king-book-awards
	Mildred L. Batchelder Award	www.ala.org/awardsgrants/mildred-l-batchelder-award
	Pura Belpré Award	www.ala.org/awardsgrants/pura-belpr%C3%A9-award
	Stonewall Book Awards: Mike Morgan & Larry Romans Children's & Young Adult Literature Award	www.ala.org/awardsgrants/stonewall-book-awards-mike-morgan-larry-romans-children%E2%80%99s-young-adult-literature-award
Association of Jewish Libraries	Sydney Taylor Book Award	jewishlibraries.org/content.php?page=Sydney_Taylor_Book_Award&bypassCookie=1
Government of Sweden	Astrid Lindgren Memorial Award	www.alma.se/en
International Board on Books for Young People	Hans Christian Andersen Awards	www.ibby.org/index.php?id=273
Jane Addams Peace Association	Jane Addams Children's Book Awards	www.janeaddamspeace.org/jacba/about.shtml
National Council for the Social Studies	Carter G. Woodson Book Awards	www.socialstudies.org/awards/woodson
United States Board on Books for Young People	USBBY Outstanding International Books List	www.usbby.org/list_oibl.html

settings, and illustrations; and how readers from within the culture view the book. References can help document authenticity and accuracy.

- *Translation:* For works originally written in another language, translation must preserve the integrity of the original work yet sound natural and be understandable to the target audience.

A complete discussion and list of these criteria has been provided by Lehman, Freeman, and Scharer (2010), and using them will help when reading multicultural and global children's literature.

Reading Multicultural and Global Literature

As readers may quickly discern from the previously discussed evaluation criteria, an issue arises when we read books, as we often should, outside our own culture. How can we judge, especially, the accuracy and authenticity of books that relate to cultures and settings with which we're unfamiliar? What may seem innocuous to outsiders can be very controversial for cultural insiders. What may be puzzling, distasteful, or simply incomprehensible to readers can be entirely acceptable to persons from within the culture of the story. How do I evaluate material if my own values are opposed to it? How do I keep my biases from interfering with my judgment of a book? Is that even possible?

The answer to these and other conundrums is not to give up and retreat into one's own comfort zone. Rather, we need more than ever to read, read, read, but to do so responsibly. Hade (1997) calls for what he terms "reading multiculturally" (p. 233) when encountering multicultural literature, and my colleagues and I (Lehman et al., 2010) extend that concept to "reading globally" (p. 22). We define this type of reading in two ways: reading widely and reading critically. *Reading widely* simply means reading a lot. No single book (no matter how authentic) or author (no matter how much of a cultural native) can represent or speak for an entire culture. Mistaking that they can—known as "the danger of the single story" (Adichie, 2009, para. 1)—is what contributes to essentializing, as described earlier. Therefore, one of the best ways to learn about both a culture and its literature is by reading quantities of it. As readers, we gain knowledge about the history, values, practices, settings, and ways of life that define a culture and our familiarity with its literary traditions if we immerse ourselves in as many titles as possible. Reading widely provides a better sense of what is authentic and accepted by the culture. This is a threshold on which we can then begin to read fairly and critically.

Botelho and Rudman (2009) use the term "critical multicultural analysis" (p. 5) to describe this type of reading, and it's where we bring to bear our ability to recognize our own biases and think about literature through a different lens. It involves reading against the grain of our taken-for-granted assumptions about what seems normal. It requires consideration of what the author's biases and ideology may be and his or her intentions, often as revealed through the focalization of the story (i.e., whose story it is), what's included and omitted, what the power relationships are in the story, and how the reader is positioned by the author. It also incorporates recognition of the social contexts of the author, subject, and reader.

All of this is harder work than simply absorbing more books unquestioningly and passively, but it's essential and worth the effort as we grow in our ability to be critical readers, a vital aspect of becoming literate. Every set of educational standards for literacy learning includes critical reading as an important competency and one that most assessment systems try to measure. Fortunately, literature of diversity offers many opportunities, as well as challenges, for continually practicing and improving in this important kind of reading. Ultimately, thinking and reading critically is at the heart of becoming informed citizens and democratic participants and can lead to action for social justice.

Paired Books: A Strategy for Reading Multiculturally, Globally, Critically

Critical multicultural and global reading can, and does, happen when we read single texts, but often it works better when reading and comparing texts. Paired books is a strategy for juxtaposing two books that invite thought-provoking comparisons across one or more dimensions. (Grouping several books in this manner makes a text set, which also creates rich potential for critical reading but is more complex to develop and manage.) In this context, pairing two multicultural or global books can help illuminate similarities and differences across cultures and make the foreign seem more familiar. This is particularly important for young readers whose knowledge base is more limited and who may relate better when they identify commonalities with their own experiences. In turn, teachers may find that pairing books helps them teach students how to naturally read more critically. Here I describe the paired book reading strategy with two titles that share a number of intriguing similarities.

Comparing a Book Pair

Thank You, Mr. Falker is beloved author Patricia Polacco's (1998) tribute to her real teacher, Mr. Felker. In this story, Trisha loved books as a young girl and couldn't wait to learn to read when she entered school. However, that goal was thwarted as she struggled to make sense of print. Each year in school, she fell further and further behind her classmates, who began to treat her cruelly; her disability became more acute; and she became more discouraged and "began to feel dumb" (n.p.). None of her teachers seemed able to help her overcome, or perhaps even notice, her lack of reading ability. Even moving to a new school across the country didn't solve Trisha's problem. One boy in particular tormented her daily and made her dread going to school, and Trisha began to believe the demeaning names he called her. It wasn't until her fifth-grade year that she encountered Mr. Falker, a different kind of teacher who not only didn't tolerate the bullying but also praised her artistic talent. He also wasn't fooled by Trisha's coping strategies to pretend that she could read. He found help for her with a special reading teacher and worked tirelessly with her every day after school, always believing that she could succeed. Then, one day, she finally broke through and became a reader, an event that literally changed her life.

In a story that resonates with many of Trisha's experiences, Niki Daly (2003) presents Sarie's dilemma in *Once Upon a Time*. Set in the Little Karoo of South

Africa, this young girl also struggles with reading and dreads going to school, where her classmates make fun of her when she stumbles over words while reading aloud. In this case, however, it's a boy, Emile, who befriends her and doesn't join in on the teasing. The person who ultimately helps Sarie the most is her neighbor Ou Missus, with whom Sarie loves to spend time sitting in an old car listening to stories and sharing her troubles at school. One day they find an old book of stories, which Ou Missus helps her learn to read by repeating the stories many times and gently supplying words when Sarie needs assistance. Overall, Ou Missus conveys her confidence that Sarie will succeed, and indeed, with practice, Sarie does. On the day when she demonstrates her newly acquired mastery in school, Emile accompanies her home, and they both join Ou Missus in an imaginary game of "once upon a time."

A major theme in these books is the power of literacy, both to open realms of knowledge and imagination for readers and to be used by others as a weapon to humiliate those who lack it. Botelho and Rudman (2009) assert that literacy is "a sociocultural, multiple, and political practice" (p. 44) with the power to both transform and repress or silence individuals (or groups of people), depending on who's wielding it. For example, many U.S. states denied African Americans the right to literacy to maintain their status as slaves before the Civil War and their lack of access to political and economic power afterward. In the case of struggling readers such as Trisha and Sarie, all too often school policies maintain the status quo and actually contribute to their reading disabilities, rather than help provide a solution. For critical readers, these texts invite examination beyond the individual, personal level of dealing with bullies—which, of course, is an important concern for many children—to the institutional context of neglect or the use of inappropriate practices and standardized mandates that may actually exacerbate struggling readers' problems. Children are not too young to think about these issues if teachers help them notice what the adults are doing (or not) in stories.

In the case of struggling readers..., all too often school policies maintain the status quo and actually contribute to their reading disabilities.

Another important theme is the agency of the protagonists. Who is the problem solver? Although initially both Trisha and Sarie appear to be victims and their problems require adult intervention to solve, their strengths also ultimately support their successes. In the case of Trisha, her artistic talent garners praise from Mr. Falker as he publicly recognizes her ability. That encouragement may help her trust him when he launches a plan to teach her to read, and his belief in her undoubtedly contributes to her self-confidence and sense of agency. Likewise, Ou Missus encourages Sarie's gift for imagination and dramatic play, which helps her feel successful and, beyond that, strengthens her sense of story, a good foundation from which to build her interest in reading and her ability to read.

Furthermore, these adult characters are not only sympathetic assistants to the protagonists, but they also refuse to accept the status quo by challenging the girls' and others' assumptions about their lack of ability. The adults employ strategies that help rather than hinder the girls' literacy acquisition. Young readers will have enough experience to recognize how these adults are different from others in the stories. These two books also offer positive models of intergenerational relationships in which adults pay attention to and treat the child characters with respect.

Another literacy-related theme in *Once Upon a Time* is that other valid means to literacy acquisition exist outside school, such as the importance of building on Sarie's competence with imaginary play to support her literacy learning in school. Children such as Sarie come to school with many skills that provide a foundation for learning school discourse. Teachers need to recognize, honor, and capitalize on these language modes.

For many young readers, the protagonists are characters with whom they can identify. Eagerly anticipating learning how to read (as Trisha did) and then finding it such a struggle touches the lives of many children—if not with reading, then something else. Dreading going to school, or any setting where one feels unsuccessful, is a common response. Fearing and facing bullies is another typical childhood experience. Seeing characters overcome obstacles to finally succeed can provide catharsis and insight to nearly everyone. These two girls—both with similar disabilities and one from another country and culture—share many commonalities with children around the world, even if their specific circumstances differ from those of readers.

However, focusing only on similarities between the two books overlooks an important opportunity to compare the different settings. Trisha first lives in Michigan on the family farm, and it's clear that her extended family includes grandparents and probably other relatives. Later, her mother moves Trisha and her brother to California to take a teaching position there. For many U.S. children, these will be familiar locations, as is the ethnic diversity portrayed in Polacco's illustrations. Clearly, Mr. Falker, with his flair for stylish clothes, is not the stereotypical teacher either.

The first sentence of *Once Upon a Time* identifies its setting as the Little Karoo, and the double-page illustration shows Sarie trudging on an unpaved road across a vast, dry plain with rocky outcrops reminiscent of a Southwestern U.S. state. But here the ranching is with sheep, the plain is referred to as "the veld" (Daly, 2003, n.p.), Sarie wears a school uniform, and the steering wheel in Ou Missus's old car is on the right-hand side. In addition, if one is reading the South African version of the text rather than an American imprint, there will be different spellings and names (e.g., "Ou Missus" instead of "Aunty Anna"). So, where are we, some readers may wonder. All the characters, except possibly Ou Missus, are clearly depicted as nonwhite, and Sarie's family works "long, hard hours on the sheep farm" (n.p.), but these could be similar attributes of many settings in the

United States. And the story Sarie reads with Ou Missus is identified as Cinderella. Paying close attention to all of these clues and doing a bit of research provides a fertile opportunity to look through a cultural and national window into another place and to expand what we know about the world. Thus, if we only consider the similarities between these paired books, we miss the chance to critically analyze their cultural and geographic contexts and to gain new knowledge.

Finally, it is essential to examine the authors' qualifications in general and with respect to these titles. Patricia Polacco is a prolific author/illustrator, whose books are hugely popular with children. She also has received numerous awards and honors for her work, including the Jane Addams Children's Book Award and the Sydney Taylor Book Award. *Thank You, Mr. Falker*, a Parents' Choice Award winner, is an authentic representation of reading disability because it's an autobiographical account of Polacco's own struggle with learning to read. Thus, she is widely acclaimed by both literary critics and young readers, and this title meets the criterion of authenticity and accuracy.

Likewise, author/illustrator Niki Daly is prolific and widely known in South Africa and internationally. His talent has been recognized with many prestigious citations, both within South Africa and abroad. Being a native South African, he's well qualified to create books set in that country. He knows its cultures and landscapes well, although he's not of the same ethnicity as that portrayed in *Once Upon a Time* and doesn't live in the Little Karoo. In this instance, he must rely on his experiences with persons from Sarie's culture, as well as research. Because I'm a cultural outsider, albeit one who has visited the Little Karoo, I have to count on South African readers to address the criterion of authenticity and accuracy. My own Internet search of book reviews uncovered no objections based on the title's cultural content. I must remain mindful, however, that such opinions may exist.

Implementing the Paired Books Strategy

Having discussed these two titles in detail, I now use that background to describe how to implement the strategy in elementary literacy instruction. First, I would introduce the two books (possibly on different days) and draw out children's prior knowledge of and experience with the authors. For example, if we've read other books by these authors, I would make sure the students recalled those. I'd ask children about their frustrations with trying to learn something and what they did to succeed. Before reading *Once Upon a Time*, I also would introduce them to the location of South Africa on a map and show photographs (the Internet offers plenty of examples, if needed) of diverse scenes from that country and also ones specific to the Little Karoo region.

Next, I would read the books aloud—first *Thank You, Mr. Falker* and then *Once Upon a Time*—possibly on different days. Listeners could ask questions at any point during the reading, and at the end, we would discuss whatever the children had to say about the stories, including their personal connections to them. After rereading both stories on another day, we could discuss any questions children raised and then develop together a T-chart to compare and contrast the stories' features: plot, characters, problems and solutions, settings, and so forth. (Alternatively, small groups of students could each focus on a different feature and then report back to the whole group.) Once the chart is complete, we would discuss our findings, which could lead to more critical questions.

Here, the teacher's strategic and sensitive guidance can lead to deeper analysis of some of the issues posed in the previous section: the power of literacy and who wields that power, how to deal with bullying, the agency of characters and why some have more than others, how school helps or hinders that agency, how school-based literacy learning and use compares with children's literacy experiences outside school, how readers identified with the protagonists and why, how much readers knew about each setting, and how authentic the stories seem and how effectively the authors created them. Such analysis could lead to further reading and research in other sources.

This would be a good point to introduce a text set of additional titles related to various aspects of the original book pair (e.g., exploring more about South Africa, other examples of learning to read or of the portrayal of teachers in children's books, works by these authors), thus expanding the intertextual connections readers make between texts. I could read aloud Jacqueline Woodson's (2012) *Each Kindness*, a picture book with an African American protagonist who shuns a new girl in her class, whose ragged clothing marks her as poorer than Chloe and her friends. The theme of kindness toward others extends in this book to economic status, and children, like Chloe and her classmates, can discuss the effects of their actions. Students could read additional books in small groups, pairs, or individually and report back what they learned or experienced to the whole class. The culmination of this study could lead to further actions, as will be subsequently posed.

> *The teacher's strategic and sensitive guidance can lead to deeper analysis of some of the issues posed.*

Additional Paired Books

Each Kindness does not give background information about Maya, the new girl, but her name and the fact that she arrives and departs from the school rather unexpectedly could mean that she's part of a migrant family who follows farm work wherever the harvest is. Such circumstances are common in many parts of the United States, and many children will have firsthand experience with them. That theme of migration and immigration relates to the demographic facts, cited at the beginning of this chapter, regarding the United States, as well as around the world. If children's books are ambassadors, they also migrate from one location and culture to another. Here I focus on that theme, using additional pairs of books as examples.

The story of some of the first immigrants to North America, the Pilgrims, is recounted from two perspectives in Jean Craighead George's (1993) *The First Thanksgiving* and in *Squanto's Journey: The Story of the First Thanksgiving* by Joseph Bruchac (2000). George's account, written in an objective voice by a European American, begins with a focus on the Pawtuxets and Squanto but then shifts to the Pilgrims' story until they all come together several years later. In contrast, Bruchac, of Abenaki descent, tells Squanto's story from a first-person point of view and includes an extensive author's note in which he also addresses his relationship to the Native American culture being depicted. The difference in these two books' perspectives is clearly symbolized by the front cover illustrations: for *The First Thanksgiving*, the European immigrants are placed in the foreground with Indians approaching from the distance (almost as if they're arising from the sea behind them), whereas for *Squanto's Journey*, Squanto is pictured in the foreground with the *Mayflower* sailing in the background. This book pair will invite thoughtful critical discussion regarding the sociopolitical implications of their different presentations of one of our most iconic national stories.

More current immigrants, this time refugees from a war-torn nation, are featured in the book pair *Drita, My Homegirl* by Jenny Lombard (2006) and Katherine Paterson's (2009) *The Day of the Pelican*. In both cases, the protagonists are ethnic Albanians from Kosovo, where they were routed out of their homes and often massacred by ethnic Serbs. *Drita* alternates voices between Drita, the immigrant, and Maxie, the African American ringleader of a gang of girls who tease Drita for being different. Meli's story in *The Day of the Pelican* begins in Kosovo, and her family's flight from one refuge to another until they finally reach the United States constitutes much of the narrative and provides considerable background information about the Kosovo conflict. However, Meli, too, encounters new classmates in Vermont who mistreat her and especially hold inaccurate stereotypes of Muslims in the immediate aftermath of September 11, 2001. The attitude of Americans who have a longer history in the United States toward newcomers is an important theme to examine with these titles.

Finally, because stories are migrants, too, especially folktales, different variants of the same tale offer fruitful comparisons. Stories that originate in one culture often are retold in another, with both benefits and potential problems, as noted by Hsieh and Matoush (2012) in their critical analysis of retellings of the Mulan ballad published in the United States. Two versions—*The Ballad of Mulan* retold by Song Nan Zhang (1998) and *Fa Mulan* retold by Robert D. San Souci (1998)—highlight some essential differences when stories are conveyed by persons from within the culture (Zhang) or as an outsider (San Souci). Hsieh and Matoush explore these issues and note that Zhang's version shows careful attention to historical accuracy, even including the Tang poem in Chinese calligraphy alongside the translated text, whereas San Souci's version is a much more freely adapted story. In particular, his account emphasizes Mulan the woman warrior and possible romance motifs—both themes that resonate well for a U.S. audience. In contrast, Zhang centers his retelling on the theme of filial piety. The books' illustrations convey these differences as well. Beyond these two versions, as noted by Hsieh and Matoush, even more remarkable comparisons can be drawn with Disney's fairytale princess version of the story. Young readers can easily grasp the issues surrounding different variants by examining books such as these. Once they begin to engage in this type of critical reading, they may see a need for further action.

Reading the (Real) World: Literacy Learning and Action for Social Justice

When critical reading inspires children to take social action (see Short, 2012), the endeavor can be a valuable means of linking literacy learning to the real world. Continuing to build on the migration/immigration theme, which impacts nearly every community in the United States in some way, I offer here a few examples that may initiate action for social justice. For younger readers, *The Color of Home* by Mary Hoffman (2002) recounts Hassan's experience as a refugee from Somalia, from which his family had to flee violence. Although first published in Great Britain, this story is equally relevant in the United States, where large immigrant communities of Somalis reside. It's a poignant depiction of the terror that drives many migrants from their homelands and their deep longing for the place they left behind. It also is a narrative that may lead students to explore how they can reach out to these new immigrants and make them feel more accepted in their new country. These actions may include "adopting" a new immigrant family, inviting immigrants to share their experiences with classes, researching what services are most needed by new immigrants and how well those are provided in the community, and taking other actions to help create a more open, welcoming environment.

At the higher end of the reading and interest level, Christopher Paul Curtis's (2012) *The Mighty Miss Malone*, set during the Great Depression, is a powerful, moving account of migration within the United States due to lack of employment opportunities. Deza and her family slip from a marginal, but manageable, economic status into poverty, which disrupts the formerly strong family unit and poses serious safety risks for all members of the family. Their struggles are not far different from those of many poor and homeless people today and most certainly can be a catalyst for exploring ways for students to take action, such as visiting homeless shelters, working in food banks, and even seeking ways to redress the causes of poverty in our local and broader society. As Curtis states in the Afterword,

> I want this [book] to be a springboard for young people to ask questions and do more research on some of the themes the book explores, in this case the Great Depression and poverty in general....I hope that Deza can serve as a voice for the estimated fifteen million American children who are poor, who go to bed hungry and whose parents struggle to make a dignified living to feed and care for them. (p. 303)

This is real-world literature study, and it would make literacy learning relevant for contemporary young readers. Children gain agency if they understand an issue in society, believe they can make a difference, and take action to be part of the solution. Often, books are the best messengers of these issues.

Conclusion

Great literature portrays the enormous diversity of our world, not only reflecting readers' own lives but also introducing them to other experiences that enrich and enlarge their vision and understanding. Jeannie Baker's (2010) double narrative *Mirror* aptly symbolizes cross-cultural exchange—in the form of a carpet going from Morocco to Australia—to illustrate how two boys from opposite sides of the globe share commonalities. However, to benefit the most from such literature, we must read multiculturally and globally—that is, both widely and critically. The world will be a better place if every generation builds these bridges and if literacy teachers play a vital role in nurturing this development.

REFERENCES

Adichie, C.N. (2009). *The danger of a single story* [Video speech]. Retrieved from www.ted.com/talks/chimamanda_adichie_the_danger_of_a_single_story

Bishop, R.S. (1994). Introduction. In R.S. Bishop (Ed.), *Kaleidoscope: A multicultural booklist for grades K–8* (pp. xiii–xxii). Urbana, IL: National Council of Teachers of English.

Botelho, M.J., & Rudman, M.K. (2009). *Critical multicultural analysis of children's literature: Mirrors, windows, and doors.* New York, NY: Routledge.

Cai, M., & Bishop, R.S. (1994). Multicultural literature for children: Towards a clarification of the concept. In A.H. Dyson & C. Genishi (Eds.), *The need for story: Cultural diversity in classroom and community* (pp. 57–71). Urbana, IL: National Council of Teachers of English.

Freeman, E., & Lehman, B. (2001). *Global perspectives in children's literature.* Boston, MA: Allyn & Bacon.

Hade, D.D. (1997). Reading multiculturally. In V.J. Harris (Ed.), *Using multiethnic literature in the K–8 classroom* (pp. 233–256). Norwood, MA: Christopher-Gordon.

Hazard, P. (1944). *Books, children and men* (M. Mitchell, Trans.). Boston, MA: Horn Book.

Hsieh, I.H., & Matoush, M.M. (2012). Filial daughter, woman warrior, or identity-seeking fairytale princess: Fostering critical awareness through Mulan. *Children's Literature in Education, 43*(3), 213–222. doi:10.1007/s10583-011-9147-y

Kiefer, B.Z. (2010). *Charlotte Huck's children's literature* (10th ed.). Boston, MA: McGraw-Hill.

Lehman, B.A., Freeman, E.B., & Scharer, P.L. (2010). *Reading globally, K–8: Connecting students to the world through literature.* Thousand Oaks, CA: Corwin.

Lepman, J. (2002). *A bridge of children's books: The inspiring autobiography of a remarkable woman* (E. McCormick, Trans.). Dublin, Ireland: O'Brien. (Original work published 1969)

Short, K.G. (2012). Children's agency for taking action. *Bookbird, 50*(4), 41–50.

Tomlinson, C.M. (1998). International children's literature and this bibliography. In C.M. Tomlinson (Ed.), *Children's books from other countries* (pp. 3–6). Lanham, MD: Scarecrow.

U.S. Census Bureau. (2010). *How do we know? America's foreign born in the last 50 years.* Retrieved from https://www.census.gov/how/pdf//Foreign-Born--50-Years-Growth.pdf

CHILDREN'S LITERATURE CITED

Baker, J. (2010). *Mirror.* Somerville, MA: Candlewick.

Bruchac, J. (2000). *Squanto's journey: The story of the first Thanksgiving.* San Diego, CA: Silver Whistle.

Curtis, C.P. (2012). *The mighty Miss Malone.* New York, NY: Wendy Lamb.

Daly, N. (1999–2009). Jamela [Series]. New York, NY: Farrar, Straus & Giroux.

Daly, N. (2003). *Once upon a time.* London, UK: Frances Lincoln.

Erdrich, L. (2003). *Sacagawea.* Minneapolis, MN: Carolrhoda.

George, J.C. (1993). *The first Thanksgiving.* New York, NY: Philomel.

Hoffman, M. (2002). *The color of home.* New York, NY: Phyllis Fogelman.

Lombard, J. (2006). *Drita, my homegirl.* New York, NY: G.P. Putnam's Sons.

Paterson, K. (2009). *The day of the pelican.* New York, NY: Clarion.

Polacco, P. (1998). *Thank you, Mr. Falker.* New York, NY: Philomel.

Ryan, P.M. (2000). *Esperanza rising.* New York, NY: Scholastic.

San Souci, R.D. (1998). *Fa Mulan.* New York, NY: Hyperion Books for Children.

Williams-Garcia, R. (2010). *One crazy summer.* New York, NY: Amistad.

Woodson, J. (2012). *Each kindness.* New York, NY: Nancy Paulsen.

Yin. (2001). *Coolies.* New York, NY: Philomel.

Zhang, S.N. (1998). *The ballad of Mulan.* Union City: CA: Pan Asian.

OTHER RECOMMENDED CHILDREN'S BOOKS RELATED TO THE THEME OF MIGRATION/IMMIGRATION

Multicultural

Alvarez, J. (2009). *Return to sender.* New York, NY: Alfred A. Knopf.

Cofer, J.O. (2004). *Call me María: A novel in letters, poems, and prose.* New York, NY: Orchard.

Lai, T. (2011). *Inside out & back again.* New York, NY: Harper.

Park, L.S. (2010). *A long walk to water: Based on a true story.* Boston, MA: Clarion.

Weatherford, C.B. (2002). *Remember the bridge: Poems of a people.* New York, NY: Philomel.

Williams, K.L., & Mohammed, K. (2009). *My name is Sangoel.* Grand Rapids, MI: Eerdmans Books for Young Readers.

International

Daly, J. (2010). *Sivu's six wishes.* Grand Rapids, MI: Eerdmans Books for Young Readers.

Diakité, B.W. (1999). *The hatseller and the monkeys.* New York, NY: Scholastic.

Jacobson, S., & Colón, E. (2010). *Anne Frank: The Anne Frank House authorized graphic biography.* New York, NY: Hill and Wang.

Naidoo, B. (2011). *Aesop's fables.* London, UK: Frances Lincoln Children's.

Ohi, R. (2013). *Kenta and the big wave.* Toronto, ON, Canada: Annick.

Poole, J. (2005). *Anne Frank.* New York, NY: Alfred A. Knopf.

ABOUT THE AUTHOR

 Barbara A. Lehman is a professor emerita of teaching and learning at The Ohio State University, Mansfield Campus, USA, where she taught courses in children's literature and literacy. Her scholarly interests focus on multicultural and global children's literature and child-centered literary criticism. She coedited *Teaching With Children's Books: Paths to Literature-Based Instruction* (National Council of Teachers of English, 1995) and *Creating Books for the Young in the New South Africa: Essays on Authors and Illustrators of Children's and Young Adult Literature* (McFarland, 2014), coauthored *Global Perspectives in Children's Literature* (Allyn & Bacon, 2001) and *Reading Globally, K–8: Connecting Students to the World Through Literature* (Corwin, 2010), and wrote *Children's Literature and Learning: Literary Study Across the Curriculum* (Teachers College Press, 2007).

Barbara's articles have appeared in the *ChLA Quarterly*, *Children's Literature in Education*, and the *Journal of Children's Literature*, among others. She has coedited the *Journal of Children's Literature* and *Bookbird*. She was president of the United States Board on Books for Young People in 2011 and the 2009 recipient of the IRA Arbuthnot Award. Barbara was a Fulbright Scholar in South Africa in 2004–2005 and now lives in Columbus, Ohio. She can be contacted at lehman.1@osu.edu.

CHAPTER 9

"That Isn't Fair!"/"¡No Es Justo!" Process Drama for Children

Learning to Think Critically About Picture Books in English and Spanish

Nancy Roser, Deborah Palmer, & Erin Greeter, *University of Texas at Austin*

Miriam Martinez, *University of Texas at San Antonio*

Deborah A. Wooten, *University of Tennessee, Knoxville*

SARA:	*I wouldn't do nothing what he says 'cause he's not my principal or my teacher.*
CRUZ:	*You'll have more and more bad...Bad stuff happen to you...A lie doesn't bring you your dad.*
MS. ALANIS:	*You are Pedro. You are 9 years old! What will you do?*

—Second graders and their teacher "stepping into"
The Composition by Antonio Skármeta (2000b)

For as far back as histories of reading instruction reach, teachers have gathered children around texts to monitor their comprehension—most typically by raising questions at the end of passages (e.g., Mathews, 1976; Smith, 2002). Well before there was guided reading (Fountas & Pinnell, 1996), Betts (1946) proposed an instructional frame that he called directed reading, characterized by the teaching acts of building readers' background for the text, setting purposes for reading, and stopping readers to check their comprehension. Later, Stauffer (1975) added thinking to the notion of directed reading, calling his revised frame Directed

Reading–Thinking Activity. Stauffer advocated meaning-based reader predictions, the testing of those predictions (by reading), and the subsequent confirmation or rejection of one's hypotheses (through sharing thinking at selected points). The procedures for a Directed Reading–Thinking Activity deliberately varied the amount of reading children did before they stopped to share their thinking. For example, readers were asked to predict from the title clues and to stop again for prediction after reading the first page, after three pages, and again after completing about five pages.

In classrooms, reading instruction could feel, as one first grader put it, like "start–stop reading." That young reader was mildly protesting the continuous interruptions. Listeners on the story rug sometimes resist, too: "Just *read!*" young children sometimes complain when their teacher stops a compelling story to make room for talk. As university researchers and classroom teachers, we argue here for the potential of a well-chosen (and limited) stopping point in children's reading. We are proposing the story's turning point—just before a central character makes a critical decision and the plot elements begin to resolve—as a place for stopping to invite deeper meanings through talk and drama. We provide evidence of the thinking children engage in when invited into the story at that fecund moment—to live in another's world, to deliberately experience what one may have never been asked to experience, and to enact the repercussions of decisions characters face at critical moments. Stories resolved can be reacted to more easily than they can be shaped, whereas stories unresolved are filled with possibilities for shaping. Stepping in and taking action before a story is finished, while simultaneously accepting the plot's constraints and assumptions, is what we call process drama (i.e., creating narrative) as distinct from acting out stories (i.e., interpreting narrative). Process drama, as described by its proponents (Heathcote & Bolton, 1995; O'Neill, 1995), allows players to step into the role of characters faced with a real dilemma and work their way through the muddle. From inside a story world, for example, children can pose and try out original and varied solutions to a central problem before discovering how the author solved the problem in the story. As teachers and university researchers, we have been inviting children into drama by stopping at the turning point of culturally sensitive picture books as one way for readers to cross borders and occupy others' perspectives.

> *Stories resolved can be reacted to more easily than they can be shaped, whereas stories unresolved are filled with possibilities for shaping.*

Choosing Drama for the Reading Curriculum

Researchers continue to demonstrate how well-chosen literature can provide for discussion that supports children's connections to diverse characters and unfamiliar events (Edmiston & Enciso, 2002; Leland & Harste, 2005; Lysaker, Tonge, Gauson, & Miller, 2011; Short, 1992). Although still not pervasive in U.S. classrooms, drama has a strong base of evidence for its effects on comprehension (Pellegrini & Galda, 1982), language development (Mages, 2008), literary understandings (Adomat, 2007; Edmiston, 1993; Sipe, 2002), and playful interpretations (Paley, 1981; Rowe, 1998; Wohlwend, 2009). But although discussions of socially conscious and language-diverse children's literature have informed theory and practice (e.g., Martínez-Roldán & López-Robertson, 1999; Rogers & Mosley, 2004), there has been less systematic inquiry into the potential of stopping within stories to make meanings through process drama (Adomat, 2010; Roser, Martinez, Carrell Moore, & Palmer, 2014). In support of dual-language learners' willingness to empathize with diverse characters and more deeply understand events, we describe in this chapter classroom opportunities to read and think critically, to pose and then try out dramatic solutions when children are stopped at the turning point in culturally sensitive stories and invited into the story world.

We chose the active, invitational, and challenging nature of process drama as the vehicle to support deepened understandings for children who are already crossing borders in their dual-language classrooms. We hoped that the combination of culturally sensitive texts and opportunities to explore new terrains would support these children's language learning, comprehension, critical thinking, and empathy. We were aware that picture books with culturally sensitive themes could foster discussions of bigotry, class, cultures, gender, language, human conflict, ethnicity, and race, so process drama seemed a sensible choice to both the teachers and university-based researchers in our efforts to support children's restorying of issue-centric picture books in critically conscious ways (Clarke & Whitney, 2009; Medina, 2006; Rogers & Mosley, 2010) and within the languages of home and school (Martínez-Roldán, 2003).

We found that children could move most comfortably toward process drama in baby steps, first displaying the "transparent" and "performative" responses that Sipe (2008, p. 86) theorized from his observations of children's storytime talk. He described transparent responses as those occurring at moments of great story intensity in which children might be compelled to address the text or its characters or even join in the action by speaking original lines. Performative responses are those in which the children take over the story, "hijacking it" (p. 174) in ways that manipulate and even control the text. This hijacking—taking up and over the story—is much like process drama. But initially, teachers invited and made room for children's interpretive facial expressions and gestures from their seated positions. We wanted to build comfort with nonverbal participation in meaning making before inviting talk, movement, and finally, the full-blown stepping into character that would allow for trying out alternate solutions that children posed during discussion at the turning point. All of us were intent on observing, listening, recording, and making sense of children's interactions and critical insights as they thought, talked, played, and took over the story, (re)shaping the action toward ends they could justify.

Setting Drama Within Two-Way Dual-Language Education

Although we believe that engaging the body and mind in dramatic exploration of authentic, multicultural picture books can help all children access deeper and more critical understandings of text and world, we intentionally explored these strategies with a group of emergent bilingual[1] students in a two-way dual-language program. These programs in the United States are increasingly popular models of bilingual education in which children from both English-dominant and minority-language–dominant families (in most cases, Spanish) learn together bilingually in the same classroom.

As part of a multiyear ethnography set in a Southwestern dual-language elementary school, we documented the talk and dramatic responses of first and second graders as they and their teachers discussed and stepped into selected multicultural children's literature, often offered in English and Spanish. At least half the instructional day is conducted in the non-English language and the rest in English (Howard, Sugarman, Christian, Lindholm-Leary, & Rogers, 2007). Children learn other students' dominant languages through content instruction, working together to support one another in the classroom. The explicit goals of two-way dual-language programs are to develop in all children bilingualism and biliteracy, high academic achievement, and cross-cultural competencies. These programs appear to be powerful spaces for success for English learners in terms of both English-language acquisition and academic achievement, while offering enrichment opportunities in a second language to English-dominant children (Lindholm-Leary, 2001; Thomas & Collier, 2002). Given the large and growing population of English learners in U.S. schools and the increasingly multilingual/multicultural global society, such innovative programs seem imperative.

For dual-language programs to meet their goals, they must not only engage children in thoughtful and carefully designed content instruction through two languages but also integrate critical multicultural perspectives into the curriculum (Freeman, 1998; Palmer, 2008). In particular, the development of cross-cultural competencies in children requires a challenging and critical curriculum offering diverse cultural perspectives and a range of narratives (Fránquiz & Salinas, 2011; Ladson-Billings, 1994). Thus, drama is well matched with the goals of language learning, and the teachers and children were enthusiastic participants. The affordances of drama meant that teachers and children could draw on all of their linguistic and cultural resources to make sense of new texts and contexts, supporting one another to build bilingualism while developing their critical comprehension.

We grounded our collaborative project in a sociocultural view of learning (Gutiérrez, Bien, Selland, & Pierce, 2011; Street, 2003; Vygotsky, 1978) in that we believe that working toward meaning, acquiring discourses, and developing multicultural understandings through drama are all inherently social and culturally situated practices, enacted with tools and texts (including languages themselves).

Making Meanings Through Drama

In the five first- and second-grade classrooms in which we observed and participated, the first language of approximately half of the children was Spanish, and the other half spoke primarily English. Because the school leadership was in search of an enlivened curriculum for dual-language learners, we offered teachers hands-on support for drama, including professional readings and resources, and (through the resources of a small materials grant) choices from a set of picture books with culturally and critically conscious themes, many of the titles in both Spanish and English. See Table 9.1 for the

---

Table 9.1. Principles That Guided Our Book Choices

- Are there central social and ethical issues within the stories (e.g., power, fairness, race, class, identity) for children to question and reflect on? Exploring the central issues helps children step into less familiar situations, whether because of geography, culture, gender, or other borders.
- Are there characters of about the children's ages who could benefit from advice or a shift in perspective? Because understandings of character are often preliminary to dramatization and central to entering into the world of the "other," it is important for children to explore dynamic characters who experience a wide range of emotions, moods, and relationships as the plot unfolds.
- Do characters face a critical decision or dilemma that might seem beyond the characters' control? Stories with a need for decisive action create space for children to think critically and defend their positions.
- Is there sufficient ambiguity in the story, allowing for multiple and even conflicting points of view? Conflicts without definitive answers or solutions position children to "take over" the story and see how their own sense of justice can be enacted.
- Are the picture books available in multiple languages so children can draw on their diverse resources to engage in play and make meaning?

---

criteria we used for selecting books that are respectful of the "life experiences, traditions, histories, values, worldviews, and perspectives of the diverse cultural groups that make up a society" (Grant & Ladson-Billings, 1997, p. 185). (A reproducible version of Table 9.1 is also provided at the end of this chapter for teacher use.)

To get started, teachers gave children opportunities to step into the turning points of traditional and familiar literature but with (perhaps) more active provocateurs. For example, taking the role of Grasshopper in Aesop's fable The Ant and the Grasshopper, the teacher pleaded with the ants (the children) for forgiveness and understanding, asking them to remember a time when having fun was so important that their own chores went undone. Some ant children forgave and took in the cold, hungry insect; others held firm and denied the grasshopper food he didn't work for; and still others posed alternative solutions (involving grasshopper penance). All ants expressed the reasoning behind their decision. It was important to remind ourselves that we valued the options children constructed and played into at the turning point rather than enactment of the correct ending to the fable.

As children became more comfortable playing into familiar story scenes (although there were still squirmers, resisters, and gigglers), the teachers invited children into the chosen pieces of culturally sensitive literature at a preselected turning point—the decisive moment in the story in which the protagonist faces a crisis and must act. The turning point would serve as the stopping place. To prepare for this phase, we worked to identify the turning points of our collection. (See Table 9.2 for a list of culturally sensitive picture books. Table 9.3 offers links to additional booklists, as well as other resources related to process drama.) To avoid the dreaded start–stop reading, we also agreed that we would never identify more than two such decisive points. For example, we settled on a turning point in *Henry and the Kite Dragon* by Bruce Edward Hall (2004) after the 11th opening. At that point, the Chinese American children must decide whether to confront the Italian American children who have been throwing rocks at their kites. As another example, in *My Name Is Yoon* by Helen Recorvits (2003), a turning point occurs when the immigrant child, Yoon, must decide whether she will write her name in the English way her teacher expects of her or use the characters of her Korean home language that seem right and "happy" (n.p.) to her. In *The Composition* by Antonio Skármeta (2000b), children experiencing a repressive political regime must decide whether to obey military orders by writing honest essays that reveal their parents' civil disobedience, or lie to protect their parents.

Having identified each story's likely place for stopping to discuss, problem solve, and try on solutions, we slipped a small card into the turning point page

Table 9.2. Culturally Conscious Books for Process Drama

Book	Illustrator
Cohn, D. (2002). *¡Sí, se puede!/Yes, we can! Janitor strike in L.A.* El Paso, TX: Cinco Puntos.	Francisco Delgado
González, R. (2005). *Antonio's card/La tarjeta de Antonio.* San Francisco, CA: Children's Book.	Cecilia Concepción Álvarez
Hall, B.E. (2004). *Henry and the kite dragon.* New York, NY: Philomel.	William Low
Harrington, J.N. (2004). *Going north.* New York, NY: Farrar, Straus & Giroux.	Jerome Lagarrigue
Lacámara, L. (2010). *Floating on Mama's song/ Flotando en la canción de Mamá.* New York, NY: Katherine Tegen.	Yuyi Morales
Landowne, Y. (2004). *Sélavi: A Haitian story of hope.* El Paso, TX: Cinco Puntos.	Youme Landowne
Medina, J. (1999). *My name is Jorge on both sides of the river: Poems in English and Spanish.* Honesdale, PA: Wordsong.	Fabricio Vanden Broeck
Naylor, P.R. (1991). *King of the playground.* New York, NY: Atheneum Books for Young Readers.	Nola Langner Malone
Park, F., & Park, G. (2000). *The royal bee.* Honesdale, PA: Boyds Mills.	Christopher Zhong-Yuan Zhang
Polacco, P. (2009). *The butterfly.* New York, NY: Puffin.	Patricia Polacco
Recorvits, H. (2003). *My name is Yoon.* New York, NY: Frances Foster.	Gabi Swiatkowska
Skármeta, A. (2000). *La composición.* Caracas, Venezuela: Ekare.	Alfonso Ruano
Skármeta, A. (2000). *The composition* (E. Amado, Trans.). Toronto, ON, Canada: Groundwood.	Alfonso Ruano
Vamos, S.R. (2011). *The cazuela that the farm maiden stirred.* Watertown, MA: Charlesbridge.	Rafael López
Wiles, D. (2001). *Freedom summer.* New York, NY: Aladdin.	Jerome Lagarrigue
Williams, K.L., & Mohammed, K. (2007). *Four feet, two sandals.* Grand Rapids, MI: Eerdmans Books for Young Readers.	Doug Chayka
Winter, J. (2005). *The librarian of Basra: A true story from Iraq.* San Francisco, CA: Harcourt.	Jeanette Winter
Woodson, J. (2001). *The other side.* New York, NY: G.P. Putnam's Sons.	E.B. Lewis

Table 9.3. Internet Resources Related to Process Drama

Website	URL
Cooperative Children's Book Center	ccbc.education.wisc.edu/books/detailListBooks .asp?idBookLists=77
Drama-Based Instruction Network	www.utexas.edu/cofa/dbi
Goodreads (sublist of social justice and peace picture books)	www.goodreads.com/group/bookshelf/40108-peace-and-social-justice?shelf=picture-book
The Kennedy Center: ArtsEdge	https://artsedge.kennedy-center.org/educators/how-to/from-theory-to-practice/process-drama
Morea Steinhauer: Children's Books on Social Justice Issues	www.moreasteinhauer.com/2008/06/childrens-books-on-social-justice-issues

(see Table 9.4 for sample card content). Because our picture book selection largely dealt with sensitive social issues, included dynamic characters, and involved important moral/ethical decisions that could turn the action, the books themselves made for valid and vocal disagreements among children. That was a plus. Yet, like Short (2011), we were concerned that we were sometimes sharing only one-sided stories or providing only one view of a community—a minus. We recognized that representing only one instance of a culture fails to offer the diversity and complexity of a people and place. We risked, for example, presenting only one view of a war-damaged area (e.g., *The Librarian of Basra: A True Story From Iraq* by Jeanette Winter, 2005; *Four Feet, Two Sandals* by Karen Lynn Williams and Khadra Mohammed, 2007) that might evoke compassion but not further a broad understanding. Discussion helped fill gaps, but we were determined to introduce more than one side of a story.

Teachers shared each picture book across two days. On the first day, the teachers introduced the book and read aloud from its opening to a preidentified turning point. Stopping at a character's decision point made for speculative talk, the proffering of solutions, and the first steps toward trying out some ideas from inside the story. Process drama means that teachers, too, step into and speak from a role, such as a kite-making grandfather who feels certain no kite is worth fighting over or a teacher who wants to ensure that all of her students can write in English. O'Neill (1995) defines this teacher activity as providing the pretext from which the group will work together. A mutually agreed-upon pretext helps set the stage for the action.

To signal the stopping point for deliberative talk, teachers often turned the book upside down on their laps and waited for children to weigh in with proposals for action that seemed logical, likely, useful, or fair. At this point, the children

Table 9.4. Examples of Turning Point Invitations

Book	Pretext	Stopping/Turning Point	Invitation
▪ Anzaldúa, G. (1997). *Friends from the other side/Amigos del otro lado*. San Francisco, CA: Children's Book.	Consider the book's title together: ▪ "What is the 'other' side?" ▪ "What would be 'other' if you lived somewhere else?" ▪ "Name or play how people decide someone is different."	After a neighbor woman shouts, "¡La migra!" (n.p.)	▪ "Take on the role of Prietita and play her decision." ▪ The teacher and other students can be neighbors asking about the decision.
▪ Hall, B.E. (2004). *Henry and the kite dragon*. New York, NY: Philomel.	▪ Discuss a time when students disagreed or misunderstood another. ▪ "Name or play how they resolved the conflict."	After reading opening 11: "'Come on!' I shouted, and led my friends down eight flight of stairs and out onto the street, leaving Grandfather Chin and the giant dragon kite on the roof, alone." (n.p.)	▪ "As friends of Henry, what are you going to do? Are you going to follow?" ▪ Invite students to play what Henry and Tony might say to each other.
▪ Hoffman, M. (1994). *Amazing Grace*. New York, NY: Dial Books for Young Readers. ▪ Hoffman, M. (1996). *La asombrosa Graciela*. New York, NY: Dial Books for Young Readers.	▪ Discuss a time when students achieved a goal. ▪ "What happens when you put your mind to something?"	After reading opening 7: One day Grace's teacher said they would do the play *Peter Pan*. Grace knew who she wanted to be. When she raised her hand, Raj said, "You can't be Peter—that's a boy's name." (n.p.)	▪ "What are you going to say in response to Raj?" ▪ Invite students, as Grace, to explain why they want to play a boy character.
▪ Skármeta, A. (2000). *La composición*. Caracas, Venezuela: Ekare. ▪ Skármeta, A. (2000). *The composition* (E. Amado, Trans.). Toronto, ON, Canada: Groundwood.	Ask and discuss with students, "Is it right to lie?"	After reading opening 10: "Take out your notebooks....Take out your pencils.... Now write!" (n.p.)	▪ "What are you going to write?" ▪ Invite students to become Pedro and explain or show what they might do to protect their family.

were unaware of how the actual plot resolves. To test the likely implications of a proposed solution, children stepped into the crisis, took on the character roles, and attempted to be convincing about their decided courses of action. Playing out different solutions in different ways—from chorused protests to full-blown overturning of the plot—allowed not only divergent courses of action but also exploration of the ramifications of those choices.

The goals for stopping at a critical juncture were to recollect the problem, collect the largest range of opinions toward generating and testing potential solutions, and challenge with logic and text evidence. By contrast, the goal was not to correctly predict the story ending.

Thinking Critically Through Process Drama

If young children have a nearly inherent link to critical literacy, it may be through their sense of fairness. That is, primary graders may not question the origin of societal power structures, the history of oppression, the silencing of voices, or their own roles in change, but they do seem to have a nearly inborn sense of justice ("That's not fair!"/"¡No es justo!"). Across the read-alouds, children seemed most ready to speak back to instances of unfairness, bullying, or inequity. With an eye toward fairer solutions, they contributed to plans and defended ideas. Perhaps it was this burgeoning sense of equity that accounted for children's passion as they demonstrated their understandings of characters' perspectives, pushed back, were swayed by others (at times), and drew from personal and cultural experiences to reason. In the following sections, we offer the evidence (through language) of what children seemed ready to do with drama-based support for critical thinking. We conclude with a close look at the role and moves of teachers that seemed to elicit children's thoughtful participation.

Speaking Back to Injustice Through Drama

Perching a green elfin hat on her head, Ms. Salinas closed *La Asombrosa Graciela* by Mary Hoffman (1996; see Hoffman, 1994, for the English version, *Amazing Grace*) and, assuming the voice of the lead character, sadly declared that because she's a girl, she'll never be allowed to play the coveted role of Peter Pan in the school play. Children took on the challenge with gusto, gestures, exclamations, justifications, and vehement counters to her declaration, providing reasons that Graciela (Grace in the English version), who is both female and black, could play Peter Pan or any other role. Still in the role of Graciela, Ms. Salinas asked some children to play the perspectives of characters who believed that only boys should play boy roles, while others played the roles of children who had ideas for what should happen next in Graciela's classroom (and why). As children played into the pretext, their voices overlapped:

GABRIELA: *¡Pero, yo puedo hacer!* (But, I can do it!)

ÁNGELA: *¡No importa!* (It's not important!)

CAROLINA: *¿Por qué una niña no puede ser Peter Pan?* (Why can't a girl be Peter Pan?)

ÁNGELA: *¡Si puedo hacer en mi casa, yo puedo hacer aquí también!* (If I can do it in my house, I can do it here [in the classroom], too!)

We listened for the use of first person, a signal that children were speaking from within the story world (rather than from a more dispassionate spectator stance). From inside Graciela's emotions and experience, many students seemed eager to address bullying and discrimination. The conflict at the story's turning point generated lively responses among Ms. Salinas's first graders. Graciela's allies stood up for her, reasoning that they, too, could do anything that they set their minds to. Displaying her comprehension of the story before the turning point, one child (assuming Graciela's role) recalled that she had played many social and imaginary roles outside of school: "*¡Si puedo hacer en mi casa, yo puedo hacer aquí también!*" ("If I can do it in my house, I can do it here [in the classroom], too!"). Books with culturally sensitive themes and the need for decisive action seemed instrumental to children's speaking and playing against injustice.

Reasoning, Justifying, Arguing From Evidence Through Drama

As described previously, *The Composition* (see Skármeta, 2000a, for the Spanish version, *La Composición*) is set in an unidentified country in which an imposing army captain demands that schoolchildren write essays revealing what their parents do with their free time. Third-grade protagonist Pedro and his classmates must decide whether they'll tell the truth in their compositions or lie to protect their families. Ms. Alanis paused for the first time in her reading of *The Composition* as a dissident is arrested and hauled away. The arrested character is the father of one of Pedro's classmates, Daniel. At that point, Ms. Alanis set the stage for her second graders to imagine the presence of an imposing military figure in the classroom—one who demands that children betray family secrets:

TEACHER: You saw what happened to Daniel's dad yesterday. You talk to your parents. Suddenly, this captain is in here. What are you gonna do? What are you gonna write on your paper?

MARIANA:	I would write on my paper, "When I come home from school, I do my work, and then me and my parents eat, and then we listen to the radio, and then we go to bed."
LANCE:	Well, you shouldn't write that they listen to the radio, because then they will ask, "What type of radio?"
TEACHER:	Oh, Lance is (describing) a good point. Say it again, Lance.
MARIANA:	They listen to music.
LANCE:	If you write—if you write about the radio [turns to Mariana and extends his hand], someone will think, will say, "What type of radio?"
MARIANA:	I'll say, I'll write, "It's a *music* radio. They just listen to *music*, and then we all go to bed."
CRUZ:	No, they'll come at night, and they'll take your family.

Proposing what they will (and will not) reveal in their compositions moved the children to think deeply into the threat and weigh its seriousness against the junta's promises of prizes and acclaim for honest writing. Posing, justifying, and listening to others' responses help shape ideas and become the fodder for the drama: Mariana explaining her lie, with Lance helping to tighten it, as well as Cruz's contention that lying may not be the solution. Lance's comment showed sophisticated reasoning; he questioned Mariana's idea of writing about the radio, constructing a theory that radio broadcasts might stir more suspicions. Ms. Alanis requested that Lance restate his point ("Say it again, Lance"), which called the children's attention to the detail of his rationale. Lance broadened the talk in making his peers aware of the trouble that Mariana's writing may cause. His point allowed for Mariana to present her plan with more detail and authority. Dialogic exchanges in preparation for process drama often seemed to demonstrate children's active involvement. Discussion seemed to build necessary preparation for the stepping in.

Changing Perspectives Through Drama

In some cases, understandings shifted as the children engaged in conversation or participated in the drama. Because of the plot twist in *Henry and the Kite Dragon*, children's shifts in perspective were made evident. Set in New York City in the 1920s, Henry and the children from Chinatown must decide what to do when the children from Little Italy repeatedly destroy Grandfather Chin's handmade kites by flinging rocks. Across classrooms that read *Henry and the Kite Dragon* aloud, the teachers stopped reading at the decision point. While still seated, teachers asked children to step in: "If you were out there with Henry, and he said, 'C'mon, let's go! Let's go to the park!' would you go?" Students immediately accepted the invitation to problem solve:

GREG: I'm just gonna go there and do something about it [smiles]!

HAILEY: I would be kind of, like, scared to get there, but I would be angry because they would…

JULIE: They'd keep on throwing rocks, and they're trying to throw rocks at our dragon!

TOM: Maybe they just think it's not fair that he can make so much good kites, that he can make better kites…

GREG: I think that they are just going to make friends.

HAILEY: I would probably just use my words, just say like, "I don't like when you throw rocks at my kite 'cause I worked really hard on them."

Most children initially stood in Henry's corner, expressing feelings of anger and a desire for retribution. Greg, Hailey, and Julie's sense of an undeserved attack was countered by Tom's perspective, as he tried to understand the motivations of the rock-throwing children from Little Italy. Tom offers the possibility that the Italian American children might have been motivated by jealousy (they were unable to make such amazing kites). Greg took up Tom's remark, adding expectations for a friendly reconciliation and countering his own earlier threat of physical action. Hailey, having first admitted how torn she felt (both "scared" and "angry"), seemed to borrow experiential knowledge to communicate her plan, explaining that she would "just use my words." The perspectives meant different plans could be tried out and feelings examined. When the story line shifts, providing the explanation for the Italian American children's actions, children weighed into their decisions again.

Drawing on Personal Experiences, Cultural Knowledge, and Language Resources for Making Meaning

Stepping into a story is not a culturally neutral act. Children bring their lives, languages, interests, personal experiences, and cultural knowledge to the interpretive act of meaning making. While discussing *Friends From the Other Side/Amigos del Otro Lado* by Gloria Anzaldúa (1997), Ms. Johnson provided space for students to share relevant personal and cultural experiences in connecting to the story of Prietita, who helps Joaquín, an undocumented immigrant from Mexico, hide from *la migra* (immigration officials). When Ms. Johnson asked, "What are you thinking?" Josué offered his own story:

JOSUÉ: One time, my grandma [inaudible] the police called another police, *y la llevaron pa'trás a Texas* (and they took her back to Texas).

MS. JOHNSON: *¿A Texas o a México?* (To Texas or to Mexico?)

JOSUÉ: *A Texas.*

MS. JOHNSON: Did y'all hear what Josué said? Is it OK if I tell them what you just said?

JOSUÉ: [nods OK]

MS. JOHNSON: Josué said that one time his—*abuelita o abuelito* (grandmother or grandfather)?

JOSUÉ: *Abuelita.* (Grandmother.)

MS. JOHNSON: His *abuelita* was here in Texas, and they got stopped in the car. Yes?

JOSUÉ: [nods in affirmation]

MS. JOHNSON: They got stopped in the car, and the police officer called another police officer. Who do you think that other police officer was?

TESSA: The border patrol.

MS. JOHNSON: [to Josué] The border patrol?

JOSUÉ: [nods in affirmation]

MS. JOHNSON: And what did they do, Josué?

JOSUÉ: *La mandaron pa'trás.* (They sent her back.)

MS. JOHNSON: *La mandaron pa'trás.* (They sent her back.)

JOSUÉ: *Porque no tenía el esticker del carro.* (Because she didn't have the [registration] sticker on her car.)

TESSA: But where did they send her?

MS. JOHNSON: *Pa'trás.* (Back.)

Josué's cultural resources, gained through family experiences, supported his connection to the story, including his knowledge of immigration procedures, deportation risks, and transnational travel. Linking the scene in the text to a relevant personal situation enabled not only Josúe but also his classmates to empathize with Joaquín's plight and fears. Josué demonstrated that as children participate in the planning of the drama, in the action, or in the reflection, they draw from wellsprings that enable them to inhabit characters and to exercise their own powerful sense of connection and identity.

Because the children had varying proficiencies in English and Spanish, there were differences in the amount of talk and action. This is not uncommon in any classroom, but it's especially true of linguistically diverse dual-language contexts (Palmer, 2011). Even so, drama allows for a range of participation, becoming a scaffold for emergent bilinguals who are developing their verbal skills in their second language. Children who didn't frequently participate verbally when stories were read in English registered responses through mime, facial expressions, and/or gestures. For example, while reading *Friends From the Other Side/Amigos del Otro Lado*, Ms. Johnson invited the class to play into their understandings of how Joaquín felt when he crossed the Mexican border with his mother. The children used their bodies to express emotions of exhaustion, fear, and hope and then froze into tableaux. Talk isn't typically part of a tableau, but the frozen moments often spark critical reflection. Postperformance, one child spontaneously expressed an understanding that he had gained through the drama: "¡Yo todavía soy Mexicano!" ("I'm still Mexican!"). The child had identified with the story world character so closely that few words were necessary to express an appreciation of identity and heritage language.

Inviting Children to Drama: Teachers' Roles

The teachers in this dual-language school relied on literature to open spaces for children to engage with powerful ideas, even as those children were developing increased proficiency in two languages. Further, across classrooms, all teachers accepted the range of ways children stepped into stories (from gesture to movement to fully enacted scenes). If empathy and a sense of social justice stem from knowing and understanding others, we believe that the most important discovery we made was that of asking children to become the character. A deceptively simple teacher directive to become the character at a turning point ("You are Pedro. What are you going to do?") seemed to transform thought, talk, and play. When children became the character, their language shifted from the sidelined, "If I were Pedro...," to the discourse and actions of a fully immersed character, with its consistent use of first person and its identity ("I will not lie."). A teacher's request, "What are you going to do?" seemed to help children shift from speculating about characters to positioning themselves within the story world. This shift seemed to have the most promise for taking on new understandings and perspectives.

But teachers made other moves toward ensuring their students' deep engagement and ever more thoughtful responses through drama. For example, teachers took an active role in the drama, often initiating the scene and sometimes provoking the resultant action (as when Ms. Alanis became the military might in a classroom, or Ms. Salinas became the amazing Graciela). Teachers sometimes pushed back against the players' proposed plans, arguing their likelihood or raising possible consequences for actions. For example, during a turning point scene from

Henry and the Kite Dragon, Ms. Alanis troubled a friendly resolution between characters at odds with one another when she asked, "Do you think you'll just suddenly say, 'Let's just be friends?'" Gentle reality checks seemed to give students a nudge to think more deeply about their roles (Wolf, Edmiston, & Enciso, 1997).

Teachers also worked to scaffold children's participation in drama. For example, as O'Neill (1995) suggests, teachers can support participation by reestablishing the premise of the story, setting up an event, or reminding children of the problem the character(s) faces. Encouraging talk before action prepares children to step in and play out their ideas for decisive action. In nearly every classroom, teachers collected evidence from children about what a character feels and understands—before they stepped into roles. Further, by choosing or arranging scenes that involve a group of children, teachers ensured that nearly all the children participated in the drama rather than simply serving as the audience. And when children have played a scene in several ways, some teachers guided reflections on the action, encouraging the players to rethink their ideas, drawing from text and the drama experience. Finally, teachers helped children clarify the rationale for their actions from a character's vantage point.

In Table 9.5, we describe teacher moves, illustrated with examples of language to demonstrate how each invitation to drama might sound for a selected book, *The Composition*. We don't offer these examples as procedural but rather as a demonstration of the beginnings of a discursive tool kit that teachers may consider when working into process drama.

Although the teacher accounted for the majority of moves into stories, not all movements toward drama were teacher initiated. Sometimes the story itself, its suspense or its conflicts, became so compelling that the students spoke directly to the action or illustration. Drama requires teachers to actively listen to children's spontaneous responses, from expulsions or intakes of air to taking on character roles, as the story is shared. These moments generate openings for children to think into their spontaneous responses.

Conclusion

Teachers need not be fluent in a language to recognize the value of that language to students and to affirm its role in their learning (Fránquiz & de la Luz Reyes, 1998). Neither must teachers be thespians or hams to help children step into texts toward deepened understandings. All teachers can encourage emergent bilingual children to enter the conversation and draw on their full linguistic and cultural repertoires, inviting children to respond in the language varieties they choose. Moreover, all teachers can increase the likelihood that children will make deep and lasting meanings from the bridges they construct with well-chosen literature.

In general, drama has been credited with supporting children's engagement, language, and comprehension. Even so, drama is not a part of most elementary

Table 9.5. Examples of Teacher Moves

Teacher Move	Teacher Language During Class Discussion of *The Composition*[a]
The teacher invites talk that gathers or clarifies understandings of characters (traits, actions, or feelings).	"What do we know about Pedro?"
The teacher sets the scene for the students to enter the story world as themselves.	"You just saw what happened to Daniel's dad yesterday. You talk to your parents. Suddenly, this captain is in here. What are you gonna do? What are you gonna write on your paper?"
The teacher asks the students to take a character's perspective to make decisions and to offer a rationale from the character's vantage point.	"If you were Pedro, what would you be thinking right now?"
The teacher steps into role and tries to persuade students to think differently.	"But he [the captain] says that you get a gold medal, but instead you get this colorful sash to wear. You get to carry something in the parade."
The teacher reasons and pushes back by pointing out the realities or consequences of the students' proposed actions.	"Is it right to lie? What happens when you lie?"
The teacher invites movement or action in response to the story.	"Show me the face. What face do you think his parents are making right now?"
The teacher lifts text into students' own lives to garner deeper reflection.	"Close your eyes for a minute. If you knew something bad might happen to your family and you knew they might come and take your mom or your dad away, would you lie?"

[a]Skármeta, A. (2000). *The composition* (E. Amado, Trans.). Toronto, ON, Canada: Groundwood.

curricula. Its premises and preparation may seem intimidating, and its freedoms can seem to threaten classroom decorum and the business of learning. Yet, process drama in these beginners' classrooms wasn't traditional reenactment of a story (e.g., playing the role of Goldilocks) but rather a form of authoring or constructing an event or set of events with peers toward solving a problem. When a text is unfinished, it is malleable and the drama offers its players active coauthorship. The most successful dramatizations occurred when there were multiple propositions for action. Through drama, teachers and children occupy the story world as participants, speaking out from the setting, the issues, and the times and assuming that their decisions and actions can make a real difference in the events being portrayed. With and without teacher invitations, turning points seem like the "just right" stopping places (in just the right amounts) for the players to take on the perspectives of characters and try varying and innovative ways for understanding others and solving problems. Turning point stops can provide opportunities for engagement, the stretching of perspectives, invitations to language, and a place for critical thought (DeNicolo & Fránquiz, 2006).

Process drama, under the guidance of teachers, invites exploratory participation from all students, makes room for personal and collaborative thinking, and creates opportunities for negotiation and agency with language. Under the aegis of teachers and in the presence of carefully chosen books, children understand the world differently, their roles within it, and the thinking required of them for fair play.

Consider finding a turning point and stepping into the drama.

NOTE

[1]The term *emergent bilingual*, as defined by García (2009), refers to children who are developing bilingual skills, and can include English learners as well as learners of other languages.

REFERENCES

Adomat, D.S. (2007). Through characters' eyes: How drama helps young readers understand stories from the "inside out." In D.W. Rowe, R.T. Jiménez, D.L. Compton, D.K. Dickinson, Y. Kim, K.M. Leander, & V.J. Risko (Eds.), *56th yearbook of the National Reading Conference* (pp. 68–80). Oak Creek, WI: National Reading Conference.

Adomat, D.S. (2010). Dramatic interpretations: Performative responses of young children to picturebook read-alouds. *Children's Literature in Education, 41*(3), 207–221. doi:10.1007/s10583-010-9105-0

Betts, E. (1946). *Foundations of reading instruction*. New York, NY: American Book.

Clarke, L.W., & Whitney, E. (2009). Walking in their shoes: Using multiple-perspectives texts as a bridge to critical literacy. *The Reading Teacher, 62*(6), 530–534. doi:10.1598/RT.62.6.7

DeNicolo, C.P., & Fránquiz, M.E. (2006). "Do I have to say it?": Critical encounters with multicultural children's literature. *Language Arts, 84*(2), 157–170.

Edmiston, B. (1993). Going up the beanstalk: Discovering giant possibilities for responding to literature through drama. In K.E. Holland, R.A. Hungerford, & S.B. Ernst (Eds.), *Journeying: Children responding to literature* (pp. 250–266). Portsmouth, NH: Heinemann.

Edmiston, B., & Enciso, P. (2002). Reflections and refractions of meaning: Dialogic approaches to classroom drama and reading. In J. Flood, D. Lapp, J.R. Squire, & J.M. Jensen (Eds.), *Handbook of research on teaching the English language arts* (2nd ed., pp. 868–880). Mahwah, NJ: Erlbaum.

Fountas, I.C., & Pinnell, G.S. (1996). *Guided reading: Good first teaching for all children*. Portsmouth, NH: Heinemann.

Fránquiz, M.E., & de la Luz Reyes, M. (1998). Creating inclusive learning communities through English language arts: From Chanclas to Canicas. *Language Arts, 75*(3), 211–220.

Fránquiz, M.E., & Salinas, C.S. (2011). Newcomers developing English literacy through historical thinking and digitized primary sources. *Journal of Second Language Writing, 20*(3), 196–210. doi:10.1016/j.jslw.2011.05.004

Freeman, R.D. (1998). *Bilingual education and social change*. Philadelphia, PA: Multilingual Matters.

García, O. (2009). Emergent bilinguals and TESOL: What's in a name? *TESOL Quarterly, 43*(2), 322–326.

Grant, C.A., & Ladson-Billings, G. (Eds.). (1997). *Dictionary of multicultural education*. Phoenix, AZ: Oryx.

Gutiérrez, K.D., Bien, A.C., Selland, M.K., & Pierce, D.M. (2011). Polylingual and polycultural learning ecologies: Mediating emergent academic literacies for dual language learners. *Journal of Early Childhood Literacy, 11*(2), 232–261. doi:10.1177/1468798411399273

Heathcote, D., & Bolton, G. (1995). *Drama for learning: Dorothy Heathcote's mantle of the expert approach to education*. Portsmouth, NH: Heinemann.

Howard, E.R., Sugarman, J., Christian, D., Lindholm-Leary, K.J., & Rogers, D. (2007). *Guiding principles for dual language education* (2nd ed.). Washington, DC: Center for Applied Linguistics.

Ladson-Billings, G. (1994). *The dreamkeepers: Successful teachers of African American children*. San Francisco, CA: Jossey-Bass.

Leland, C.H., & Harste, J.C. (with Huber, K.R.). (2005). Out of the box: Critical literacy in a first-grade classroom. *Language Arts, 82*(5), 257–268.

Lindholm-Leary, K.J. (2001). *Dual language education*. Tonawanda, NY: Multilingual Matters.

Lysaker, J.T., Tonge, C., Gauson, D., & Miller, A. (2011). Reading and social imagination: What relationally oriented reading instruction can do for children. *Reading Psychology, 32*(6), 520–566.

Mages, W.K. (2008). Does creative drama promote language development in early childhood? A review of the methods and measures employed in the empirical literature. *Review of Educational Research, 78*(1), 124–152. doi:10.3102/0034654307313401

Martínez-Roldán, C.M. (2003). Building worlds and identities: A case study of the role of narratives in bilingual literature discussions. *Research in the Teaching of English, 37*(4), 491–526.

Martínez-Roldán, C.M., & López-Robertson, J.M. (1999). Initiating literature circles in a first-grade bilingual classroom. *The Reading Teacher, 53*(4), 270–281.

Mathews, M.M. (1976). *Teaching to read, historically considered*. Chicago, IL: University of Chicago Press.

Medina, C.L. (2006). Critical performative literacies: Intersections among identities, social imaginations and discourses. In J.V. Hoffman, D.L. Schallert, C.M. Fairbanks, J. Worthy, & B. Maloch (Eds.), *55th yearbook of the National Reading Conference* (pp. 182–194). Oak Creek, WI: National Reading Conference.

O'Neill, C. (1995). *Drama worlds: A framework for process drama*. Portsmouth, NH: Heinemann.

Paley, V.G. (1981). *Wally's stories: Conversations in the kindergarten*. Cambridge, MA: Harvard University Press.

Palmer, D.K. (2008). Building and destroying students' 'academic identities': The power of discourse in a two-way immersion classroom. *International Journal of Qualitative Studies in Education, 21*(6), 647–667. doi:10.1080/09518390701470537

Palmer, D. (2011). The discourse of transition: Teachers' language ideologies within transitional bilingual education programs. *International Multilingual Research Journal, 5*(2), 103–122. doi:10.1080/19313152.2011.594019

Pellegrini, A.D., & Galda, L. (1982). The effects of thematic-fantasy play training on the development of children's story comprehension. *American Educational Research Journal, 19*(3), 443–452. doi:10.3102/00028312019003443

Rogers, R., & Mosley, M. (2004). Learning to be just: Interactions of white working-class peers. In E. Gregory, S. Long, & D. Volk (Eds.), *Many pathways to literacy: Young children learning with siblings, grandparents, peers and communities* (pp. 142–154). New York, NY: RoutledgeFalmer.

Rogers, R., & Mosley, M. (2010). Read-alouds as spaces for the deliberation of public sphere issues. In R.T. Jiménez, V.J. Risko, M.K. Hundley, & D.W. Rowe (Eds.), *59th yearbook of the National Reading Conference* (pp. 102–116). Oak Creek, WI: National Reading Conference.

Roser, N., Martinez, M., Carrell Moore, H., & Palmer, D. (2014). *Reinvite drama into classrooms, part 2: Exploring stories through process drama* [IRA E-ssentials series]. Newark, DE: International Reading Association. doi:10.1598/e-ssentials.8062

Rowe, D.W. (1998). The literate potentials of book-related dramatic play. *Reading Research Quarterly, 33*(1), 10–35. doi:10.1598/RRQ.33.1.2

Short, K.G. (1992). Researching intertextuality within collaborative classroom learning environments. *Linguistics and Education, 4*(3/4), 313–333. doi:10.1016/0898-5898(92)90006-I

Short, K.G. (2011). Children taking action within global inquiries. *The Dragon Lode, 29*(2), 50–59.

Sipe, L.R. (2002). Talking back and taking over: Young children's expressive engagement during storybook read-alouds. *The Reading Teacher, 55*(5), 476–483.

Sipe, L.R. (2008). *Storytime: Young children's literary understanding in the classroom.* New York, NY: Teachers College Press.

Smith, N.B. (2002). *American reading instruction* (Special ed.). Newark, DE: International Reading Association.

Stauffer, R.G. (1975). *Directing the reading–thinking process.* New York, NY: Harper & Row.

Street, B. (2003). What's "new" in New Literacy Studies? Critical approaches to literacy in theory and practice. *Current Issues in Comparative Education, 5*(2), 77–91.

Thomas, W.P., & Collier, V.P. (2002). *A national study of school effectiveness for language minority students' long-term academic achievement.* Santa Cruz, CA: Center for Research on Education, Diversity & Excellence.

Vygotsky, L.S. (1978). *Mind in society: The development of higher psychological processes* (M. Cole, V. John-Steiner, S. Scribner, & E. Souberman, Eds. & Trans.). Cambridge, MA: Harvard University Press.

Wohlwend, K.E. (2009). Damsels in discourse: Girls consuming and producing identity texts through Disney princess play. *Reading Research Quarterly, 44*(1), 57–83. doi:10.1598/RRQ.44.1.3

Wolf, S., Edmiston, B., & Enciso, P. (1997). Drama worlds: Places of the heart, head, voice, and hand in dramatic interpretation. In J. Flood, S.B. Heath, & D. Lapp (Eds.), *Handbook of research on teaching literacy through the communicative and visual arts* (pp. 492–505). New York, NY: Macmillan Library Reference USA.

CHILDREN'S LITERATURE CITED

Anzaldúa, G. (1997). *Friends from the other side/Amigos del otro lado.* San Francisco, CA: Children's Book.

Cohn, D. (2002). *¡Sí, se puede!/Yes, we can! Janitor strike in L.A.* El Paso, TX: Cinco Puntos.

González, R. (2005). *Antonio's card/La tarjeta de Antonio.* San Francisco, CA: Children's Book.

Hall, B.E. (2004). *Henry and the kite dragon.* New York, NY: Philomel.

Harrington, J.N. (2004). *Going north.* New York, NY: Farrar, Straus & Giroux.

Hoffman, M. (1994). *Amazing Grace.* New York, NY: Dial Books for Young Readers.

Hoffman, M. (1996). *La asombrosa Graciela.* New York, NY: Dial Books for Young Readers.

Lacámara, L. (2010). *Floating on Mama's song/Flotando en la canción de Mamá.* New York, NY: Katherine Tegen.

Landowne, Y. (2004). *Sélavi: A Haitian story of hope.* El Paso, TX: Cinco Puntos.

Medina, J. (1999). *My name is Jorge on both sides of the river: Poems in English and Spanish.* Honesdale, PA: Wordsong.

Naylor, P.R. (1991). *King of the playground.* New York, NY: Atheneum Books for Young Readers.

Park, F., & Park, G. (2000). *The royal bee.* Honesdale, PA: Boyds Mills.

Polacco, P. (2009). *The butterfly.* New York, NY: Puffin.

Recorvits, H. (2003). *My name is Yoon.* New York, NY: Frances Foster.

Skármeta, A. (2000a). *La composición.* Caracas, Venezuela: Ekare.

Skármeta, A. (2000b). *The composition* (E. Amado, Trans.). Toronto, ON, Canada: Groundwood.

Vamos, S.R. (2011). *The cazuela that the farm maiden stirred.* Watertown, MA: Charlesbridge.

Wiles, D. (2001). *Freedom summer.* New York, NY: Aladdin.

Williams, K.L., & Mohammed, K. (2007). *Four feet, two sandals.* Grand Rapids, MI: Eerdmans Books for Young Readers.

Winter, J. (2005). *The librarian of Basra: A true story from Iraq.* San Francisco, CA: Harcourt.

Woodson, J. (2001). *The other side.* New York, NY: G.P. Putnam's Sons.

OTHER RECOMMENDED CHILDREN'S BOOKS WITH MOMENTS FOR REFLECTION AND DRAMA

Boelts, M. (2007). *Those shoes.* Somerville, MA: Candlewick.

Choi, Y. (2001). *The name jar.* New York, NY: Dell Dragonfly.

DiSalvo-Ryan, D. (1994). *City green.* New York, NY: Morrow Junior.

Johnson, J.C. (2010). *Seeds of change: Planting a path to peace.* New York, NY: Lee & Low.

Lorbiecki, M. (2000). *Sister Anne's hands.* New York, NY: Puffin.

Thong, R. (2010). *Fly free!* Honesdale, PA: Boyds Mills.

Tonatiuh, D. (2014). *Separate is never equal: Sylvia Mendez & her family's fight for desegregation.* New York, NY: Abrams Books for Young Readers.

van Mol, S. (2011). *Meena.* Grand Rapids, MI: Eerdmans Books for Young Readers.

Woodson, J. (2012). *Each kindness.* New York, NY: Nancy Paulsen.

ABOUT THE AUTHORS

Nancy Roser is a professor of language and literacy studies, the Flawn Professor of Early Childhood, and a Distinguished Teaching Professor at the University of Texas at Austin, USA. A former elementary teacher, she teaches undergraduate elementary reading and language arts, as well as classes on children's literature. Nancy's research interests include the close inspection of children's book conversations in classrooms. She can be contacted at nlroser@utexas.edu.

Deborah Palmer is an associate professor of bilingual/bicultural education in the Department of Curriculum and Instruction at the University of Texas at Austin, USA. A former two-way dual-language fourth- and fifth-grade teacher in California, she now teaches courses in the foundations of bilingual and dual-language education, teaching in bilingual/ESL settings, discourse analysis, and second-language acquisition. Deborah's research interests include bilingual education policy and politics, two-way bilingual education, and teacher leadership in bilingual/ESL education. She can be contacted at debpalmer@austin.utexas.edu.

Erin Greeter is a doctoral candidate at the University of Texas at Austin, USA, and a former elementary bilingual teacher. She is completing her doctorate in language and literacy with a focus on the meaning-making processes of bilingual children learning through drama. Erin can be contacted at egreeter@gmail.com.

Miriam Martinez is a professor of literacy in the Department of Interdisciplinary Learning and Teaching at the University of Texas at San Antonio, USA, where she teaches classes in reading and children's literature. She is a coeditor of the *Journal of Children's Literature*. Miriam's research interests focus on children's literary understanding and on textual factors that shape that understanding. She can be contacted at miriam.martinez@utsa.edu.

Deborah A. Wooten is an associate professor of reading in the Department of Theory and Practice in Teacher Education at the University of Tennessee, Knoxville, USA. Before joining the university faculty, she taught elementary school for 23 years. After earning her PhD from New York University, she continued to teach in the elementary classroom for 10 years to research practical new methods for using children's literature to foster connections across content areas while scaffolding students to think metacognitively.

Deborah has served on children's and young adult book award committees and is currently a board member for the Children's Literature Assembly. She is an author and editor of numerous books, chapters, and articles, including coediting and contributing to *The Continuum Encyclopedia of Young Adult Literature* (Continuum, 2005) and *Children's Literature in the Reading Program: An Invitation to Read* (third edition; International Reading Association, 2009). Deborah can be contacted at dwooten1@utk.edu.

Guidelines for Selecting Books
That Children Can Step Into

- Are there central social and ethical issues within the stories (e.g., power, fairness, race, class, identity) for children to question and reflect on? Exploring the central issues helps children step into less familiar situations, whether because of geography, culture, gender, or other borders.

- Are there characters of about the children's ages who could benefit from advice or a shift in perspective? Because understandings of character are often preliminary to dramatization and central to entering into the world of the "other," it is important for children to explore dynamic characters who experience a wide range of emotions, moods, and relationships as the plot unfolds.

- Do characters face a critical decision or dilemma that might seem beyond the characters' control? Stories with a need for decisive action create space for children to think critically and defend their positions.

- Is there sufficient ambiguity in the story, allowing for multiple and even conflicting points of view? Conflicts without definitive answers or solutions position children to "take over" the story and see how their own sense of justice can be enacted.

- Are the picture books available in multiple languages so children can draw on their diverse resources to engage in play and make meaning?

CHAPTER 10

Selecting Engaging Texts for Upper Elementary Students Who Avoid Reading or Find Reading Difficult

Elizabeth A. Swaggerty, *East Carolina University*

I n grades 3–5, the majority of students are able to decode most words and use a variety of strategies to navigate and enjoy various types of text. Yet, they still have much to learn about reading, especially as they encounter increasingly sophisticated text types and varying purposes for reading. Clearly, some will be further along than others on the path to independent reading of a variety of texts, but some intermediate-grade students fall behind in their ability to read. These students might develop behaviors that convey the appearance of reading or avoid reading altogether. By fourth grade, one- or two-year lags in reading achievement are common, and by sixth or ninth grade, three- or four-year lags are, too (Allington, 2008).

These readers are labeled "at risk," "struggling," or "in need of intervention," and their reading motivation often declines as they progress through elementary and middle school. This decline in motivation to read is problematic because more reading leads to better readers, and conversely, when intermediate readers struggle with reading or avoid it for other reasons, reading achievement is threatened (Allington, 2012). For this reason, matching students with texts that they can and want to read is an important consideration, especially if developing the habit of reading and fostering lifelong readers is the goal.

This chapter details both student and text considerations for matching intermediate-grade students (grades 3–5), particularly those who find reading difficult or are reluctant to read, to books that they can and want to read. Teaching tips for supporting engaged reading are also included.

Children's Literature in the Reading Program: Engaging Young Readers in the 21st Century (4th ed.), edited by Deborah A. Wooten & Bernice E. Cullinan. © 2015 by the International Literacy Association.

Know Your Students

Developmentally, students in grades 3–5 should read a variety of long and short texts in a variety of genres for various purposes. They should read silently most of the time but be able to read fluently and expressively when reading aloud, interpret and use illustrations and visual aids in texts, use and build background knowledge when reading, analyze and discern the meaning of multisyllable words, make textual connections, sustain reading of lengthy texts over several days or weeks, and read a variety of text types and formats (Fountas & Pinnell, 2001). To foster the continued development of reading skills and strategies, as well as engagement with texts, students' preferences in reading materials and their reading abilities should be considered.

Consider Students' Preferences

When students have agency in making their own text choices, they're more motivated to engage in reading and more likely to finish reading the text. Choice in reading materials is a motivating factor for readers of all ages (Flowerday, Schraw, & Stevens, 2004; Krashen, 2011) and a particularly important consideration for children who find reading difficult.

However, struggling readers may not be as knowledgeable about the types of texts they prefer because they often lack experience with text. Libraries filled with stacks of books can be overwhelming for students. Teachers and librarians are perfectly positioned to investigate students' interests and help them find texts that match their interests, offering support until students are able to choose their own texts (Reutzel, Jones, & Newman, 2010; Sanden, 2014). This scaffolding can be provided by sharing a variety of texts in small groups and with the whole class through book talks and read-alouds or on an individual basis. For example, if a teacher knows that a particular student is interested in Star Wars, sharing a copy of *Star Wars Jedi Academy: Return of the Padawan* by Jeffrey Brown (2014) might entice the student to read. Exposure to interesting texts can serve as a hook that reluctant and struggling readers need to connect to texts. Adults providing such guidance should value students' initial interests but also encourage students to investigate a variety of options, thereby broadening the topics, genres, and formats they read.

Consider Students' Reading Abilities

Student agency in choosing texts can be a very powerful motivating factor for reading, but educators should also be mindful of students' reading abilities when selecting texts. Students who find reading difficult, in particular, should approach a text feeling capable of successfully reading it independently (Hinchman, Alvermann, Boyd, Brozo, & Vacca, 2004). In other words, students should think, I want to and I *can* read this text. Thus, students' reading abilities and text difficulty should be considerations when selecting books.

Most educators know the value of matching readers to text for independent reading that's on or near their independent reading levels as identified by reading assessments. As far back as 1946, researchers suggested that if reading for meaning, students should be reading texts in which they were able to read at least 90% of the words and comprehending at least 75% of the information (Betts, 1946). That is, students should be reading with ease when reading independently.

Students' reading abilities can be measured with a variety of reading assessments, and the resulting reading levels are represented with grade-level, lettered, or other leveling systems. Although reading-level frameworks offer a helpful structure for matching books to readers, they should be used with care. When assessing students to determine reading levels, several factors might skew the validity of designated levels: Decoding ability and comprehension ability don't always align, some students are more successful silent than oral readers, and difficult text doesn't always lead to frustration (Halladay, 2012). Thus, some flexibility in using assessment results and text-leveling systems to match readers to texts is advised.

For example, when students are motivated to read a particular book, they can often transcend reading-level labels (Hunt, 1970). Some readers will power through a difficult text because they're motivated to read it because the topic interests them or because a friend is reading it, too. To support student success with texts that might be too difficult for them, teachers can read the first part of the text to students so they can become familiar with the text, gain understandings about pronunciation of keywords, and hopefully gain enough momentum to continue reading.

Another consideration is that when struggling students are relegated to read only books on their reading level, they might be stuck with below-grade-level basal texts and "baby books" recommended or assigned by teachers that don't interest them and that they're embarrassed to read. Conversely, texts that are characterized by a lower reading level but maintain a higher interest level (sometimes called high/low texts) can help children feel more confident and experience more success with the texts they're reading (see the Appendix). Online tools such as the Scholastic Book Wizard (www.scholastic .com/bookwizard) can aid in estimating both reading and interest levels of books, but no leveling system is flawless. It's important that levels assigned to books are considered estimates.

Texts that are characterized by a lower reading level but maintain a higher interest level (sometimes called high/low texts) can help children feel more confident and experience more success.

Know Your Texts

Knowing students and their preferences is important when selecting texts for intermediate-grade students to read independently, but it isn't enough for fostering reading engagement. Educators must also know a variety of texts to match students to texts they might like and actually read. Educators can gain familiarity with series books, magazines, picture books, nonfiction, graphic novels, and high-interest/lower level books that are especially appropriate for and of interest to intermediate-grade students. Each of these is explored next.

Series Books

Series books have been a popular reading staple for centuries (Worthy, 1996). This popularity has resulted in wide availability, with books on just about every reading level, topic, and genre imaginable. Such books appeal to readers because students are able to gain mastery over the formulaic conventions of the text with similar characters, language, and content from book to book.

"I noticed you finished reading your book. That's great! Did you know that this is a series, with more books that feature the same characters? Would you like to check out the second book?"

Teachers should tap into the potential of series books for students who are reluctant to read or find it difficult. Once students read the first book in a series and become familiar with the conventions of the text, they're likely to get hooked and engage in reading subsequent books in the series. After a student finishes reading the first book in a series, the teacher might say something like this: "I noticed you finished reading your book. That's great! Did you know that this is a series, with more books that feature the same characters? Would you like to check out the second book?"

Teachers can take it a step further, too, by recommending a similar series that might be more challenging, scaffolding students into reading more difficult texts. Dav Pilkey's books are perfectly suited for this type of support because there are several series options from which to choose and they're all off the wall, featuring two fourth-grade students who hypnotize their principal to become a superhero in his underwear who fights off talking toilets, Dr. Diaper, and Wedgie Woman, to name a few. Students can begin by reading the *The Adventures of Super Diaper Baby* or *The Adventures of Ook and Gluk, Kung-Fu Cavemen From the Future* (Pilkey, 2002, 2010), which are composed of more accessible comic-style writing characterized by less text and more illustrations. Then, the student can be encouraged to read Pilkey's (1997–2014) Captain Underpants novel series, which is more challenging and includes more narrative writing and fewer illustrations.

Locating a cache of series books that are of interest to students and feature text written on lower, more accessible reading levels can aid in matching struggling readers to texts they can and want to read. MAXimum Boy by Dan Greenburg (2001–2003), The Amazing Days of Abby Hayes by Anne Mazer (2000–2009), and After Happily Ever After by Tony Bradman (2009–2014) are examples of popular series for students in the intermediate grades that are accessible to struggling readers in terms of reading-level designations. The After Happily Ever After series, in particular, is written on approximately a second-grade level, but the text appeals to readers in grades 3–5, too. These short chapter books have many pictures to support the text's meaning and aren't intimidating in length, at about 60 pages long each.

Magazines

Magazines are legitimate reading materials that are sometimes marginalized or absent in classrooms, especially in terms of valued reading material for independent reading times. They appeal to intermediate-grade students because they are interesting, address current topics, contain a large amount of graphic material, feature short articles, and reflect a format typically chosen by older readers. Magazines are often available at public libraries, or subscriptions can be purchased for individuals, classrooms, or school libraries.

Highlights (for ages 6–12) and *Cricket* (for ages 9–14) are illustrated literary magazines written for students in the intermediate grades. There are also magazine options that are especially appropriate for students in the intermediate grades and have a more narrow focus on a specific subject, such as science, the arts, sports, and social studies. Here are some good examples:

- *Ask:* Nonfiction for ages 6–10 that focuses on the arts and science
- *Dig:* For ages 9 and up, with a focus on archaeology
- *Muse:* Nonfiction for ages 10 and up that focuses on the arts and science
- *National Geographic Kids:* For ages 6–14, with a focus on geography, adventure, wildlife, and science
- *Ranger Rick:* Focuses on the natural world for ages 7–12
- *Sports Illustrated Kids:* Sports coverage for ages 8–14
- *Zoobooks:* For ages 8–12, with articles about animals, birds, reptiles, and insects

The following magazines are more gender specific and geared to students in grades 3–5:

- *Boys' Life:* For boys 6 and up, with articles on topics such as history, the outdoors, science, and technology

- *Girls' Life:* For girls 10 and up, with a focus on a variety of preteen and teen issues

- *Discovery Girls:* For girls 9–12, with articles on a variety of topics, such as bullying, technology, and positive body image

Two companies that sell popular toys for children in grades 3–5 publish the following magazines:

- *American Girl:* About the American Girl dolls, for girls 8–12

- *LEGO Club Magazine:* Free, for ages 6 and up, with comics, games, and puzzles about LEGOs

Teachers might add magazine subscriptions to the classroom wish list for parents to purchase at the beginning of the school year. As the year progresses and teachers get to know students, teachers can make magazine recommendations to both students and parents. For example, a teacher might notice that one student regularly wrote about horses in her journal and shared stories of her uncle's horse on several occasions. When the new issue of *Zoobooks* comes out, a horse might be on the front cover or a feature in an article. The teacher might say, "Oh my goodness, Sara, look what this issue of *Zoobooks* is about! Would you like to have a look? I know how much you love horses, and I'd love to hear what you think about this issue!" Matching struggling students to magazines that align with their interests can be a powerful way to encourage actual reading.

> *Matching struggling students to magazines that align with their interests can be a powerful way to encourage actual reading.*

Picture Books

Some intermediate-grade teachers or students might think they've outgrown picture books, but many of them feature more advanced or sophisticated concepts, issues, and/or vocabulary and are better suited for older, more mature readers. Picture books are especially appropriate for struggling readers because they tend to be brief in length and contain illustrations and pictures that can support word-solving dilemmas.

For example, *Each Kindness* by Jacqueline Woodson (2012) is a picture book about a cheerful new girl whom classmates nickname "Never New" because of her secondhand clothing and shoes. This text requires inference making, and its themes of bullying, friendship, empathy, rejection, and kindness make it appropriate for readers in grades 3–5. However, the text is written on a third-grade level and the pictures can support word-solving dilemmas, making it more accessible to readers in grades 4 and 5 who find reading difficult. After *Each*

Kindness is read, the student could be introduced to other books written by Jacqueline Woodson, and ideally, the texts might increase in difficulty. In this way, the student can gain confidence with the successful reading of the first text and have the momentum to navigate subsequent, more difficult texts. The teacher might say something like, "Since you read *Each Kindness* and enjoyed it so much, why don't you try *Show Way* [Woodson, 2005] next? It's written by the same author, and I'd like to know what you think about it." The teacher might even recommend partner reading one of Woodson's (2002) chapter books, such as *Maizon at Blue Hill*.

Nonfiction

Nonfiction is an umbrella term for texts that present factual information (Maloch & Bomer, 2013). Duke and Tower (2004) further divide nonfiction into informational text, concept books, procedural texts, biographies, and reference materials. These texts allow readers to learn about the real world and can be invaluable when written about a specific topic that appeals to a reader's interests.

Recently published nonfiction books for children reveal an emphasis on visuals, accurate information, and a more engaging writing style than their predecessors. However, most have high literacy demands in terms of both text structure and vocabulary. Locating on-level nonfiction text is a challenge, and when it can be located, the reading level is typically noted in a highly visible way on the front or back cover, which can be a deterrent for a struggling reader who already feels behind peers in terms of reading ability. Educators should take the time to locate nonfiction texts that are of interest to students, accessible in terms of text difficulty, and feature pictorial supports.

Books packed with illustrations and information, such as the *2014 Scholastic Book of World Records* by Jennifer Carr Morse (2013) and the *Encyclopedia of Animals* by DK Publishing (2006), allow the reader to select the title and then portions of the text that are of particular interest, without requiring commitment to reading the entire book. After a student reads portions of an animal fact book, the teacher might recommend an associated nonfiction text, such as National Geographic Society's (2010–2014) Weird but True! series. Each of these texts focuses on one topic, and students can be encouraged to read each book in its entirety. For example, a teacher might say, "I noticed you've been reading that awesome book of animal facts. I bet you're learning a lot. Check out this book called *Ape Escapes! and More True Stories of Animals Behaving Badly* [by Aline Alexander Newman, 2012]. I think it might be right up your alley."

When a struggling reader is interested in a nonfiction text that appears to be above his or her reading level, a quick preview of the text, particularly in terms of the keywords and text structure, might aid in the student's understanding of the text, especially if he or she is motivated to read about the topic. Pointing out the organization of the text, important word meanings, graphics, headings, and so forth can aid in preparing the student to successfully read the text, feeding his or her curiosity about the topic of interest.

Graphic Novels

Graphic novels are additional text options for children in the intermediate grades. Botzakis (2010) explains that graphic novels are similar to comic books, but graphic novels tend to be contained in one single narrative as compared with the serial stories told in comic books. Graphic novels have been in print since the 1950s but have gained popularity in the last decade. They offer complex combinations of text and images that are attractive to some readers. Readers use the pictures to determine the author's meaning and the text's meaning, which can be more intuitive or apparent to students who are more drawn to visuals. Also, more illustrations means less text, which makes the book appear longer and more advanced, yet it can be read quickly, with the likely outcome of both completion and enjoyment.

Another consideration for students who find reading difficult is that some graphic novels reflect lower readability levels, yet they appeal to readers of a wide span of ages and abilities. For example, Doug TenNapel's (2011) *Bad Island* comprises text written on approximately a second- or third-grade level but appeals to children in grades 2–9. Squish by Jennifer Holm and Matthew Holm (2011– 2014) is a graphic novel nonfiction series written on approximately a third-grade level about a goofy grade school amoeba who goes to school and tries to save the world "one cell at a time!" (Holm & Holm, 2011, back cover).

When introducing a graphic novel to a student who finds reading difficult or is reluctant to read, the teacher can take a few minutes to explain how graphic novels work. The teacher might say, "Graphic novels are like comic books, but the whole book is one story. Pay close attention to the illustrations *and* the text because they work together to tell the story. The words don't make sense without the images, and the images don't make sense without the words."

Sometimes students need help figuring out which direction to read the text, so the teacher can show the student how to navigate and read the first couple of pages, thinking aloud while doing so: "I'm going to start reading here and go across the page. But look, here on this page, it switches, and you read top to bottom. I can tell because I started reading left to right, and it wasn't making any sense!"

E–Books and Internet Reading

Many of the texts described previously are available in digital formats, which may increase students' interest. E-books are available through a number of electronic devices, or e-readers/tablets, many of which are now available in classrooms and school libraries (e.g., Kindle, Nook, Nexus). Downloading texts is instant and often less expensive than purchasing print versions. Not all published texts are available in digital format, but the list of those that are continues to grow. Many e-book services allow downloads on multiple devices, and current page bookmarking is kept track of through Wi-Fi or cellular networks. For intermediate-grade students, TumbleBookLibrary (www.tumblebooks.com/library/asp/about_tumblebooks.asp) offers early chapter books and is available through many school and public libraries. Scholastic offers many affordable e-books for the intermediate grades through Storia (www.scholastic.com/storia-school).

Bookmarking these sites on school computers can assist students in locating them quickly during independent reading time, and sharing them with parents can foster at-home engagement with the same sites.

Additionally, innumerable other reading options for students in the intermediate grades exist on the Internet. Beginning with students' interests helps adults narrow text options and increase reading motivation. For example, if a student likes sports, the Sports Illustrated Kids website (www.sikids.com) features up-to-date information about a variety of sports in a kid-friendly format. The National Geographic Kids website (kids.nationalgeographic.com) features engaging videos and information about animals, the environment, and science. Hosted by the University of Illinois at Urbana–Champaign, Just for Kids (urbanext.illinois .edu/kids/index.cfm) is another option that features content and activities related to a wide variety of science and social studies topics. Bookmarking these sites on school computers can assist students in locating them quickly during independent reading time, and sharing them with parents can foster at-home engagement with the same sites.

More Classroom Strategies to Set Students Up for Success

Once teachers have considered students' interests and abilities and matched them to texts that they can and want to read, what's next? The following strategies can be employed by classroom teachers to aid in setting students up for success with the kinds of books discussed in this chapter for independent reading. Employment of these strategies with the students who find reading difficult or are reluctant to read can increase the likelihood that they'll experience success with reading now and throughout their schooling in later years.

Why Am I Reading This?

Comprehension is strengthened if the reader sets a purpose before reading. Talk briefly with the student about why he or she is reading the text. Is the reading for pleasure/leisure? Will there be a quiz? Is the student reading the text for information (to learn something)?

Connect

After the student selects a text to read, help him or her connect to the text before diving into the first page. Find out what the student knows about the genre, topic, author, and so forth. Help him or her establish a connection(s) to the text to aid comprehension right from the start.

Jump-Start

To help the student feel comfortable and successful reading the text independently, take a few minutes to read the first page or two of a picture book or the first couple chapters of a longer book aloud to the student while he or she follows along with you. This aids in setting the tone for the book and models pronunciation of characters, places, and so on. After reading, have a brief conversation about what was read to check for understanding and model how good readers make predictions about what might happen next in the text. Then, encourage the student to make those predictions as he or she continues reading.

Book Talk

Brief book talks (individual, small-group, or whole-class) can be instrumental in marketing various books to students and broadening their typical text choices. As the year progresses, students can be encouraged to do book talks, too. Peer marketing can be powerful. Book trailers (similar to movie trailers) are also popular and can be found for many books online. Here's a trailer featuring author/ illustrator Dav Pilkey (2013) talking about his book *Captain Underpants and the Revolting Revenge of the Radioactive Robo-Boxers*: www.youtube.com/ watch?v=qz6O8HFzcGA.

Check In

If students are reading longer or more difficult texts, check in with them periodically to inquire about the status of the reading, to check for understanding, and to see if the students need assistance. A quick conversation can reveal comprehension difficulties, fake reading, or the abandonment of the text altogether. The teacher can provide more support or encouragement or aid the student in finding an alternative book that's more appropriate.

Final Thoughts

With motivation to read and access to texts that they can and want to read, all students in upper elementary school can experience a successful trajectory in terms of reading achievement and reading motivation. It's important that teachers accept the challenge to provide all students, especially those who find reading difficult or are reluctant to read, with accessible reading materials in school settings so students can develop the attitude and skills necessary to become habitual readers. This challenge also applies to guardians outside of school settings. When adults consider the preferences and abilities of children and gain familiarity with a variety of texts, they're better equipped to match children to texts, which makes a difference in fostering a lifelong positive reading habit.

NOTE
I would like to extend my appreciation to fifth-grade teacher Renee Whitaker and third-grade teacher Kenyada Pretlow for their feedback on this chapter.

REFERENCES

Allington, R.L. (2008). *What really matters in Response to Intervention: Research-based designs.* Boston, MA: Pearson.

Allington, R.L. (2012). *What really matters for struggling readers: Designing research-based programs.* Boston, MA: Pearson.

Betts, E.A. (1946). *Foundations of reading instruction.* New York, NY: American Book.

Botzakis, S. (2010). A book by any other name? Graphic novels in education. *The ALAN Review, Summer,* 60–64.

Duke, N.K., & Tower, C. (2004). Nonfiction texts for young readers. In J.V. Hoffman & D.L. Schallert (Eds.), *The texts in elementary classrooms* (pp. 125–144). Mahwah, NJ: Erlbaum.

Flowerday, T., Schraw, G., & Stevens, J. (2004). The role of choice and interest in reader engagement. *The Journal of Experimental Education, 72*(2), 93–114. doi:10.3200/JEXE.72.2.93-114

Fountas, I.C., & Pinnell, G.S. (2001). *Guiding readers and writers, grades 3–6: Teaching comprehension, genre, and content literacy.* Portsmouth, NH: Heinemann.

Halladay, J.L. (2012). Revisiting key assumptions of the reading level framework. *The Reading Teacher, 66*(1), 53–62. doi:10.1002/TRTR.01093

Hinchman, K.A., Alvermann, D.E., Boyd, F.B., Brozo, W.G., & Vacca, R.T. (2004). Supporting older students' in- and out-of-school literacies. *Journal of Adolescent & Adult Literacy, 47*(4), 304–310.

Hunt, L.C., Jr. (1970). The effect of self-selection, interest, and motivation upon independent, instructional, and frustration levels. *The Reading Teacher, 24*(2), 146–151.

Krashen, S.D. (2011). *Free voluntary reading.* Santa Barbara, CA: Libraries Unlimited.

Maloch, B., & Bomer, R. (2013). Informational texts and the Common Core Standards: What are we talking about, anyway? *Language Arts, 90*(3), 205–213.

Reutzel, D.R., Jones, C.D., & Newman, T.H. (2010). Scaffolded silent reading: Improving the conditions of silent reading practice in classrooms. In E.H. Hiebert & D.R. Reutzel (Eds.), *Revisiting silent reading: New directions for teachers and researchers* (pp. 129–150). Newark, DE: International Reading Association. doi:10.1598/0833.08

Sanden, S. (2014). Out of the shadow of SSR: Real teachers' classroom independent reading practices. *Language Arts, 91*(3), 161–175.

Worthy, J. (1996). A matter of interest: Literature that hooks reluctant readers and keeps them reading. *The Reading Teacher, 50*(3), 204–212.

CHILDREN'S LITERATURE CITED

Benton, J. (2004–2014). Dear dumb diary [Series]. New York, NY: Scholastic.

Bradman, T. (2009–2014). After happily ever after [Series]. Mankato, MN: Stone Arch.

Brown, J. (2014). *Star Wars Jedi Academy: Return of the Padawan*. New York, NY: Scholastic.

Buckley, M. (2005–2012). The sisters Grimm [Series]. New York, NY: Amulet.

Christopher, M. (2007). *Double play at short*. Boston, MA: Little, Brown.

Clements, A. (1998). *Frindle*. New York, NY: Atheneum Books for Young Readers.

Dahl, M. (2009–2014). Dragonblood [Series]. Mankato, MN: Stone Arch.

DiTerlizzi, T., & Black, H. (2003–2014). The Spiderwick chronicles [Series]. New York, NY: Simon & Schuster Books for Young Readers.

DK Publishing. (2006). *Encyclopedia of animals*. New York, NY: Author.

Gerstein, M. (2007). *The man who walked between the towers*. New York, NY: Square Fish.

Graff, L. (2008). *The thing about Georgie*. New York, NY: HarperTrophy.

Greenburg, D. (2001–2003). MAXimum boy [Series]. New York, NY: Scholastic.

Gutman, D. (2007–2014). My weird school [Series]. New York, NY: HarperCollins.

Holm, J.L., & Holm, M. (2011). *Squish: Super Amoeba*. New York, NY: Random House Children's.

Holm, J.L., & Holm, M. (2011–2014). Squish [Series]. New York, NY: Random House Children's.

Hunter, E., (Kate Cary, Cherith Baldry, & Tui Sutherland). (2003–2015). Warriors [Series]. New York, NY: HarperCollins.

Jenkins, S. (2014). *Eye to eye: How animals see the world*. Boston, MA: Houghton Mifflin Harcourt.

Kessler, L. (2003–2012). Emily Windsnap [Series]. Cambridge, MA: Candlewick.

Kibuishi, K. (2008–2014). Amulet [Series]. New York, NY: Graphix.

Kinney, J. (2007–2014). Diary of a wimpy kid [Series]. New York, NY: Amulet.

Krosoczka, J.J. (2009–2014). Lunch Lady [Series]. New York, NY: Alfred A. Knopf.

Krulik, N. (2006–2009). How I survived middle school [Series]. New York, NY: Scholastic.

Mazer, A. (2000–2009). The amazing days of Abby Hayes [Series]. New York, NY: Scholastic.

McDonald, M. (2000–2014). Judy Moody [Series]. Cambridge, MA: Candlewick.

Morse, J.C. (2013). *2014 Scholastic book of world records*. New York, NY: Scholastic.

National Geographic Society. (2010–2014). Weird but true! [Series]. Washington, DC: Author.

Newman, A.A. (2012). *Ape escapes! and more true stories of animals behaving badly*. Washington, DC: National Geographic Society.

Palacio, R.J. (2012). *Wonder*. New York, NY: Alfred A. Knopf.

Park, B. (1992–2013). Junie B. Jones [Series]. New York, NY: Random House Children's.

Patterson, J., & Tebbetts, C. (2011). *Middle school: The worst years of my life*. New York, NY: Little, Brown.

Peirce, L. (2010–2015). Big Nate [Series]. Kansas City, MO: Andrews McMeel.

Pilkey, D. (1997–2014). Captain Underpants [Series]. New York, NY: Scholastic.

Pilkey, D. (2002). *The adventures of Super Diaper Baby*. New York, NY: Blue Sky.

Pilkey, D. (2010). *The adventures of Ook and Gluk, kung-fu cavemen from the future*. New York, NY: Blue Sky.

Pilkey, D. (2013). *Captain Underpants and the revolting revenge of the Radioactive Robo-Boxers*. New York, NY: Scholastic.

Rand, J. (2001–2014). American chillers [Series]. Topinabee Island, MI: AudioCraft.

Riordan, R. (2008–2011). The 39 clues [Series]. New York, NY: Scholastic.

Riordan, R. (2010–2014). Heroes of Olympus [Series]. New York, NY: Disney·Hyperion.

Rowling, J.K. (1998–2007). Harry Potter [Series]. New York, NY: Arthur A. Levine.

Russell, R.R. (2009–2014). Dork diaries [Series]. New York, NY: Aladdin.

Scieszka, J. (2014–2015). Frank Einstein [Series]. New York, NY: Amulet.

Scieszka, J., & Smith, L. (1992). *The Stinky Cheese Man and other fairly stupid tales.* New York, NY: Viking.

Smith, J. (1991–2004). Bone [Series]. New York, NY: Graphix.

Snicket, L. (Daniel Handler). (1999–2006). A series of unfortunate events [Series]. New York, NY: HarperCollins.

Stilton, G. (Elisabetta Dami). (2004–2015). Geronimo Stilton [Series]. New York, NY: Scholastic.

TenNapel, D. (2010). *Ghostopolis.* New York, NY: Graphix.

TenNapel, D. (2011). *Bad island.* New York, NY: Graphix.

Woodson, J. (2002). *Maizon at Blue Hill.* New York, NY: Puffin.

Woodson, J. (2005). *Show Way.* New York, NY: G.P. Putnam's Sons.

Woodson, J. (2012). *Each kindness.* New York, NY: Nancy Paulsen.

ABOUT THE AUTHOR

 Elizabeth A. Swaggerty has taught third- and seventh-grade English language arts. She is certified to teach elementary (K–6) and reading (K–12). She earned her PhD in literacy studies at the University of Tennessee, Knoxville, USA, and is currently an associate professor of reading education at East Carolina University in Greenville, North Carolina, USA, where she teaches both graduate and undergraduate courses.

Elizabeth has authored numerous articles and book chapters on reading in the intermediate and middle grades, teacher action research, preservice teacher education, and academic writing. She is actively involved in her local IRA reading council and currently serving as cochair of the IRA Task Force for Literacy Teacher Preparation. Elizabeth and her husband, Andy, and their two children, Ben and Maya, stay busy with trips to the Outer Banks, sporting events, and, of course, reading. She can be reached at swaggertye@ecu.edu.

APPENDIX

This table features a sampling of high-interest texts for intermediate-grade readers. Note that the chart is certainly not all-inclusive.

Book	Series	Graphic Novel	Picture Book	High/Low[a]	Nonfiction
Benton, J. (2004–2014). Dear dumb diary [Series]. New York, NY: Scholastic.	X	X			
Bradman, T. (2009–2014). After happily ever after [Series]. Mankato, MN: Stone Arch.	X			X	
Buckley, M. (2005–2012). The sisters Grimm [Series]. New York, NY: Amulet.	X				
Christopher, M. (2007). Double play at short. Boston, MA: Little, Brown.				X	
Clements, A. (1998). Frindle. New York, NY: Atheneum Books for Young Readers.				X	
Dahl, M. (2009–2014). Dragonblood [Series]. Mankato, MN: Stone Arch.	X			X	
DiTerlizzi, T., & Black, H. (2003–2014). The Spiderwick chronicles [Series]. New York, NY: Simon & Schuster Books for Young Readers.	X				
DK Publishing. (2006). Encyclopedia of animals. New York, NY: Author.			X		X
Gerstein, M. (2007). The man who walked between the towers. New York, NY: Square Fish.			X	X	X
Graff, L. (2008). The thing about Georgie. New York, NY: HarperTrophy.				X	
Greenburg, D. (2001–2003). MAXimum boy [Series]. New York, NY: Scholastic.	X			X	
Gutman, D. (2007–2014). My weird school [Series]. New York, NY: HarperCollins.	X			X	

[a]These books are high interest and characterized by lower reading-level text.

(continued)

Book	Series	Graphic Novel	Picture Book	High/Low[a]	Nonfiction
Holm, J.L., & Holm, M. (2011–2014). Squish [Series]. New York, NY: Random House Children's.	X	X		X	X
Hunter, E., (Kate Cary, Cherith Baldry, & Tui Sutherland). (2003–2015). Warriors [Series]. New York, NY: HarperCollins.	X				
Jenkins, S. (2014). *Eye to eye: How animals see the world*. Boston, MA: Houghton Mifflin Harcourt.			X		X
Kessler, L. (2003–2012). Emily Windsnap [Series]. Cambridge, MA: Candlewick.	X				
Kibuishi, K. (2008–2014). Amulet [Series]. New York, NY: Graphix.	X	X		X	
Kinney, J. (2007–2014). Diary of a wimpy kid [Series]. New York, NY: Amulet.	X	X			
Krosoczka, J.J. (2009–2014). Lunch Lady [Series]. New York, NY: Alfred A. Knopf.	X	X		X	
Krulik, N. (2006–2009). How I survived middle school [Series]. New York, NY: Scholastic.	X				
Mazer, A. (2000–2009). The amazing days of Abby Hayes [Series]. New York, NY: Scholastic.	X			X	
McDonald, M. (2000–2014). Judy Moody [Series]. Cambridge, MA: Candlewick.	X			X	
Morse, J.C. (2013). *2014 Scholastic book of world records*. New York, NY: Scholastic.			X		X
National Geographic Society. (2010–2014). Weird but true! [Series]. Washington, DC: Author.	X		X		X
Newman, A.A. (2012). *Ape escapes! and more true stories of animals behaving badly*. Washington, DC: National Geographic Society.				X	X

[a]These books are high interest and characterized by lower reading-level text.

(continued)

Book	Series	Graphic Novel	Picture Book	High/ Low[a]	Nonfiction
Palacio, R.J. (2012). *Wonder*. New York, NY: Alfred A. Knopf.				X	
Park, B. (1992–2013). Junie B. Jones [Series]. New York, NY: Random House Children's.	X			X	
Patterson, J., & Tebbetts, C. (2011). *Middle school: The worst years of my life*. New York, NY: Little, Brown.		X		X	
Peirce, L. (2010–2015). Big Nate [Series]. Kansas City, MO: Andrews McMeel.	X	X			
Pilkey, D. (1997–2014). Captain Underpants [Series]. New York, NY: Scholastic.	X	X			
Rand, J. (2001–2014). American chillers [Series]. Topinabee Island, MI: AudioCraft.	X			X	
Riordan, R. (2008–2011). The 39 clues [Series]. New York, NY: Scholastic.	X			X	
Riordan, R. (2010–2014). Heroes of Olympus [Series]. New York, NY: Disney·Hyperion.	X			X	
Rowling, J.K. (1998–2007). Harry Potter [Series]. New York, NY: Arthur A. Levine.	X				
Russell, R.R. (2009–2014). Dork diaries [Series]. New York, NY: Aladdin.	X			X	
Scieszka, J. (2014–2015). Frank Einstein [Series]. New York, NY: Amulet.	X			X	
Scieszka, J., & Smith, L. (1992). *The Stinky Cheese Man and other fairly stupid tales*. New York, NY: Viking.			X		
Smith, J. (1991–2004). Bone [Series]. New York, NY: Graphix.	X	X		X	

[a]These books are high interest and characterized by lower reading-level text.

(*continued*)

Book	Series	Graphic Novel	Picture Book	High/Low[a]	Nonfiction
Snicket, L. (Daniel Handler). (1999–2006). A series of unfortunate events [Series]. New York, NY: HarperCollins.	X				
Stilton, G. (Elisabetta Dami). (2004–2015). Geronimo Stilton [Series]. New York, NY: Scholastic.	X			X	
TenNapel, D. (2010). *Ghostopolis.* New York, NY: Graphix.		X		X	
TenNapel, D. (2011). *Bad island.* New York, NY: Graphix.		X		X	
Woodson, J. (2002). *Maizon at Blue Hill.* New York, NY: Puffin.				X	
Woodson, J. (2005). *Show Way.* New York, NY: G.P. Putnam's Sons.			X		X
Woodson, J. (2012). *Each kindness.* New York, NY: Nancy Paulsen.			X	X	

[a]These books are high interest and characterized by lower reading-level text.

PART IV

Visiting a Rich Reading and Writing Classroom

CHAPTER 11

Creating Classroom Libraries for Grades K–5

Jonda C. McNair, *Clemson University*

Comprehensive literacy frameworks feature numerous reading and writing activities that provide children with varying levels of teacher support. Although many teachers focus particular attention on certain aspects of this comprehensive framework, such as word study and guided reading, Fountas and Pinnell (1996) maintain that the most important component of this framework is reading aloud. They write, "Reading aloud is the foundation of the early literacy framework" (p. 25). Reading aloud, which should take place every day, has numerous benefits, such as helping children view reading as a pleasurable and worthwhile activity, showing them how stories work, "build[ing] up a repertoire of text structures and literary language structures that will support them in their independent reading" (p. 26), and exposing them to books that they aren't yet able to read independently. Independent reading is another important component of the framework that should take place every day. The classroom library plays a major role in supporting reading aloud, independent reading, and even other components, such as independent writing. This chapter provides suggestions on how to create, furnish, and organize classroom libraries in K–5 settings. It also provides examples of how books in the classroom library can work together and support and enhance instruction in a number of ways.

First Steps to Creating a First-Rate Classroom Library

The arrangement of the classroom library should be such that it is a focal point in the room, which will send a message that books are important. It should also be inviting and easily accommodate five to eight children browsing at the same time. There can be posters or bulletin boards about reading on the nearby walls, stuffed animals, comfortable seating, and various bookshelves that allow for titles to be shelved and displayed—some with the covers showing. Additional items that can be included in classroom libraries include flannel or felt storyboards and aprons with props from stories, materials for writing and responding to books, and books on CD-ROMs, along with a CD player (Beeler, 1993). Book baskets can be used to

Children's Literature in the Reading Program: Engaging Young Readers in the 21st Century (4th ed.), edited by Deborah A. Wooten & Bernice E. Cullinan. © 2015 by the International Literacy Association.

organize some titles in a variety of ways. For example, books can be organized by genre, subgenre, author, illustrator, and subject.

Teachers can also display their creativity when decorating and organizing libraries. For example, as a classroom teacher, I purchased a hammock to place all of my stuffed animals in it so children could read to them. In addition to general stuffed animals, teachers can also include plush dolls and puppets created for literary characters featured in notable titles, such as Frog and Toad, Scaredy Squirrel, Elephant and Piggie, and Cassie from *Tar Beach* by Faith Ringgold (1991). Some teachers choose various themes for their classroom libraries and incorporate them into the setting. In Diller's (2008) book titled *Spaces and Places: Designing Classrooms for Literacy*, there are libraries that have themes such as gardens and beaches. As an example, the garden-themed library features white picket fences attached to the backs of plastic shelves, indoor/outdoor carpeting resembling grass, and plants.

There needs to be some method for allowing children to take books home. As a primary-grade teacher, I only allowed paperback books to go home, but hardbacks could be taken home if it was a child's birthday. It's up to teachers to decide how and what books they'll allow children to check out. I used index cards that were stored in a box with alphabet tabs. Students were instructed on how to write their name, date, and the title of the book on an index card. Once a book was returned, they could check out another title. Now there are technological tools that can facilitate book checkout. For example, an inexpensive app called Book Retriever allows teachers to create a database of all of the books in their classroom libraries. By simply scanning the barcode on the back of the book, the app will add the title to the database, along with the author, illustrator, cover image, number of titles available, and even the current price.

To protect paperback copies and have them last longer, as a classroom teacher, I purchased rolls of clear contact paper and wrapped the books while placing pieces of heavy-duty packing tape on the inside pages where the staples holding the pages together were visible. Doing this led to some books surviving for many years.

How Many and What Kinds of Books?

Although books should be visible throughout the entire classroom, such as in various content area centers, the vast majority of them should be in the classroom library. Some experts contend that elementary classroom libraries should contain five to eight books per child (Christie, Enz, Vukelich, & Roskos, 2013), so a classroom with an average of 25 students should have at least 125 titles. I believe that classroom libraries should have approximately 300 titles (or more) so as to engage a large number of children with varying interests over a period of one year. In addition, books from the classroom library can support units of study on various topics, studies of numerous authors and illustrators, and so forth. Next, I provide information about types of books and materials as well as key factors that should be considered when putting together a first-rate classroom library.

Racial Diversity

The race of the authors and illustrators should be considered when selecting books for classroom libraries so children will be able to see images of themselves and others. Bishop (1990) notes,

> Books are sometimes windows, offering views of worlds that may be real or imagined, familiar or strange. These windows are also sliding glass doors, and readers have only to walk through in imagination to become part of whatever world has been created or recreated by the author. When lighting conditions are just right, however, a window can also be a mirror. Literature transforms human experience and reflects it back to us, and in that reflection we can see our own lives and experiences as part of the larger human experience. Reading, then, becomes a means of self-affirmation, and readers often seek their mirrors in books. (p. ix)

There are some children's literature awards that have race-related criteria, such as the Coretta Scott King Book Awards, Pura Belpré Awards, Tomás Rivera Mexican American Children's Book Award, American Indian Youth Literature Award, and Asian/Pacific American Award for Literature. Selecting books that have won these awards will lead to a more diverse library in terms of race. Also, becoming familiar with these awards will assist teachers in getting to know well-established and up-and-coming authors and illustrators of color. Although statistics note the low numbers of books published each year about and by people of color (Cooperative Children's Book Center, n.d.), teachers who take the time can compile books published over many years by authors of colors and add them to their collections, along with some of the newer titles published each year.

The race of the authors and illustrators should be considered when selecting books for classroom libraries so children will be able to see images of themselves and others.

Magazines

Magazines are important to include as well. A few of my favorites include *Ranger Rick* and *Big Backyard* (formerly called *Your Big Backyard*), two award-winning publications created by the National Wildlife Federation. Both magazines feature engaging photographs of animals, interesting stories, and jokes, as well as writing samples and artwork submitted by children. Other magazines that might be of interest to children in grades K–5 include *National Geographic Little Kids*, *National Geographic Kids*, *Zoobooks*, *Footsteps*, *American Girl*, *New Moon Girls*, and *Boys' Life*, the official publication of the Boy Scouts of America.

Multiple Genres

It's important for children to read across various genres, such as poetry, informational texts, biographies, fantasy, and realistic (historical and contemporary) fiction (see Figure 11.1). By reading across genres, children become familiar with the differences across texts and receive benefits from each. For instance, poetry exposes children to the power of words and the imagery that language can evoke, whereas when reading informational texts, they gain information about the natural and social worlds while learning to navigate their distinct features (e.g., table of contents, topical vocabulary, graphs, diagrams, glossary). Fantasy allows children to imagine what if and extend the realms of what they consider generally possible. *The Adventures of Sparrowboy* by Brian Pinkney (1997) allows children to

Figure 11.1. Genres Bulletin Board

imagine what it might be like to be a comic book hero. Historical fiction provides children with opportunities to learn about the past while seeing that some human emotions are common across time and place. *The All-I'll-Ever-Want Christmas Doll* by Patricia C. McKissack (2007) is set during the Great Depression and is about a young girl who wants a doll for Christmas even though her family has little money. Yearning for Christmas gifts is something to which many children can easily relate.

There are also a number of subgenres, such as alphabet books, wordless books, graphic novels, and predictable books. The repetition, supportive illustrations, rhyme, and patterns in predictable books such as *Tuck Me In!* by Dean Hacohen (2010), for example, can provide support for emergent readers. It's a delightful story about baby animals who all need to be tucked in for bedtime. The pages feature flaps with blanket and quilt designs covering each animal in bed. Also, the endpapers at the front of the book feature all of the animals with their eyes wide open, but at the end of the book, all eyes are closed.

Picture Book Apps

The prevalence of mobile devices (e.g., smartphones, e-readers) in our everyday lives has impacted the field of children's literature. There are now many picture books that have been developed into apps, and they should be made available in K–5 classrooms. Kirkus Reviews (https://www.kirkusreviews.com) now even publishes an annual list of the best apps for children. Some apps have a number of special effects. For example, The Magic School Bus: Oceans allows children to tap the multitouch screen and hear a child's voice reading some of the science reports that students have written about the ocean. They can also tap the screen to hear the children's speech bubble comments. In addition, the app features numerous videos (with sound) of animals found in the ocean. See Table 11.1 for a listing of some my favorite picture book apps.

Classics

Most teachers would agree that *Millions of Cats* by Wanda Gág (1928/1996), *Charlotte's Web* by E.B. White (1952/2012), *Where the Wild Things Are* by Maurice Sendak (1963/2013), and *The Polar Express* by Chris Van Allsburg (1985) are indeed classics. Exceptional literature that has stood the test of time should be shared with readers. In an article titled "Why Children Should Read the Classics," Winfield (1986) writes, "Good literature stimulates thinking, evokes images, creates mental images, and engages the emotions. Good books also encourage children to read more deeply and more often. The classics provide this for readers of all ages" (p. 26).

However, too often, when the term *classic* is used, it generally excludes books written by and about authors of color (McNair, 2010). Harris (1990) writes, "Few texts written by African Americans or other groups of color are designated classics, even though many exhibit extraordinary merit, expand or reinterpret literary forms,

Table 11.1. Recommended Picture Book Apps

App Name	Picture Book Author	App Developer
Animalia	Graeme Base	The Base Factory and AppBooks
Boats	Byron Barton	Oceanhouse Media
Cinderella		Nosy Crow
Don't Let the Pigeon Run This App!	Mo Willems	Disney
Freight Train	Donald Crews	Curious Puppy
Goosed-Up Rhymes		Brain Freeze
Journey Into the Deep: Discovering New Ocean Creatures	Rebecca L. Johnson	Lerner Digital
Little Red Riding Hood		Nosy Crow
The Monster at the End of This Book	Jon Stone	Callaway Digital Arts
Planes	Byron Barton	Oceanhouse Media
Press Here	Hervé Tullet	Chronicle Books
Spot the Dot	David A. Carter	Ruckus Media
The Three Little Pigs: A 3-D Fairy Tale		Nosy Crow
Trains	Byron Barton	Oceanhouse Media
Trucks	Byron Barton	Oceanhouse Media

or provide a forum for voices silenced or ignored in mainstream literature" (pp. 540–541). My vision of classics is more broadly defined. I believe that books such as *Morning Girl* by Michael Dorris (1992), *Everett Anderson's Goodbye* by Lucille Clifton (1983), *The Watsons Go to Birmingham—1963* by Christopher Paul Curtis (1995), and *Dragon's Gate* by Laurence Yep (1993) are also classics, and I believe that good, well-rounded classroom libraries should include titles such as these.

Transitional Chapter Books

Good classroom libraries should have titles that will accommodate readers with varying ability levels. This means having not only picture books but also novels and transitional chapter books. Transitional chapter books are designed for beginning readers who want to read novels but aren't yet ready for more sophisticated novels that are longer and more complex. Most transitional chapter books have approximately 100 pages of text, larger font sizes, shorter chapters, a table of contents, and a focus on topics that are important for children ages 8–10 (Graves & Liang, 2004; McNair & Brooks, 2012). The topics include friendship, fitting in with peers, and school-related events (e.g., field day, bullies, spelling tests). Some of my favorite transitional chapter books, which often come in a series, are *Make Way for Dyamonde Daniel* by Nikki Grimes (2009), *Ling & Ting: Not Exactly the Same!* by Grace Lin (2010), *Nikki & Deja* and *Dog Days* by Karen English (2007, 2013), *Kiki: My Stylish Life* by Kyla May (2013), *The Notebook of Doom: Rise of the Balloon Goons* by Troy Cummings (2013), and *Monkey Me and the Golden Monkey* by Timothy Roland (2014).

Awards

Most teachers know the mainstream awards, including the John Newbery Medal and Randolph Caldecott Medal, but there are additional ones that they should be aware of, including the abovementioned race-based children's literature awards and others, such as the Geisel Award, Lee Bennett Hopkins Poetry Award, NCTE Orbis Pictus Award for Outstanding Nonfiction for Children, Batchelder Award, and Schneider Family Book Award. The Schneider, for example, is given to outstanding books that feature characters with disabilities. The 2014 children's book winner is *A Splash of Red: The Life and Art of Horace Pippin* by Jen Bryant (2013), which is a biography of a painter with a maimed hand.

In addition to these awards, several magazines that review children's books, such as *The Horn Book Magazine* (www.hbook.com/horn-book-magazine-2/#_) and *The Bulletin of the Center for Children's Books* (bccb.lis.illinois.edu), note titles of distinction in all issues published throughout the year. Subscribing to magazines such as these are good ways for teachers to learn about new titles being published. Reading these magazines also helps teachers learn to critically evaluate books for themselves.

Where to Obtain Books

Acquiring 300 titles for a classroom library, considering that most hardback books now cost around $18.00, can be a daunting task. Luckily, there are more affordable ways that teachers can obtain books that aren't this expensive. First, teachers can use discounted websites for ordering books online, such as Amazon (www.amazon.com) and Book Outlet (bookoutlet.com), one of my favorite places to shop. Amazon offers books at reduced prices and also allows for the purchase of used copies of out-of-print titles, sometimes as low as 1 cent (plus $3.99 shipping). Hardback copies ordered via Book Outlet cost around $7.00 or $8.00, and paperback copies are around $3.00 or $3.50. Also, Scholastic Reading Club Online (https://clubs2.scholastic.com) is a way to acquire inexpensive paperback copies, although it should be noted that books by authors and illustrators of color are often lacking (McNair, 2008), so teachers will have to obtain racially diverse books from other sources. Over the years, I have also found copies of used books in good condition at stores like Goodwill and the Salvation Army. Although I've had to wade through lots of books that I wouldn't recommend, knowing about notable authors and illustrators, as well as awards, allowed me to find some exceptional titles, such as *Esperanza Rising*, a winner of the Pura Belpré written by Pam Muñoz Ryan (2000). Checking out books from public and school libraries is also another way to obtain books that can remain in the library for at least a few weeks, allowing for books to be regularly rotated.

A Few Ways Books From the Classroom Library Can Work Together

Studies of Authors and Illustrators

As a former classroom teacher of grades K–2, one of my favorite ways to share books with students was through studies of authors and illustrators. Each week, I focused on a different author or illustrator (or team) and lined a dry-erase board ledge with 10–15 books by this person. I made sure to read or share at least one book by this individual during our daily read-aloud time. On Mondays, I would introduce the author or illustrator by sharing biographical information about him or her, brief summaries of some of his or her books, and photographs of the author or illustrator. I created a bulletin board with photos of all of the individuals studied over the course of the year. Here's a sampling of authors and illustrators worthy of study in grades K–5: Arnold Adoff, Aliki, George Ancona, Molly Bang, Ashley Bryan, Floyd Cooper, Donald Crews, Leo and Diane Dillon, Lois Ehlert, Denise Fleming, Douglas Florian, Gail Gibbons, Nikki Grimes, Yumi Heo, Lee Bennett Hopkins, Rachel Isadora, Angela Johnson, Ann Jonas, E.B. Lewis, J. Patrick Lewis, Leo Lionni, Patricia C. McKissack, Kadir Nelson, Andrea Davis Pinkney and Brian Pinkney, Jerry Pinkney, James Ransome, Pam Muñoz Ryan, Cynthia Rylant, Allen Say, Seymour Simon, Gary Soto, Janet S. Wong, Audrey and Don Wood, and Jacqueline Woodson.

Pairing of Informational and Fictional Texts

Another way that books can work together is through pairing informational texts and fictional stories on the same topic so children will learn about the differences between these two genres. One example would be the pairing of *Owl Babies* by Martin Waddell (1992) and *Owls* by Gail Gibbons (2005). The first story is about three baby owls who awake one night to discover that their mother is gone. They worry that something has happened to her and anxiously await her return. The second title provides factual information about owls. It also contains textual features that are typical in informational texts, such as topical vocabulary (e.g., *owlet, raptors, talons, brood*), realistic photographs and images, pronunciation keys (e.g., for *incubation*, "in·kew·BAY·shun"; Gibbons, 2005, n.p.), and labels and diagrams providing details about an owl's body. Taberski (2001) writes, "By reading both a fiction and nonfiction book on a common topic, children can draw comparisons between the genres and learn the different purposes for which they're written" (p. 26). Two other examples of texts that would work well together in this way are *Papa, Please Get the Moon for Me* by Eric Carle (1986) paired with *The Moon Book* by Gail Gibbons (1997), and *Froggy Gets Dressed* by Jonathan London (1992) paired with *Frogs* by Nic Bishop (2008).

Units of Study

Having a solid core collection of books in the classroom library can make it easier to pull books together for units of study or to place them in centers around the room. For example, if a teacher wants to introduce his or her students to various aspects of art, he or she could feature books about artists, such as *Diego Rivera: His World and Ours* by Duncan Tonatiuh (2011), *Fabulous! A Portrait of Andy Warhol* by Bonnie Christensen (2011), and *Me and Uncle Romie: A Story Inspired by the Life and Art of Romare Bearden* by Claire Hartfield (2002). Two other recommended books on the subject of art are *Meet Me at the Art Museum: A Whimsical Look Behind the Scenes* by David Goldin (2012) and *Look! Look! Look!* by Nancy Elizabeth Wallace (2006).

Conclusion

Having a first-rate classroom library is undoubtedly a challenge for teachers, but it's a valuable one. There are many factors to be considered when choosing books to fill the shelves, such as the race of the authors and illustrators, whether there are books across various genres and subgenres, and how to acquire many titles without spending huge amounts of money. However, the benefits will make all the effort worthwhile when children read on a regular basis within the classroom and beyond. Reading is like any other skill: The more one practices, the better one will become. Having a first-rate classroom library that will engage children will certainly encourage them to read and perhaps lay the foundation for them to become avid and lifelong readers.

REFERENCES

Beeler, T. (1993). *I can read! I can write! Creating a print-rich environment.* Cypress, CA: Creative Teaching.

Bishop, R.S. (1990). Mirrors, windows, and sliding glass doors. *Perspectives, 6*(3), ix–xi.

Christie, J.F., Enz, B.J., Vukelich, C., & Roskos, K.A. (2013). *Teaching language and literacy: Preschool through the elementary grades* (5th ed.). Boston, MA: Pearson.

Cooperative Children's Book Center. (n.d.). *Children's books by and about people of color published in the United States: Statistics gathered by the Cooperative Children's Book Center, School of Education, University of Wisconsin–Madison.* Retrieved from ccbc.education.wisc.edu/books/pcstats.asp

Diller, D. (2008). *Spaces and places: Designing classrooms for literacy.* Portland, ME: Stenhouse.

Fountas, I.C., & Pinnell, G.S. (1996). *Guided reading: Good first teaching for all children.* Portsmouth, NH: Heinemann.

Graves, B., & Liang, L.A. (2004). Transitional chapter books: An update. *Book Links*, *13*(5), 12–16.

Harris, V.J. (1990). African American children's literature: The first one hundred years. *The Journal of Negro Education*, *59*(4), 540–555. doi:10.2307/2295311

McNair, J.C. (2008). The representation of authors and illustrators of color in school-based book clubs. *Language Arts, 85*(3), 193–201.

McNair, J.C. (2010). Classic African American children's literature. *The*

Reading Teacher, 64(2), 96–105. doi:10.1598/RT.64.2.2

McNair, J.C., & Brooks, W.M. (2012). Transitional chapter books: Representations of African American girlhood. *The Reading Teacher, 65*(8), 567–577. doi:10.1002/TRTR.01084

Taberski, S. (2001). Fact and fiction: Read aloud. *Instructor, 110*(6), 24–26, 105.

Winfield, E.T. (1986). Why children should read the classics. *PTA Today, 11*(6), 26–27.

CHILDREN'S LITERATURE CITED

Bishop, N. (2008). *Frogs*. New York, NY: Scholastic.

Bryant, J. (2013). *A splash of red: The life and art of Horace Pippin*. New York, NY: Alfred A. Knopf.

Carle, E. (1986). *Papa, please get the moon for me*. Natick, MA: Picture Book Studio.

Christensen, B. (2011). *Fabulous! A portrait of Andy Warhol*. New York, NY: Christy Ottaviano.

Clifton, L. (1983). *Everett Anderson's goodbye*. New York, NY: Henry Holt.

Cummings, T. (2013). *The notebook of doom: Rise of the balloon goons*. New York, NY: Scholastic.

Curtis, C.P. (1995). *The Watsons go to Birmingham—1963*. New York, NY: Yearling.

Dorris, M. (1992). *Morning girl*. New York, NY: Hyperion.

English, K. (2007). *Nikki & Deja*. New York, NY: Clarion.

English, K. (2013). *Dog days*. New York, NY: Clarion.

Gág, W. (1996). *Millions of cats*. New York, NY: Penguin Putnam Books for Young Readers. (Original work published 1928)

Gibbons, G. (1997). *The moon book*. New York, NY: Holiday House.

Gibbons, G. (2005). *Owls*. New York, NY: Holiday House.

Goldin, D. (2012). *Meet me at the art museum: A whimsical look behind the scenes*. New York, NY: Abrams Books for Young Readers.

Grimes, N. (2009). *Make way for Dyamonde Daniel*. New York, NY: G.P. Putnam's Sons.

Hacohen, D. (2010). *Tuck me in!* Somerville, MA: Candlewick.

Hartfield, C. (2002). *Me and Uncle Romie: A story inspired by the life and art of Romare Bearden*. New York, NY: Dial Books for Young Readers.

Lin, G. (2010). *Ling & Ting: Not exactly the same!* New York, NY: Little, Brown.

London, J. (1992). *Froggy gets dressed*. New York, NY: Viking.

May, K. (2013). *Kiki: My stylish life*. New York, NY: Scholastic.

McKissack, P.C. (2007). *The all-I'll-ever-want Christmas doll*. New York, NY: Schwartz & Wade.

Pinkney, B. (1997). *The adventures of Sparrowboy*. New York, NY: Simon & Schuster Books for Young Readers.

Ringgold, F. (1991). *Tar beach*. New York, NY: Dragonfly.

Roland, T. (2014). *Monkey me and the golden monkey*. New York, NY: Scholastic.

Ryan, P.M. (2000). *Esperanza rising*. New York, NY: Scholastic.

Sendak, M. (2013). *Where the wild things are* (50th anniversary ed.). New York, NY: HarperCollins. (Original work published 1963)

Tonatiuh, D. (2011). *Diego Rivera: His world and ours*. New York, NY: Abrams Books for Young Readers.

Van Allsburg, C. (1985). *The Polar Express*. Boston, MA: Houghton Mifflin.

Waddell, M. (1992). *Owl babies*. Cambridge, MA: Candlewick.

Wallace, N.E. (with Friedlaender, L.K.). (2006). *Look! Look! Look!* New York, NY: Marshall Cavendish.

White, E.B. (2012). *Charlotte's web*. New York, NY: HarperTrophy. (Original work published 1952)

Yep, L. (1993). *Dragon's gate*. New York, NY: HarperTrophy.

OTHER RECOMMENDED PICTURE BOOKS

Alarcón, F.X. (1998). *From the Bellybutton of the Moon and other summer poems/ Del Ombligo de la Luna y otros poemas de verano*. San Francisco, CA: Children's Book.

Barton, B. (2001). *My car*. New York, NY: Greenwillow.

Brown, M. (2011). *Marisol McDonald doesn't match/Marisol McDonald no combina*. New York, NY: Children's Book.

Chin, J. (2009). *Redwoods*. New York, NY: Flashpoint.

Choung, E. (2008). *Minji's salon*. La Jolla, CA: Kane Miller.

Clement, N. (2008). *Drive*. Honesdale, PA: Boyds Mills.

Clement, N. (2011). *Job site*. Honesdale, PA: Boyds Mills.

Crews, D. (1991). *Bigmama's*. New York, NY: Greenwillow.

Deedy, C.A. (2007). *Martina, the beautiful cockroach: A Cuban folktale*. Atlanta, GA: Peachtree.

Ehlert, L. (2005). *Leaf Man*. Orlando, FL: Harcourt.

Fleming, D. (2002). *Alphabet under construction*. New York, NY: Henry Holt.

Florian, D. (1998). *Insectlopedia*. Orlando, FL: Harcourt.

Florian, D. (2007). *Comets, stars, the moon, and Mars*. Orlando, FL: Harcourt.

Garland, M. (2013). *Car goes far*. New York, NY: Holiday House.

Gibbons, G. (2006). *Ice cream: The full scoop*. New York, NY: Holiday House.

Grimes, N. (1994). *Meet Danitra Brown*. New York, NY: Mulberry.

Harjo, J. (2000). *The good luck cat*. Orlando, FL: Harcourt.

Hoban, T. (1997). *Look book*. New York, NY: Greenwillow.

Jenkins, S. (1995). *Biggest, strongest, fastest*. New York, NY: Houghton Mifflin.

Jenkins, S. (2004). *Actual size*. Boston, MA: Houghton Mifflin.

Jenkins, S. (2013). *The animal book: A collection of the fastest, fiercest, toughest, cleverest, shyest—and most surprising— animals on earth*. New York, NY: Houghton Mifflin Harcourt.

Kalan, R. (1978). *Rain*. New York, NY: Greenwillow.

Khan, H. (2012). *Golden domes and silver lanterns: A Muslim book of colors*. San Francisco, CA: Chronicle.

Lewis, J.P. (Ed.). (2012). *National Geographic book of animal poetry: 200 poems with photographs that squeak, soar, and roar!* Washington, DC: National Geographic Society.

Mack, J. (2012). *Good news, bad news*. San Francisco, CA: Chronicle.

McKissack, P.C. (1986). *Flossie & the fox*. New York, NY: Dial Books for Young Readers.

McKissack, P.C. (1988). *Mirandy and Brother Wind*. New York, NY: Alfred A. Knopf.

McLeod, B. (2006). *Superhero ABC*. New York, NY: HarperCollins.

Morales, Y. (2008). *Just in case: A trickster tale and Spanish alphabet book*. New York, NY: Roaring Brook.

Morales, Y. (2013). *Niño wrestles the world*. New York, NY: Roaring Brook.

Nelson, K. (2008). *We are the ship: The story of Negro league baseball*. New York, NY: Jump at the Sun.

Nelson, K. (2011). *Heart and soul: The story of America and African Americans*. New York, NY: Balzer + Bray.

Nelson, V.M. (2009). *Bad news for outlaw: The remarkable life of Bass Reeves, deputy U.S. marshal*. Minneapolis, MN: Carolrhoda.

Pinkney, A.D. (1996). *Bill Pickett: Rodeo-ridin' cowboy*. San Diego, CA: Harcourt Brace.

Pinkney, B. (1995). *JoJo's flying side kick.* New York, NY: Simon & Schuster Books for Young Readers.

Roessel, M. (1995). *Songs from the loom: A Navajo girl learns to weave.* Minneapolis, MN: Lerner.

Savage, S. (2011). *Where's walrus?* New York, NY: Scholastic.

Simon, S. (2001). *Animals nobody loves.* New York, NY: SeaStar.

Swentzell, R. (1992). *Children of clay: A family of Pueblo potters.* Minneapolis, MN: Lerner.

Tonatiuh, D. (2010). *Dear Primo: A letter to my cousin.* New York, NY: Abrams Books for Young Readers.

Weatherford, C.B. (2008). *Before John was a jazz giant: A song of John Coltrane.* New York, NY: Henry Holt.

Yaccarino, D. (2009). *The fantastic undersea life of Jacques Cousteau.* New York, NY: Alfred A. Knopf.

Yum, H. (2011). *The twins' blanket.* New York, NY: Frances Foster.

OTHER RECOMMENDED TRANSITIONAL CHAPTER BOOKS AND UPPER ELEMENTARY–GRADE NOVELS

Atinuke. (2011). *The N° 1 car spotter.* Tulsa, OK: Kane Miller.

Bond, V., & Simon, T.R. (2010). *Zora and me.* Somerville, MA: Candlewick.

Erdrich, L. (2012). *Chickadee.* New York, NY: Harper.

Garza, X. (2011). *Maximilian & the mystery of the Guardian Angel: A bilingual lucha libre thriller.* El Paso, TX: Cinco Puntos.

Green, M.Y. (2002). *A strong right arm: The story of Mamie "Peanut" Johnson.* New York, NY: Puffin.

Higgins, F.E. (2007). *The black book of secrets.* New York, NY: Feiwel and Friends.

Krishnaswami, U. (2011). *The grand plan to fix everything.* New York, NY: Atheneum Books for Young Readers.

Montijo, R. (2013). *The gumazing gum girl! Chews your destiny.* New York, NY: Disney·Hyperion.

Prineas, S. (2008). *The magic thief.* New York, NY: HarperTrophy.

Ryan, P.M. (2010). *The dreamer.* New York, NY: Scholastic.

Sheth, K. (2007). *Keeping corner.* New York, NY: Disney·Hyperion.

Sheth, K. (2010). *Boys without names.* New York, NY: Balzer + Bray.

Walter, M.P. (1986). *Justin and the best biscuits in the world.* New York, NY: Lothrop, Lee & Shepard.

Williams-Garcia, R. (2010). *One crazy summer.* New York, NY: Amistad.

Williams-Garcia, R. (2013). *P.S. be eleven.* New York, NY: Amistad.

ABOUT THE AUTHOR

Jonda C. McNair is an associate professor of literacy education at Clemson University, South Carolina, USA. She specializes in literature intended for youths, with an emphasis on books written by and about African Americans. She is currently the chair of the Coretta Scott King Book Awards Committee. Jonda is currently serving as a coeditor of the *Journal of Children's Literature* and as the department editor for the Children's Literature Reviews column in *Language Arts.* Her work has appeared in various journals, including *The Reading Teacher*, *Young Children*, *Review of Educational Research*, *The Journal of Negro Education*, and *Children's Literature in Education.* Jonda can be contacted at jmcnair27@aol.com.

CHAPTER 12

Young Readers Study Writers

Jane Hansen, *University of Virginia*

There's no other way to become a writer except by reading and writing.

—Lowry (Quantz, 2014, p. 9)

All writers are readers before we write a word, so there's a kinship and it's very deep.

—Tartt ("Carnegie Awards Presented," 2014, p. A5)

The quotes above show us this: Writers read. They've done so for ages, but it's something new for many young readers to learn. Eventually, however, we hear them say, "I'm reading a piece of writing every time I read." As educators, we work hard for this to happen, as it is new for some of us to realize that when our young writers read, a writer's ways with words can excite them!

Because we've only recently started to find classrooms of writers, it's also new to teach reading to writers. Most reading practices are still based on the assumption that the recipients of the teaching are only readers. Thankfully, however, as more classrooms fill with writers, we modify our reading instruction to focus on readers/writers—an innovation in teaching that's slowly spreading, even though some large-scale efforts may try to interfere (Goatley & Johnston, 2013).

When we focus on young writers, we realize that they study writers' ways with words. And, they study authors' ways with illustrations and graphics. These readers talk about what they notice, and they use professionals' ideas in their own writing.

In this chapter, I write about three general situations in which readers use their mentors' writing to inform their creations. I begin with two students who create content area assignments by borrowing, in unexpected ways, from the professionals they admire. Next, I show a teacher who starts with a tepid draft of a personal narrative and contemplates how to turn it into a draft with zest. A professional writer comes to her rescue. Finally, I write about teachers and students with open minds. They're continuously on the lookout for how and/or what to write, and ideas appear in what they read!

Children's Literature in the Reading Program: Engaging Young Readers in the 21st Century (4th ed.), edited by Deborah A. Wooten & Bernice E. Cullinan. © 2015 by the International Literacy Association.

Writers Start With Content Assignments and Enrich Them With What They Admire in the Works of Their Mentor Authors

In the kindergarten class of Betsy Carter, the children, via teacher read-alouds, have noticed that illustrations in some books only show part of a person. Maybe someone is running off the page, and only one leg shows. Maybe someone is laughing, and only the face shows. The children had been drawing entire people when they created illustrations for their writing, and their study of professional illustrators, a highly advocated practice (Ray, 2010), leads them to rethink their own drawings.

In January, when the class studied magnets, one child drew only a hand. On that day, Ms. Carter had asked the children to write about what they had learned about magnets, and Allison (all student names are pseudonyms) not only did so but also only drew the part of her body that mattered—without any prompts or reminders from her teacher about what they had noticed in illustrations. On her own, this young scientist/writer borrowed an aspect of the work of professionals that her class had discussed.

Below her hand, you see the pencil she holds, with a string wrapped around it. At the end of the string is the magnet, and the various black circles show the penny falling down.

In Allison's text, we see the word *magnet* in capital letters, a feature Allison borrowed from another book in their classroom. She's on her way as a reader who sees books as pieces of writing for her to emulate.

Importantly, she sounds like herself. Her own kindergarten voice sounds forth in her text: "the MAGNET DEDEt Like the Pene" ("The magnet didn't like the penny"; see Figure 12.1).

Similarly, the kindergarten children of Janice Novakowski (2010) study text features and use them in their science notebooks. They create labels, text boxes, and drawings in their unlined notebooks. Plus, their use of magnifying glasses informs their detailed drawings. Importantly, they make their own decisions about how they record their observations, thoughts, and questions. As advocated by Heard (2013), these young writers learn various craft tools and use them to convey the message that they decide to put forth.

Overall, writers of informational texts notice the features of the domain in which they're working. Students writing articles in the style of journalists study articles from their local news and ask questions about the sources of information that the reporters may have used (Van Sluys, 2011). To go out as reporters is a trek that several of the students may enjoy. Or, they may take other journeys, such as the one created by the following student.

In the fifth-grade class of Carolena Saunders, the children composed "Personal Passion Projects." They chose their own topics, researched them, and wrote in the genre(s) of their choice. Terran made his decision quickly, knowing right off that his topic would be geography. "Just a bit broad," advised Ms. Saunders, and Terran narrowed it to the geography of Africa. He was set, determined, and ready to go.

Terran's research question became "What do I want to know about Africa?" and he answered it by saying that he wanted to know what it's like "from the top to the bottom." Along the way, he became animated by a decision to write like J.R.R. Tolkien—who has taken his readers on great adventures! To accomplish this, Terran rewrote several phrases several times. Here's a glimpse of his work, which he researched and created on an iPad:

Figure 12.1. "The Magnet Didn't Like the Penny" by a Kindergartner

> Let's start in Morocco....we meet the Berber people, who are also traveling south....the soaring mountains slope into an immense desert called the Sahara Desert! There we meet a small group of nomads....Leaving the nomads, we turn east at the northern tip of the twisty Niger River....Passing many obstacles (snakes, heat, sand storms) we reach Sudan...the descending bank of the Nile River, rolling steadily south....Leading us down the river the man finds a boat in perfectly good shape, and provides us a bumpy way across the swift river.... A month of trudging...the Ruwenzori Mountains are now visible in the Central African Republic. We pass many cities filled with people and markets....Slowing down at the markets, we wait our turn to fill our canteens from a short hose coming from a small aquifer....We see the Orange River and eventually come to a small village near Cape Town, South Africa, where the villagers are pulling in the morning catch....A welcoming town with good food, good people and exquisite views provides us the end of a long tour through Africa. What do you think Asia would be like?

This young writer, well-schooled in the crossovers between reading and writing, enjoys the challenge of combining territories. Ms. Saunders, his teacher, sets as her goal that her students will connect their reading to their writing, and she gives them the latitude they need to read books of their choice. In conferences about those books, she notices that they often comment on a writer's style—beyond the characters, adventure, excitement, or romance. They pay attention to how the author is telling the story or relating the information. Ms. Saunders was excited about Terran's decision to intentionally try the style of a master.

Importantly, writers learn from writers (Fletcher, 2011). Yes, their immersion in the words of authors, in the masters' ways of putting words together, becomes something young writers can hear and then yearn to try. The teachers of Terran and Allison teach with the wisdom of their profession. Maloch and Bomer (2013) tell us that explicit strategy instruction is not the key to reading and writing informational texts. It must be accompanied by students' immersion in the reading and writing of texts that have been composed via those strategies. Then, the writers will use the strategies they need in the creations they're excited to create.

Some writers bring the specific features of masters to their notebooks in the midst of science, as Allison did with her close-up illustration of her hand, and Terran thought about the readability—and enjoyability—of Tolkien as he drafted his assignment. Other writers call on their mentors when they feel they must revisit a draft that sounds flat, as this next writer does.

A Writer Starts With a Tepid Draft and Sparks It With a Mentor Author's Craft

Julie Haddix, a fifth-grade teacher/writer runs a classroom in which her read-aloud reigns. Her oral reading skills are excellent, and not a day passes without Ms. Haddix sharing books—as a writer to other writers. She collects top-quality literature and reads both chapter and picture books. Ms. Haddix's students love this time of day, sandwiched between reading and writing. It's the glue that holds the two together—literally. What do we do with what we read? As writers, we use it!

Ms. Haddix demonstrated her use of reading one day when she stood in front of her class, sheets of paper in hand, and said, "I've been working on this, and here is one of my paragraphs." She read it aloud to them:

> I was glad I wasn't afraid of tight spaces as the metal door clanged shut. At least I wasn't in it alone. There were four other people packed into this small metal cage with me. We were like sardines, so tightly fit together we couldn't even raise our arms, much less move!

Then, she said, "When I read it over last night, I wondered how I could change my wording so it would be more dramatic. I decided to try Gary Paulsen's way with words, his short clips, verbs, sentences."

Ms. Haddix then read her new draft to the class:

> "Tight spaces don't bother me." Repeating this statement over and over provided me some distraction as the metal door clanged shut. At least I wasn't alone. There were four other people packed into this small cage with me. Like sardines. So tightly fit together, we couldn't even raise our arms.

A brief, energetic response followed in acknowledgment of what Ms. Haddix had done, and the class picked up their pencils to write. They were in the midst of various drafts, and they'll incorporate the short-sentence possibility sometime—maybe today, maybe next week—when it fits into their work.

It's the culture, the way of doing things in this classroom. Ms. Haddix is the leader of the overall nature of trying what other writers have tried. That notion of trying, exploring, taking adventures with words, is what these fifth graders learn from her—the teacher who writes and reads. As Rief (2014), an experienced middle school teacher, says, "The most prevalent writing advice from most writers is: Read! Read! Read!" (p. 102). Writers, as they read, notice textual features that they may use, as they are always on the lookout for new ideas for their drafts.

That's similar to what the young writers do in the following section. They go to fictional and faraway places, led by their teachers via professional writers who write in nontraditional ways.

Writers Start With Open Minds and Notice Mentor Authors' Unexpected Approaches

In the third-grade classroom of Beth Buchholz, the children studied Greece and, within that unit, read the myth about the naming of Athens in *Greek Myths*, written in graphic format by Marcia Williams (2011). According to it, the gods Athena and Poseidon quarreled over the naming of Athens. Poseidon thrust his trident into a rock on the Acropolis, seawater gushed out, and he promised the people riches through sea trade if they named the city after him. Athena planted an olive tree as her gift to the people, and they decided that she had given the more valuable gift.

Also, Ms. Buchholz read *The Iliad and the Odyssey* by Marcia Williams (2006), a book in which comic strips tell each step of Odysseus's journey—with a bit of humor in the conversations between the characters. The children loved this read-aloud, and the class studied it, as they often do with texts, in ways similar to those advocated by Newkirk (2012). The careful reading by these third-grade writers led them to understand Williams's decisions, which will help them consider wise decisions about their own writing.

"The ultimate message is that writing is the human act of making choices" (Newkirk, 2012, p. 145). More specifically, when writers create graphics, they must decide where to place both words and drawings. They create their drafts with their heads full of ideas based on what they've seen, talked about, and read. Their reading—of all the preparation they've done, "actually a specific kind of reading—is still the best writing instruction" (p. 143). It develops habits for the writers so they can be readers who read like writers—readers who notice.

In this third-grade class, Ms. Buchholz noticed the children's attention to the texts. One day, on the spot, she decided to capitalize on the importance of what these young readers were doing, so she invited them to consider bringing graphics into their own writing about Greece. Several of them created one-page comics based on the myth of the naming of Athens.

In Figure 12.2, this young writer used the spear and trident to identify which character is talking. Importantly, his voice sings in his rendition of this myth!

The writers who tried this form of writing loved creating their variations of the origin of Athens's name, thanks to their teacher's recognition of a teachable moment to invite her writers to bring various writings about Greece into their own work.

We now move to first grade, where writers are on the lookout for ideas for their own writing whenever their teacher reads to them. They take on new ways of writing without worry that what professionals have done is something they can't do. At this early time in their lives as writers, they already know that the nature of writers is to communicate by intentionally stepping out into new territory. Young children's intentional leaps forward are central to their lives as writers (Hansen, 2014).

Martin is in the first-grade classroom of Anne James, whose daily read-alouds, and the conversations around them, offer frequent invitations to the young writers. At the time of Martin's creation, Ms. James had read two books in which the authors included letters as a partial means by which to tell their story. One was *I Wanna Iguana* by Karen Kaufman Orloff (2004), and the book that Ms. James read to the class on this exact day was *Detective LaRue: Letters From the Investigation* by Mark Teague (2004). It opens with a reprint of a newspaper article, "Hibbins' Cats Missing: Dog Suspected" (n.p.). On the next page is the dog typing a letter to his owner: "I hate to disrupt your vacation, but you must return immediately! An unfortunate misunderstanding…has landed me in jail" (n.p.). The book continues with an exchange of letters.

Martin, during the class time for writing that followed the read-aloud, began a book he titled "The monster of gabbet city. The investagation." He begins, "gabbet city was a pieceful place until one Day something horrible happend." On page 2: "on the Detector it said monster But the police force did not Believe

Figure 12.2. A Third Grader's Greek Graphic Story

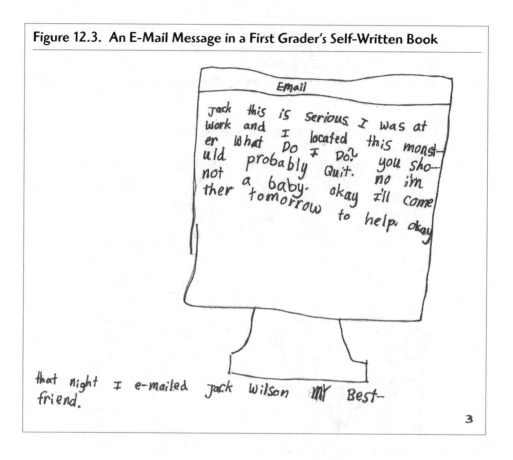

Figure 12.3. An E-Mail Message in a First Grader's Self-Written Book

> Email
>
> Jack this is serious. I was at
> work and I located this monst-
> er. What do I do? you sho—
> uld probably quit. no i'm
> not a baby. okay i'll come
> ther tomorrow to help. okay
>
> that night I e-mailed Jack Wilson my Best-
> friend.
>
> 3

it." You can see page 3 in Figure 12.3. With this move, Martin's characters can continue to communicate during the night, moving his complex story ahead at a fast pace.

Ever writing and reading, this alert young writer listens to authors' words and sees their graphics with his own possibilities in mind. Then, he's off to write with new thoughts to spark him forward. The daily infusion and reflection about professionals' ideas helps ensure Martin's ways of not only using their work but, importantly, also distinguishing himself from other writers.

Young Writers Study Writers

Overall, when young writers study writers, their intent is to move beyond. They want to move beyond themselves—to create their own paper voice. Just as they each speak forth in an oral voice that distinguishes them from all others, they want their paper voice to do likewise.

That's a complex task!

Writers not only look for what they can borrow from others but also search inside themselves for what they can do that no one else in their sphere of writers has done. One young writer, an ardent reader of riddles, challenged himself to write one in math one day. Sitting, thinking, pencil in mouth, he finally wrote one about shapes, with the answer to the riddle on the back of his paper (Hansen et al., 2010). While working, he covered his paper, and then he just had to try out his riddle on all!

Writers bare bravery. Menena Cottin (2008) did so in *The Black Book of Colors*, a book like no other. Johnston (2012) stepped out in *Opening Minds: Using Language to Change Lives*, a book of sage, strong words for teachers, and he includes children when he writes about "teachers." Finally, Allison, the first young writer in this chapter, taught us something with only one hand—and she was only in kindergarten.

REFERENCES

Carnegie awards presented to Tartt, Goodwin for books. (2014, June 30). *The Daily Progress*, p. A5.

Fletcher, R. (2011). *Mentor author, mentor texts: Short texts, craft notes, and practical classroom uses*. Portsmouth, NH: Heinemann.

Goatley, V.J., & Johnston, P. (2013). Innovation, research, and policy: Evolutions in classroom teaching. *Language Arts*, *91*(2), 94–104.

Hansen, J. (2014). First grade writers revisit their work. In A. Shillady (Ed.), *Spotlight on young children: Exploring language and literacy* (pp. 64–71). Washington, DC: National Association for the Education of Young Children.

Hansen, J., Davis, R., Evertson, J., Freeman, T., Suskind, D., & Tower, H. (2010). *The preK–2 writing classroom: Growing confident writers*. New York: Scholastic.

Heard, G. (2013). *Finding the heart of nonfiction: Teaching 7 essential craft tools with mentor texts*. Portsmouth, NH: Heinemann.

Johnston, P.H. (2012). *Opening minds: Using language to change lives*. Portland, ME: Stenhouse.

Maloch, B., & Bomer, R. (2013). Teaching about and with informational texts: What does research teach us? *Language Arts*, *90*(6), 441–450.

Newkirk, T. (2012). *The art of slow reading: Six time-honored practices for engagement*. Portsmouth, NH: Heinemann.

Novakowski, J. (2010). Nonfiction literacy in kindergarten: Young students incorporate text features into their science notebooks. *Science and Children*, *48*(3), 40–43.

Quantz, A. (2014). Lois Lowry: "I wish all events could be like this one." *VFH Views*, Spring, 9. Retrieved from virginiahumanities.org/files/2011/11/VFH-Views-Spring-NL.pdf

Ray, K.W. (2010). *In pictures and in words: Teaching the qualities of good writing through illustration study*. Portsmouth, NH: Heinemann.

Rief, L. (2014). *Read write teach: Choice and challenge in the reading-writing workshop*. Portsmouth, NH: Heinemann.

Van Sluys, K. (2011). *Becoming writers in the elementary classroom: Visions and decisions*. Urbana, IL: National Council of Teachers of English.

CHILDREN'S LITERATURE CITED

Cottin, M. (2008). *The black book of colors* (E. Amado, Trans.). Berkeley, CA: Groundwood.

Orloff, K.K. (2004). *I wanna iguana*. New York, NY: G.P. Putnam's Sons.

Teague, M. (2004). *Detective LaRue: Letters from the investigation*. New York, NY: Scholastic.

Williams, M. (2006). *The Iliad and the Odyssey*. London, UK: Walker.

Williams, M. (2011). *Greek myths*. Somerville, MA: Candlewick.

OTHER RECOMMENDED CHILDREN'S LITERATURE

Beaty, A. (2013). *Rosie Revere, engineer*. New York, NY: Abrams Books for Young Readers.

Donaldson, J. (2012). *Superworm*. New York, NY: Arthur A. Levine.

Gaiman, N. (2010). *The graveyard book*. New York, NY: Harper.

Gravett, E. (2010). *The rabbit problem*. New York, NY: Simon & Schuster Books for Young Readers.

Hosford, K. (2012). *Infinity and me*. Minneapolis, MN: Carolrhoda.

Lai, T. (2011). *Inside out & back again*. New York, NY: Harper.

Lee-Tai, A. (2006). *A place where sunflowers grow/砂漠に咲いたひまわり*. San Francisco, CA: Children's Book.

Palacio, R.J. (2012). *Wonder*. New York, NY: Alfred A. Knopf.

Park, L.S. (2010). *A long walk to water: Based on a true story*. Boston, MA: Clarion.

Rhodes, J.P. (2013). *Sugar*. New York, NY: Little, Brown.

ABOUT THE AUTHOR

Jane Hansen is a retired professor who continues to work in classrooms of young writers whose teachers love to share great writing with them. She was a professor at the University of New Hampshire, Durham, USA, for two decades and then at the University of Virginia, Charlottesville, USA, for 13 years. Before teaching on the university level, she was an elementary teacher for more than a decade. Jane has published several articles and books about writing and is currently the president of the Reading Hall of Fame. She can be contacted at jh5re@virginia.edu.

CHAPTER 13

Primary Students Writing and Reading Informational Text

Colleen P. Gilrane, *University of Tennessee, Knoxville*

Maggie Lingle Lohr, *Underwood Elementary School*

> *Donald Graves and several others deserve enormous credit for this discovery: Very young children can write before they can read, can write more than they can read, and can write more easily than they can read—because they can write anything they can say.*
>
> —Elbow (2004, p. 10)

e cannot imagine teaching young children without immersing them in the richness of a literate environment—including not only a classroom library of wonderful children's literature but also leveled books to support emergent readers' independence (Fry, 2002; Glaswell & Ford, 2011; Rog & Burton, 2001) and most especially daily writers' workshop (Calkins, 1994; Graves, 1983; Hansen, 2009; Harwayne, 2001). Our many years of learning, reading, and writing alongside children have taught us that the breadth of literature that they select won't be limited to stories, as long as we make available a wide array of genres for reading and support children's genre choices in their writing. We haven't needed new standards to infuse informational texts into our classrooms, as the children have insisted on them. We find this quote from Newkirk (1989) to be as true today as when he wrote it 25 years ago:

> On what grounds do we say that an informational book on dinosaurs is less meaningful than *Where the Wild Things Are*? My own work in elementary classes suggests that children differ considerably in the forms of writing they excel at (and the kinds of reading they prefer). A child who writes dull, conventional stories may write excellent descriptions of science displays. Others may exhibit

Children's Literature in the Reading Program: Engaging Young Readers in the 21st Century (4th ed.), edited by Deborah A. Wooten & Bernice E. Cullinan. © 2015 by the International Literacy Association.

a fluency in their letter writing that is missing from other types of writing. All of which argues for an elementary-school classroom where a range of possibilities is open to students. (p. 5)

Much support, including in this volume, is available to assist teachers in selecting informational texts (Duke, Bennett-Armistead, & Roberts, 2002; Gilrane, 2009; Hoyt, 2007; Mantzicopoulos & Patrick, 2011) and inviting children to engage with them in ways that support their literacy development (Clark, Jones, & Reutzel, 2013; Duke & Block, 2012; Maloch & Bomer, 2013b; Maloch & Horsey, 2013; Yopp & Yopp, 2006). We add our voices to the conversation in the hope of persuading you that a rich, literate environment is not complete until the writers' workshop is included so children will have the time and choice they need to compose their own informational texts and to demonstrate how they've orchestrated all of those other lessons (Graves, 1989; Newkirk, 1989). This matters not only because of the critical impact of writing on reading (Graham & Hebert, 2011) but also because our classrooms must allow every child to thrive.

> *A rich, literate environment is not complete until the writers' workshop is included.*

Equity of opportunity...resides in school programs that make it possible for students to follow their bliss, to pursue their interests, to realize and develop what they are good at....We ought to try to grasp what might be beyond our reach—or what's a heaven for? (Eisner, 1997, p. 353)

In the sections that follow, we give a brief overview of the literacy engagements available to children throughout the day in Maggie's primary classroom, share two focus units dealing with informational texts, and finally share several informational texts that children chose independently to write once the focus units were over, during their writers' workshop time.

Literacy Engagements Throughout the Day

We have worked together for many years, as coteachers and as part of a group of teacher researchers who strive to support one another "in our mutual yearning for joyful, powerful literacy and learning for all, no matter the setting or label" (Gilrane, Allen, Boyce, Lohr, & Swafford, 2013, p. 1). We're deeply committed to the importance of teacher decision making, authentic texts, and honoring our students' lives and voices as we support them in their learning (Gilrane & Lohr, in press). Although word-level work is part of the classroom routine, we describe here those portions of the day in which the focus was on engagement with complete texts: read-aloud, independent reading, shared/guided reading, and writing.

Read-Alouds

Read-alouds take place all day long! Shared poetry reading is part of the day's opening, and interactive read-alouds (Hoyt, 2007) support the children's development of literary responses and comprehension strategies. The best minilessons during writers' workshop are read-alouds of good writing: good children's literature! And at least once a day, we read aloud for the sheer joy of experiencing a book, especially when the classroom or one of the children has a new one! Informational texts are easily included in read-alouds, and it's easy to find books that fit the season of the year, the topics under study in the classroom, or the interests of the children.

Independent Reading

Whether it's called self-selected reading (Cunningham, Hall, & Defee, 1998), read to self (Boushey & Moser, 2006), or readers' workshop (Hansen, 2001) doesn't matter. The important thing is that children have time *every single day* for their own independent reading. Our school day has several opportunities for independent reading, beginning when the children arrive at school, before the opening bell rings, and engage in what Maggie calls Warm-Up Work. Four days per week, the children select a workstation from those available, but one day each table group is assigned to check in with Maggie and replace the six books in the Read to Self baggie that stays in their desk. These are leveled, so the children can manage them independently, but the titles are selected by the children. For the first half of the year, Maggie supports them by helping them decide on a specific level, based on her ongoing assessments and their own self-evaluation of how they're doing. Later in the year, the conversations become more along the lines of "How do you know when a book is easy or hard for you?" Informational texts as well as stories are available in the room, and selected by the children, along with a magazine. These books are read during Read to Self time and at any other time during the day when the children have time and choose to read (or when a teacher pulls up a chair to listen).

The Book Nook is the name of the classroom library, which contains a wide array of materials, as well as beanbag chairs and a rocking chair. It's available all day long for reference, as well as being one of the centers available to the children during the literacy block, while they aren't meeting with Maggie for small-group guided reading. It's occasionally a Warm-Up Work station, too. No limits—of genre, of level, of anything—are placed on the children's selections in the Book Nook, and informational texts are enormously popular.

Shared/Guided Reading

Shared reading is a daily whole-class activity during which genres, strategies, and topics form the basis of interactive lessons; we'll talk more about this in the next section about our units. Small groups meet with Maggie for follow-up instruction and practice during the literacy block. Informational texts are often the focus during these shared reading lessons and guided reading groups.

Writers' Workshop

Our favorite hour of the day is when the children are writing and engaged in conferences about their writing with us and with one another (Calkins, 1994; Graves, 1983; Hansen, 1983; Harwayne, 2001). Except for a few weeks during the year when we might focus on a particular genre, as we describe next, the workshop is a time when children decide what to write and how to write it, what kind of paper and writing implements to use, and whether to share and/or publish their pieces. We pull up chairs next to them and ask, "How's it going?"

Informational Text Focus Units

In this section, we share the writing and the reading that took place during a focus unit on How-To Books in December and one on "All About" Books in January. Leading up to these, the children had been immersed in all of the literary engagements described previously and were well rehearsed in making decisions both as readers and as writers in various settings. The class had also already experienced conversations about the differences between texts designed to entertain and those designed to inform, and the students had generated a list of cues that they could use to determine what kind of book they were reading or writing:

How Do We Know (Information)?	**How Do We Know (Entertainment)?**
■ Photographs	■ Laugh
■ How something works	■ Illustrations
■ Real things	■ Not real
■ True things	■ Story
■ Facts	

Although these aren't perfect or sophisticated criteria, they demonstrate the children's growing awareness of the purposes of different types of texts (Maloch & Bomer, 2013a) and indicate their readiness to focus on an informational genre as readers and writers.

December: How–To Books

Informational texts designed to teach the steps of a process are a natural fit for young children, as they allow for the blending of texts with the enactment of the processes themselves (Siegel, 2006; Wolf, Edmiston, & Enciso, 1997). Maggie began this unit by reading aloud two how-to books from the How Things Are Made series by Inez Snyder (2003–2005), *Wax to Crayons* (Snyder, 2003f) and *Grains to Bread* (Snyder, 2005b) for two days of shared reading. The interaction around these books focused on the processes themselves, of course, which fascinated the children, and went beyond to include conversation about the words the author used to explain the processes, as well as text features such as bold print for important words. Additional books from the series were available in the Book Nook and as a Warm-Up Work station and were frequently selected by the children once the series had been introduced. They were able to learn the steps involved in making some more of their favorite foods when they read Snyder's (2003a, 2003b, 2003c, 2003d, 2005a, 2005c, 2005e) *Beans to Chocolate*, *Milk to Ice Cream*, *Oranges to Orange Juice*, *Tomatoes to Ketchup*, *Berries to Jelly*, *Grapes to Raisins*, and *Sap to Syrup*. A bit more mysterious to them, but compelling, were the processes involved in *Trees to Paper* (Snyder, 2003e) and *Sand to Glass* (Snyder, 2005d).

A favorite part of this week was when the whole class made—and ate— peanut butter crackers! This became the foundation for exploring how-to books as writers, beginning with the interactive writing assignment "How to Make a Cracker Sandwich" as a language experience text. Figure 13.1 shows the class's description of the process, including their revisions (not everyone agreed on four pieces!) and their going back and circling the sequencing words that they had used, following the model of the How Things Are Made series. For the last few days of this week, during writers' workshop, each child drew and labeled the steps in the process and used these to write a personal *How to Make Peanut Butter Crackers* book.

During week 2 of this unit, writers' workshop time was devoted to each child's creation of a how-to book on a topic of his or her choice, one about which he or she was expert enough to instruct others in the process. Graphic organizers were available in case the children wished to use them, and Jamela's web (see Figure 13.2; all of the student names are pseudonyms) for *How To Tiye Your Shoow lasis together in a not* (*How to Tie Your Shoe Laces Together in a Knot*) is an example of how comfortable they were in making decisions as writers. She enlarged the bubble for step 4 and added steps 5 and 6 (complete

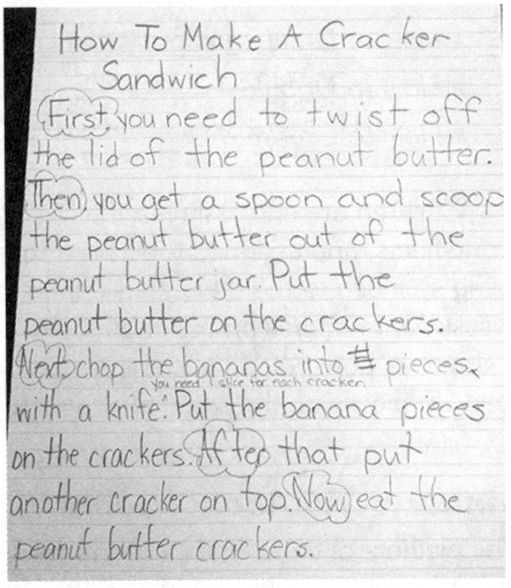

Figure 13.1. Whole-Class Text Based on Making Peanut Butter Crackers

How To Make A Cracker Sandwich
First you need to twist off the lid of the peanut butter. Then you get a spoon and scoop the peanut butter out of the peanut butter jar. Put the peanut butter on the crackers. Next chop the bananas into 4 pieces. you need 1 slice for each cracker with a knife. Put the banana pieces on the crackers. After that put another cracker on top. Now eat the peanut butter crackers.

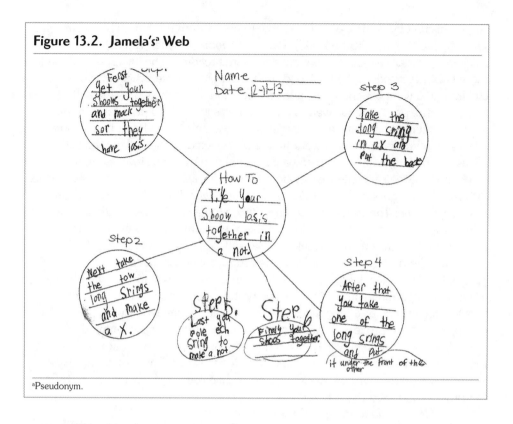

Figure 13.2. Jamela'sᵃ Web

ᵃPseudonym.

with lines for writing) rather than being constrained by the form. Other titles generated during this focus unit included the following:

- *How to Draw a Penguin*
- *How to Dribble*
- *How to Groom a Dog*

- *How to Play Poptropica*
- *How to Do a Cartwheel*
- *How to Cook a Quick Egg*

Children are endlessly fascinating! Why anyone would want workbooks, worksheets, and assigned topics is a mystery to us, when the children themselves bring so much to the table. Our experience is that even when a mandated writing assessment requires an assigned topic, our children can handle that just fine (Gilrane & Lohr, 2012) and don't need yearlong practice at prompt-writing. Why read 25 pieces on the same topic when you can read such variety as this?

January: "All About" Books

The plethora of topics and children's voices continued in late January with a focus unit on "All About" Books that invited the children to select something they know—or could learn—about in enough depth to write a chapter book. Again, Maggie began with interactive shared reading and writing lessons about features of informational texts, first with the whole class engaged with one book at a time. *Awesome Walruses* by Eric Charlesworth (2007) and *Hurricanes* by Jim Mezzanotte (2010) were both perfect selections because the children were so engaged in learning "all about" both topics that they eagerly attended to every single bit of information provided, developing authentic appreciation for the text features that the authors used to convey it.

The next step was for the children to work in pairs, each pair reading a different informational text from the Book Nook. Our list of favorites at the end of this chapter is a sample of these, but others that work well for this purpose are *First the Egg* by Laura Vaccaro Seeger (2007) and *About Fish: A Guide for Children* Cathryn Sill (2005), which capitalize on children's interest in animals, as well as *Food From Farms* by Nancy Dickmann (2011) and *How Did That Get in My Lunchbox? The Story of Food* by Chris Butterworth (2013) because foods are always favorites! Books that invite children to interpret what they sense around them, such as *Weather* by Darlene Stille (2012) and *Watching the Seasons* by Edana Eckart (2004), engage children's life experiences and draw them in. Once the pairs of children found books that they were interested in, they read them and used sticky notes to bookmark and label the features they found in their particular books (e.g., diagrams, labels, headings, captions, tables of contents, indexes) that the authors used to teach their readers "all about" their topics. Later, when the whole class came back together, each pair shared their book and its features, using the sticky notes as prompts. An emphasis this week was on the organizational strategy of chapters that focus on different aspects of the topic in question.

The children then individually selected topics to write about, and each book included a table of contents, separate chapters, and an About the Author page. In writing conferences, we engaged them in conversations designed to help them identify topics that they knew enough about that they could write in-depth material to share with others. If they had identified their topic already, the conference might be focused on appropriate chapters or on eliciting from the young writers the information to be included. Here are the titles of some of the children's books this week:

- *All About Cats*
- *All About Soccer*
- *All About Springer Spaniels*
- *All About Fishes*

- *All About Cameras*
- *All About Football*
- *All About Surfing*

Edith's book, *All About Springer Spaniels*, included four chapters. Figure 13.3 shows the beginning of Chapter 2, "What thay like to do," which is a labeled diagram showing "Thay like to Play With this Stuf." It's clear that the concept of explanatory labels to support the diagrams and text, which she was learning to use as a reader, was a writing technique that she was beginning to make sense of!

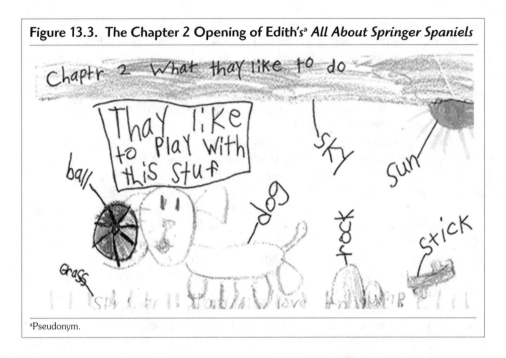

Figure 13.3. The Chapter 2 Opening of Edith's[a] *All About Springer Spaniels*

Chaptr 2 What thay like to do

Thay like to play with this stuf

ball

sky

sun

dog

rock

stick

Grass

[a]Pseudonym.

Independent Writing of Informational Texts During Writers' Workshop

We believe the children produced beautiful texts during these focus weeks, but we're even more excited by the informational texts that they chose to write when it was completely their choice, once the units were finished. It's a stronger indicator of a young author's ability to "write informative/explanatory texts to examine and convey complex ideas and information clearly and accurately through the effective selection, organization, and analysis of content" (National Governors Association Center for Best Practices & Council of Chief State School Officers, 2010, p. 18) when he or she elects to do so independently weeks and even months after the assignment than it was when everyone was doing it at the same time. Figure 13.4 lists a sampling of the informational texts that our students decided to compose during the spring semester of first grade. This ongoing self-selected writing supports Newkirk's (1989) argument "for an elementary-school classroom where a range of possibilities is open to students" (p. 5).

Edith's book, *All About Dance in Jaz*, is (despite its title) a how-to book explaining the "steps" a young dancer takes during dance class, and was written during workshop time shortly after winter break. Edith's passion for dance class and her growing knowledge of how informational texts work are clear in the

Figure 13.4. Children's Independent Informational Text Writing

Month	Author	Title
January	Edith	*All About Dance in Jazz* (a how-to book)
February/March	Alex	*All About Real Madrid* (the soccer team)
April	Heather	*How to Snap*
	Christy	*How to Take Care of a Dog*
May	Edith	*All About Dogs*
	Alex	*About Thomas Jefferson*
	Alex	*About Science*
	Edith	*All About Animals*

Note. All student names are pseudonyms.

text itself and in the illustration in an excerpt from the book shown in Figure 13.5. She used sequencing words and an explanatory diagram to support her texts, borrowing from the informational literature that she had read:

All About Dance in Jaz
by Edith

First get sined in to jazz.

Next go in the room and start doing wait the teacher tells you what to do.

She will asc you to warm up. You will have to do jumping-jax.

After that you do a dance as a groop. The techer will do it with you. She will dance in the corner.

Then you go across the flor and step clap step clap and then leep and the way you leep is do a split in the aer.

Finealea do it to the other side of the room.

Last you do a frees dance and the techer will asc you to act like something.

Before you leve you put your hand on your head and the techer will pote a sticker on your hand and she will say a magic word. The end.

Figure 13.5. Excerpt From *All About Dance in Jaz* by Edith[a]

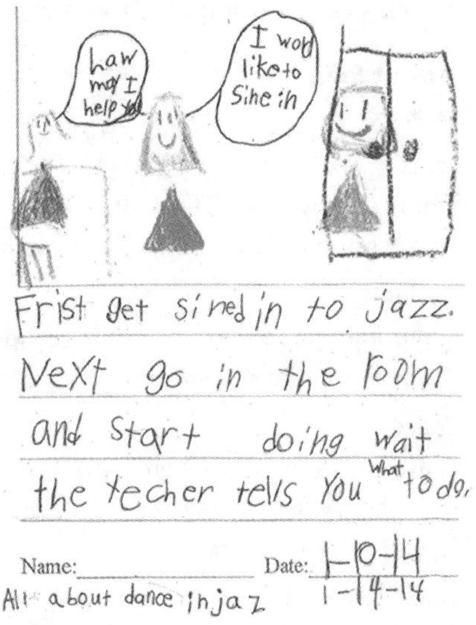

[a]Pseudonym.

Alex, who taught readers about playing the game in *All About Soccer* during the focus unit, stayed with the topic but focused on his favorite team in a book that he wrote and illustrated over several weeks in February and March. He included the kind of details that he knew his fellow soccer fans wanted to know about their favorite teams, and he defined the keyword *archenemy* as he learned authors do from his reading of informational texts:

All About Real Madrid (the soccer team)
by Alex

Real Madrid is FC Barcelona's arch inamie. Arch imnie meens they always beet them.

Real Madrid youst to have Özil but they were too many good players on Real Madrid so he left Real Madrid and Arsenal got him.

Real Madrid has Ronaldo. Ronaldo was the best player of 2013.

Cristiano Ronaldo was the best player of 2013 because he always scord on teams and beat teams and he had very good skills.

These are the players of Real Madrid—Ronaldo, Higuaín, and Pepe—and these are only a few players.

The captain of Real Madrid is Ronaldo.

The colors of the sherts on Real Madrid is gray and white.

By May, Alex was writing almost nothing but nonfiction! He wrote a book called *About Science*, blending his own sensory observations—hearkening back to *Weather* and *Watching the Seasons*—with information that he had learned in science class and during electives for its four chapters:

About Science
by Alex

Trees

Trees grow by roots. The roots are in the dirt. Trees are really tall. Trees are evrey where but mostly in forests. They are in your backyard to.

Potins

Sometimes pepole mix potins together and then they make diffrent colors. Potions are diffrent colors. Sometimes they blow up.

Leavs

Leavs have vanes. Leavs grow on trees. Leavs can die. When leavs die they fall off trees. Leavs can be tiny and big. Sometimes they come in diffrent colors.

Turtels

Turtels are reptiles. There are many kinds of turtels in the world. Turtels are green. Turtels start as babies. Turtels mostly live in South America. Turtels have shells and they are very strong.

The children's returning to informational texts as authors, all year long, requires that they also be able to return to the informational books as readers—to carry out their research, to check on text features, to double-check their information—*all year long!* It's important to keep informational books (actually, all books!) on display and available for the children throughout the year, not just during the week or two that they might be the focus of instruction. Although the books themselves may not be on the table alongside the child's writing folder—in fact, we discourage this during drafting because it interrupts the children's own ideas—the presence in their writing of text features and language forms borrowed from literature is evidence of its ever-growing influence, as long as the children have continual access to the books. The writers' workshop serves, among other things, as a laboratory for children to orchestrate everything that they've learned from teachers and books during direct lessons and independent reading time and apply it in an authentic performance task. It affords the opportunity for children to choose to use everything that they've learned from books, rather than doing so only when it's assigned by someone else.

> *The writers' workshop serves, among other things, as a laboratory for children to orchestrate everything that they've learned.*

Final Thoughts on the Centrality of Writing in the Primary Literacy Classroom

Lisa Cleaveland (Ray, 2004) describes giving a substitute teacher instructions as she prepared to leave her K–1 class to go on maternity leave. After covering a lot of material, Lisa summarized by saying, "No matter what, just let them write every day" (p. ix). We agree. Writing connects to our children's lives, it connects them to success, it connects to reading, and it connects everyone in the classroom—teachers and children—to one another (Gilrane, Adsit, & Charles, 2004).

Research tells us that writing supports reading (Graham, McKeown, Kiuhara, & Harris, 2012) and that the most powerful instructional focus for writing is inquiry (Hillocks, 1987, 2005), perhaps because

> when it is thoughtfully organized, [it] is in students' zone of proximal development. It challenges students to do more than they can on their own but provides the scaffolding to allow them to push beyond what they can already do. Most importantly, it gives students the power to work with ideas. (Hillocks, 2005, pp. 242–243)

Our own teaching and learning lives lead us to believe, along with Newkirk and Kittle (2013), that the writers' workshop at its best is inquiry in action. Shepard (2011) describes it "as both assessment tool and prompt for productive interactions,...whereby children develop an understanding of themselves as authors who receive feedback as a natural part of improving" (p. 27). These productive interactions are the scaffolding.

Why do we want our children to read and write? Certainly, not only (if at all) to pass standardized tests or to be "career ready." Rather, we want them to be full participants in a society that desperately needs thoughtful, caring citizens. As Giroux (1987) once said when introducing Donald Graves to a group of teachers and administrators,

> Democracy requires citizens who can think, challenge, and exhibit long-term thought. This means that public schools need to become places that provide the opportunity for literate occasions, that is, opportunities for students to share their experiences, work in social relations that emphasize care and concern for other, and be introduced to forms of knowledge that provide them with the opportunity to take risks and fight for a quality of life in which all human beings benefit. It is to our benefit that Donald Graves not only writes and talks about these issues, but also works with other teachers in implementing them. (p. 181)

We cannot imagine teaching young children without immersing them in the richness of a literate environment. And we cannot imagine a literate environment that doesn't include the writers' workshop, with its affordances to make the sorts of decisions that Giroux describes, informed by a wealth of excellent literature.

REFERENCES

Boushey, G., & Moser, J. (2006). *The daily 5: Fostering literacy independence in the elementary grades.* Portland, ME: Stenhouse.

Calkins, L.M. (1994). *The art of teaching writing.* Portsmouth, NH: Heinemann.

Clark, S.K., Jones, C.D., & Reutzel, D.R. (2013). Using the text structures of information books to teach writing in the primary grades. *Early Childhood Education Journal, 41*(4), 265–271. doi:10.1007/s10643-012-0547-4

Cunningham, P.M., Hall, D.P., & Defee, M. (1998). Nonability-grouped, multilevel instruction: Eight years later. *The Reading Teacher, 51*(8), 652–664.

Duke, N.K., Bennett-Armistead, V.S., & Roberts, E.M. (2002). Incorporating informational text in the primary grades. In C.M. Roller (Ed.), *Comprehensive reading instruction across the grade levels: A collection of papers from the Reading Research 2001 Conference* (pp. 40–54). Newark, DE: International Reading Association.

Duke, N.K., & Block, M.K. (2012). Improving reading in the primary grades. *The Future of Children, 22*(2), 55–72. doi:10.1353/foc.2012.0017

Eisner, E.W. (1997). Cognition and representation: A way to pursue the American Dream? *Phi Delta Kappan, 78*(5), 348–353.

Elbow, P. (2004). Writing first! *Educational Leadership, 62*(2), 9–13.

Fry, E. (2002). Readability versus leveling. *The Reading Teacher, 56*(3), 286–291.

Gilrane, C.P. (2009). So many books—how do I choose? In D.A. Wooten & B.E. Cullinan (Eds.), *Children's literature in the reading program: An invitation to read* (3rd ed., pp. 130–140). Newark, DE: International Reading Association. doi:10.1598/0699.13

Gilrane, C.P., Adsit, A., & Charles, S. (2004). "It's got to be the most important thing we do.": Three first-grade teachers reflect on the writing process. *New England Reading Association Journal, 40*(1), 35–38.

Gilrane, C.P., Allen, K.L., Boyce, K.A., Lohr, M.L., & Swafford, K.J. (2013, December). *Monday nights at Panera: Exploring the use of cultural-historical activity theory as a lens for understanding professional learning.* Paper presented at the 63rd annual meeting of the Literacy Research Association, Dallas, TX.

Gilrane, C.P., & Lohr, M.L. (2012, November). *"How to trace Piggie:" Exploring the use of mentor texts, digital video, and student expertise in teaching first-graders the genre of writing to a prompt.* Paper presented at the 62nd annual meeting of the Literacy Research Association, San Diego, CA.

Gilrane, C.P., & Lohr, M.L. (in press). *Happy Pig Day*: Following first-graders into the story world of Mo Willems. *The Dragon Lode, 33*(1).

Giroux, H.A. (1987). Critical literacy and student experience: Donald Graves' approach to literacy. *Language Arts, 64*(2), 175–181.

Glaswell, K., & Ford, M. (2011). Let's start leveling about leveling. *Language Arts, 88*(3), 208–216.

Graham, S., & Hebert, M. (2011). Writing to read: A meta-analysis of the impact of writing and writing instruction on reading. *Harvard Educational Review, 81*(4), 710–744.

Graham, S., McKeown, D., Kiuhara, S., & Harris, K.R. (2012). A meta-analysis of writing instruction for students in the elementary grades. *Journal of Educational Psychology, 104*(4), 879–896. doi:10.1037/a0029185

Graves, D.H. (1983). *Writing: Teachers and children at work.* Exeter, NH: Heinemann.

Graves, D.H. (1989). *Investigate nonfiction: The reading/writing teacher's companion.* Portsmouth, NH: Heinemann.

Hansen, J. (1983). Authors respond to authors. *Language Arts, 60*(8), 970–976.

Hansen, J. (2001). *When writers read* (2nd ed.). Portsmouth, NH: Heinemann.

Hansen, J. (2009). Young writers use mentor texts. In D.A. Wooten & B.E. Cullinan (Eds.), *Children's literature in the reading program: An invitation to read* (3rd ed., pp. 88–98). Newark, DE: International Reading Association. doi:10.1598/0699.09

Harwayne, S. (2001). *Writing through childhood: Rethinking process and product.* Portsmouth, NH: Heinemann.

Hillocks, G., Jr. (1987). Synthesis of research on teaching writing. *Educational Leadership, 44*(8), 71–76, 78, 80–82.

Hillocks, G., Jr. (2005). At last: The focus on form vs. content in teaching writing. *Research in the Teaching of English, 40*(2), 238–248.

Hoyt, L. (2007). *Interactive read-alouds, grades K–1: Linking standards, fluency, and comprehension.* Portsmouth, NH: Heinemann.

Maloch, B., & Bomer, R. (2013a). Informational texts and the Common Core Standards: What are we talking about, anyway? *Language Arts, 90*(3), 205–213.

Maloch, B., & Bomer, R. (2013b). Teaching about and with informational texts: What does research teach us? *Language Arts, 90*(6), 441–450.

Maloch, B., & Horsey, M. (2013). Living inquiry: Learning from and about informational texts in a second-grade classroom. *The Reading Teacher, 66*(6), 475–485. doi:10.1002/TRTR.1152

Mantzicopoulos, P., & Patrick, H. (2011). Reading picture books and learning science: Engaging young children with informational text. *Theory Into Practice, 50*(4), 269–276. doi:10.1080/00405841.2011.607372

National Governors Association Center for Best Practices & Council of Chief State School Officers. (2010). *Common Core State Standards for English language arts and literacy in history/social studies, science, and technical subjects.* Washington, DC: Authors.

Newkirk, T. (1989). *More than stories: The range of children's writing.* Portsmouth, NH: Heinemann.

Newkirk, T., & Kittle, P. (Eds.). (2013). *Children want to write: Donald Graves* and the revolution in children's writing. Portsmouth, NH: Heinemann.

Ray, K.W. (with Cleaveland, L.B.). (2004). *About the authors: Writing workshop with our youngest writers*. Portsmouth, NH: Heinemann.

Rog, L.J., & Burton, W. (2001). Matching texts and readers: Leveling early reading materials for assessment and instruction. *The Reading Teacher, 55*(4), 348–356.

Shepard, L.A. (2011). Assessing with integrity in the face of high-stakes testing. In P.J. Dunston, L.B. Gambrell, K. Headley, S.K. Fullerton, P.M. Stecker, V.R. Gillis, & C.C. Bates (Eds.), *60th yearbook of the Literacy Research Association* (pp. 18–32). Oak Creek, WI: Literacy Research Association.

Siegel, M. (2006). Rereading the signs: Multimodal transformations in the field of literacy education. *Language Arts, 84*(1), 65–77.

Wolf, S., Edmiston, B., & Enciso, P. (1997). Drama worlds: Places of the heart, head, voice, and hand in dramatic interpretation. In J. Flood, S.B. Heath, & D. Lapp (Eds.), *Handbook of research on teaching literacy through the communicative and visual arts* (pp. 492–505). New York, NY: Macmillan Library Reference USA.

Yopp, R.H., & Yopp, H.K. (2006). Informational texts as read-alouds at school and home. *Journal of Literacy Research, 38*(1), 37–51. doi:10.1207/s15548430jlr3801_2

CHILDREN'S LITERATURE CITED

Butterworth, C. (2013). *How did that get in my lunchbox? The story of food.* Somerville, MA: Candlewick.

Charlesworth, E. (2007). *Awesome walruses.* New York, NY: Scholastic.

Dickmann, N. (2011). *Food from farms.* Chicago, IL: Heinemann Library.

Eckart, E. (2004). *Watching the seasons.* New York, NY: Children's.

Mezzanotte, J. (2010). *Hurricanes.* Pleasantville, NY: Weekly Reader.

Seeger, L.V. (2007). *First the egg.* New Milford, CT: Frances Lincoln Children's.

Sill, C. (2005). *About fish: A guide for children.* Atlanta, GA: Peachtree.

Snyder, I. (2003a). *Beans to chocolate.* New York, NY: Children's.

Snyder, I. (2003b). *Milk to ice cream.* New York, NY: Children's.

Snyder, I. (2003c). *Oranges to orange juice.* New York, NY: Children's.

Snyder, I. (2003d). *Tomatoes to ketchup.* New York, NY: Children's.

Snyder, I. (2003e). *Trees to paper.* New York, NY: Children's.

Snyder, I. (2003f). *Wax to crayons.* New York, NY: Children's.

Snyder, I. (2003–2005). How things are made [Series]. New York, NY: Children's.

Snyder, I. (2005a). *Berries to jelly.* New York, NY: Children's.

Snyder, I. (2005b). *Grains to bread.* New York, NY: Children's.

Snyder, I. (2005c). *Grapes to raisins.* New York, NY: Children's.

Snyder, I. (2005d). *Sand to glass.* New York, NY: Children's.

Snyder, I. (2005e). *Sap to syrup.* New York, NY: Children's.

Stille, D.R. (2012). *Weather.* Chicago, IL: Raintree.

OTHER RECOMMENDED INFORMATIONAL TEXTS FOR PRIMARY CLASSROOMS

Bodach, V.K. (2007). *Flowers.* Mankato, MN: Capstone.

Bodach, V.K. (2007). *Fruits.* Mankato, MN: Capstone.

Bodach, V.K. (2007). *Leaves.* Mankato, MN: Capstone.

Bodach, V.K. (2007). *Seeds.* Mankato, MN: Capstone.

Jenkins, S. (1995). *Biggest, strongest, fastest.* New York, NY: Houghton Mifflin.

Jenkins, S. (2004). *Actual size.* Boston, MA: Houghton Mifflin.

Jenkins, S., & Page, R. (2003). *What do you do with a tail like this?* New York, NY: Houghton Mifflin.

Pallotta, J. (2012). *The sea mammal alphabet book.* Boston, MA: Bald Eagle.

Pyers, G. (2000). *Changing shape.* Barrington, IL: Rigby Education.

Sweeney, J. (1996). *Me on the map.* New York, NY: Dragonfly.

ABOUT THE AUTHORS

 Colleen P. Gilrane is an associate professor in the Department of Theory and Practice in Teacher Education at the University of Tennessee, Knoxville, USA, where she teaches courses in literacy and elementary education. Her teaching and research interests focus on working with teachers to create communities in which all learners have access to literacy that is rich, powerful, and joyful. Colleen can be contacted at cgilrane@utk.edu.

 Maggie Lingle Lohr is a National Board Certified primary-grade teacher at Underwood Elementary School in Raleigh, North Carolina, USA. She has served as a mentor teacher and allows her classroom to serve as a site for practica and observations by preservice and inservice teachers to support her and their continued professional learning. Maggie can be contacted at mlohr@wcpss.net.

PART V

Engaging With Resources in the Field

CHAPTER 14

Where Do We Go From Here?

Resources to Connect, Engage, and Inspire

James W. Stiles, *Plymouth State University*

Finding the best children's books and activities to support student learning across the curriculum can be overwhelming for teachers in the 21st century. At times, you can feel bombarded with ideas, strategies, and materials, each claiming to hold the key to your success—usually for a substantial fee. How do you decide which ones to use? Where do you begin?

This chapter provides an overview of resources to help get you started. I begin with an introduction to the key professional organizations in children's literature and the language arts. You'll see that they provide tremendous support for teachers, from lesson planning to professional education; particular focus is on special interest groups (SIGs) that support your interest in children's literature. Then, I discuss notable awards and booklists, a surprisingly simple and easy way to support instruction while capturing student interest. Next, I review some of the more useful Internet sources to help you select and use children's literature, particularly in the content areas. I conclude with suggestions for funding to support your growing interest in the world of children's literature.

Professional Organizations: An Invaluable Network

Professional organizations do more than just organize large annual conventions in major cities throughout the United States. They sponsor regional conferences, one-day seminars, webinars, and other opportunities to meet, share expertise, and build your professional network. In addition, membership often includes access to electronic resources, journal subscriptions, newsletters, and blogs. Many organizations offer special funding opportunities for research, professional development, and literacy initiatives. These organizations are a gateway to many of the resources that you'll need in your day-to-day practice, providing a network of opportunity for teachers at every stage of their career.

Children's Literature in the Reading Program: Engaging Young Readers in the 21st Century (4th ed.), edited by Deborah A. Wooten & Bernice E. Cullinan. © 2015 by the International Literacy Association.

Reading and Language Arts

International Literacy Association (ILA)

The teaching of reading and literacy is an essential part of any elementary school teacher's responsibilities. ILA (www.reading.org), formerly the International Reading Association, invites you to be part of a professional community that tackles the challenges and opportunities you face as a literacy educator in the classroom. ILA is a leading publisher of professional development materials, both in print and online. *The Reading Teacher*, one of three ILA journals, blends research with practice to encourage transformative classroom teaching. ILA's most recent initiative, ILA Bridges: Instructional Units for the Engaging Classroom, offers numerous downloadable examples of how to implement the Common Core State Standards across the curriculum. A wide range of support is also available for professional development and advocacy. Of particular note is the ILA E-ssentials series (www.reading.org/general/Publications/ e-ssentials.aspx), a member benefit that offers teachers practical tips for enhancing literacy in the classroom. More than 40 SIGs offer networking for a wide range of issues impacting teachers. A major conference is held each year in the summer. Individual membership starts at $24 per year and includes member discounts for publications and events.

> *ILA's most recent initiative, ILA Bridges: Instructional Units for the Engaging Classroom, offers numerous downloadable examples of how to implement the Common Core State Standards across the curriculum.*

National Council of Teachers of English (NCTE)

A shared love of children's literature, teaching, and the English language is what many members find through NCTE (www.ncte.org). They sponsor a number of excellent journals, including *Language Arts* for elementary interests and *Voices From the Middle*. In addition to traditional print publications, NCTE is active with online professional development, offering a wide range of on-demand webinars that bring you face-to-face with well-known authors. Specific sections of the website cater to elementary and middle school interests. A major convention is held each year in November. Membership fees start at $22.50 per year, with member discounts for publications and events.

American Library Association (ALA)

You love children's literature and are interested in using it in your classroom, but you're not a librarian. What could ALA mean for you? Plenty! Founded in 1876, ALA's (www.ala.org) mission is about making information of all sorts, including literature, accessible to everyone. ALA sponsors the two leading U.S. awards for children's literature, the Caldecott Medal and the John Newbery Medal, plus numerous others. The website provides resources for the selection and use of children's media, including the promotion of intellectual freedom. ALA's annual Banned Books Week offers teachers an opportunity to engage students in critical thinking and debate, key objectives for today's teaching standards. The association produces a wealth of classroom materials, including posters, bookmarks, e-resources, and support for reading promotion. A major conference is held each summer and a midwinter meeting every January. Membership fees start at $35 per year, with member discounts for publications and events.

National Associations to Support Content Area Instruction

National Council for the Social Studies (NCSS)

The teaching of social studies is often a favorite part of the elementary school curriculum for many teachers. NCSS (www.socialstudies.org) provides a wealth of online support, particularly with regard to accessing and teaching content. One of their journals, *Social Studies and the Young Learner*, showcases some of the most innovative practices that emphasize reading, writing, and critical thinking. Many downloadable resources are available, but most are limited to members. Individual memberships start at $40 and include a journal subscription, plus member discounts for publications and events.

National Science Teachers Association (NSTA)

This organization offers a wealth of resources to support science instruction in elementary schools. NSTA (www.nsta.org) has a sophisticated Web presence with downloadable materials, including a special packet of articles and teaching materials specifically for new teachers. The Freebies for Science Teachers section offers a searchable database of high-quality lesson plans and ideas. One of NSTA's series, Picture-Perfect Science Lessons by Karen Ansberry and Emily Morgan (2005–2013), is a superb resource (partly available for free online) that shows how to use a range of trade picture books for science lessons. The journal *Science & Children* is targeted toward elementary educators. Individual memberships start at $35 and include member discounts.

National Council of Teachers of Mathematics (NCTM)

NCTM (www.nctm.org) sees its mission as being an advocate for mathematics education and supporting teachers in their goal of helping all students learn; professional development and research in the teaching of mathematics are central to their work. Of particular interest is the Curriculum Focal Points section of the website, which identifies the critical topics that impact learning in grades K–8; downloadable lesson plans for specific skill areas are provided for each grade level. The journal *Teaching Children Mathematics* is targeted for grades K–5.

Membership starts at $44 per year, with member discounts for publications and events and a free journal subscription.

SIGs for Children's Literature

SIGs are prevalent in larger organizations, offering the opportunity to join colleagues interested in topics such as English as a second/other language, bilingual education, LGBTQ (lesbian, gay, bisexual, transgender, and queer) literature, and content area instruction. Two of the larger SIGS dedicated to children's literature are discussed in more detail here.

Children's Literature & Reading (CL/R)

ILA offers its members a SIG devoted to children's literature and reading. CL/R (www.clrsig.org) sponsors the annual Notable Books for a Global Society list for grades K–12 and publishes *The Dragon Lode*, a journal that shares viewpoints and ideas about children's literature, literacy, and effective teaching. Membership is open to all ILA members starting at $20 per year and includes a subscription to the journal.

Children's Literature Assembly (CLA)

CLA (www.childrensliteratureassembly.org) is NCTE's home for teachers, researchers, publishers, authors, and others who wish to celebrate the joy of children's literature in the lives of children. CLA sponsors the *Journal of Children's Literature*, the annual Notable Children's Books in the English Language Arts list, and numerous events at NCTE's annual convention to meet authors and illustrators, share ideas, and get involved. Membership includes journal subscription and other benefits and starts at $15 per year.

Other Organizations Dedicated to Children's Literature

Children's Literature Association (ChLA)

This organization emphasizes the academic study of children's literature. ChLA (www.childlitassn.org) hosts an annual children's literature conference and publishes books and two journals, *Children's Literature* and *Children's Literature Association Quarterly*. Membership includes subscriptions to both journals and other benefits and starts at $35 per year.

Children's Book Council (CBC)

CBC (www.cbcbooks.org) is an organization of children's book publishers that offers access to professional development, advocacy for children's literature, reading lists, and more. CBC sponsors the annual Children's Book Week and Children's Choice Book Awards.

The Center for Children's Books (CCB)

Hosted by the Graduate School of Library and Information Science at the University of Illinois at Urbana–Champaign, CCB (ccb.lis.illinois.edu) provides access to events, research, scholarly materials, and teaching resources related to the study and use of children's literature.

The Horn Book

Founded in 1924, The Horn Book (www.hbook.com) is dedicated to promoting the best in children's literature. They publish *The Horn Book Magazine* and *The Horn Book Guide*, two landmark resources in literary criticism and children's book reviews. Check your local library for archive copies and access; individual subscriptions start at $49.

International Organizations

International Board on Books for Young People (IBBY)

Children's literature provides a common interest that can cross borders. IBBY (www.ibby.org) is the world's leading organization devoted to promoting international understanding through children's literature. IBBY works to enable children access to quality children's literature, particularly in languages and regions traditionally underserved. Headquartered in Switzerland, IBBY is composed of 74 national chapters around the world. Worldwide IBBY congresses are held on even years, regional conferences on odd years. Membership is available through the national sections.

> *IBBY (www.ibby.org) is the world's leading organization devoted to promoting international understanding through children's literature.*

United States Board on Books for Young People (USBBY)

USBBY (www.usbby.org) is the U.S. chapter of IBBY. USBBY's mission is to promote international understanding through children's literature. USBBY sponsors speakers who address international and intercultural concerns in children's literature at major conventions, such as those of ILA, NCTE, and ALA. The board also organizes the biennial IBBY Regional Conference in North America, a weekend of immersion in international children's literature where authors, illustrators, teachers, and others discuss books, share ideas, and get to know one another. USBBY actively recruits teachers to join the organization through its State Ambassadors program. Membership starts at $20 per year.

Awards and Booklists: Connecting to the Best of the Best

With more than 30,000 children's books published each year in the United States ("Traditional Print Book Production Dipped Slightly in 2013," 2014), trying to remain current on the best new titles can seem overwhelming. Where do you start? This is one area where professional organizations can be of tremendous assistance. Most organizations in reading, language arts, and literature view identifying noteworthy titles, authors, and illustrators as part of their mission. Major awards and booklists are usually selected by a committee, each member appointed based on his or her knowledge, expertise, and ability to judge literature for the specific criteria. As you'll see in this section, awards and booklists reflect the wide range of text types, reading interests, and purposes.

General Awards

John Newbery Medal

Named after John Newbery, an 18th-century pioneer in the publication of books for children, this medal (www.ala.org/alsc/awardsgrants/bookmedia/newberymedal/aboutnewbery/aboutnewbery) is one of the most famous literary awards in children's literature. Each year, a committee of expert volunteers reads hundreds of submissions, then decides which book should be recognized among all U.S. children's books published that year. A single winner and one or more honor books are announced each spring. Historical booklists are available for 1922 to the present, affording a fascinating glimpse at children's literature over the decades.

Caldecott Medal

Just as well known as the Newbery, the Caldecott Medal (www.ala.org/alsc/awardsgrants/bookmedia/caldecottmedal/caldecottmedal) recognizes excellence in picture books published in the United States. This award celebrates the art and illustration of books for children, often drawing attention to remarkable qualities of imagination, innovation, and design. Named after Randolph Caldecott, a 19th-century illustrator noted for creating some of the earliest picture books, the medal is given each spring.

The Charlotte Huck Award is unique in that it seeks to honor the almost magical ability of literature in the hands of young readers.

NCTE Charlotte Huck Award for Outstanding Fiction for Children

Established in 2014, this award (www.ncte.org/awards/charlotte-huck) recognizes fiction that makes a difference in the lives of children. Charlotte Huck, a long-time professor at Ohio State University, was passionate in her belief that literature for children should have special qualities that stir the imagination and invite wonder.

The Charlotte Huck Award is unique in that it seeks to honor the almost magical ability of literature in the hands of young readers.

(Theodor Seuss) Geisel Award

Honoring the renowned Dr. Seuss, this award (www.ala.org/alsc/awardsgrants/bookmedia/geiselaward) celebrates books for very early readers. Award winners in this category are of particular interest to early childhood educators.

Nonfiction Awards

NCTE Orbis Pictus Award for Outstanding Nonfiction for Children

The Orbis Pictus Award (www.ncte.org/awards/orbispictus) is named after the first book designed and written specifically for children: *Orbis Sensualium Pictus* (*Visible World in Pictures*) by Johannes Amos Comenius in 1657 (see Comenius, 1887). This award recognizes excellence in nonfiction writing for children and is presented at the annual NCTE convention in November.

Scott O'Dell Award for Historical Fiction

The Scott O'Dell Award (www.scottodell.com/pages/scotto'dellawardforhistorical fiction.aspx), named for the author of acclaimed works such as the *Island of the Blue Dolphins* (O'Dell, 1960), recognizes the best historical fiction for children.

Robert F. Sibert Informational Book Medal

The best information books are recognized through the Robert F. Sibert Informational Book Medal (www.ala.org/alsc/awardsgrants/bookmedia/sibertmedal). Given the Common Core's emphasis on informational text literacy, this category is particularly interesting because it highlights the various ways authors and illustrators can present science, history, and technology to young readers.

International and Multicultural Awards

(Mildred L.) Batchelder Award

The Batchelder Award (www.ala.org/alsc/awardsgrants/bookmedia/batchelderaward) highlights outstanding books that have been translated into English. Using these exemplary books can help expose children to different viewpoints and literary styles.

Coretta Scott King Book Awards

Honoring the work of Dr. Martin Luther King, Jr. and his wife, Coretta Scott King, the Coretta Scott King Book Awards (www.ala.org/emiert/cskbookawards) recognize African American authors and illustrators whose work helps

> *Exemplary books can help expose children to different viewpoints and literary styles.*

young readers appreciate African American culture and human values that can be considered universal.

Pura Belpré Award
The Pura Belpré Award (www.ala.org/alsc/awardsgrants/bookmedia/belpremedal) honors Latino/a authors and illustrators who represent the Latino culture and experience in positive, affirming ways for young readers.

Hans Christian Andersen Awards
The Hans Christian Andersen Awards (www.ibby.org/index.php?id=273) recognize both an author and an illustrator for the lasting impact that their work has made in children's literature. Candidates are nominated by IBBY national sections worldwide, and the awards are presented every other year at the IBBY International Congress.

Astrid Lindgren Memorial Award
Named for the Swedish author of the treasured Pippi Longstocking series (Lindgren, 1950–2001), the Astrid Lindgren Memorial Award (www.alma.se/en) is given annually to an author and/or illustrator whose work exemplifies the highest artistic quality and humanitarian spirit of children's literature, so valued by Lindgren. Funded by the people of Sweden through the Swedish Arts Council, the monetary prize of 5 million Swedish krona (about $700,000) makes it the largest award in children's literature.

National Book Awards
An interesting source for identifying the best children's literature published in the United Kingdom is the National Book Awards website (www.nationalbookawards .co.uk). They recognize U.K. authors who have made significant contributions to children's literature and have broad appeal among readers.

Poetry and Short Story Awards
Lee Bennett Hopkins Poetry Awards
Two awards honor noted children's literature author and poet Lee Bennett Hopkins. The Lee Bennett Hopkins Poetry Award (pabook.libraries.psu.edu/activities/ hopkins) recognizes annually an outstanding new poetry book or anthology for children. Visit the award's Teaching Toolbox blog (leebennetthopkinsaward .blogspot.com) for ideas on using these remarkable books in your classroom. The ILA Lee Bennett Hopkins Promising Poet Award (www.reading.org/resources/ AwardsandGrants/childrens_hopkins.aspx) is given every three years to recognize outstanding new authors of poetry for children and adolescents up to grade 12.

ILA Short Story Award

Since 1986, a short story from a children's magazine, such as *Highlights*, *Cricket*, *Spider*, and *Boys' Life*, is annually awarded (www.reading.org/resources/ AwardsandGrants/childrens_witty.aspx). A committee considers fresh voice, authenticity, literary merit, and engagement as key factors when selecting winners.

Booklists to Inspire and Connect

Children's Choices Reading List

Do you ever wonder what books children prefer to read? Each year, ILA and the CBC orchestrate a national project that invites teams of children to read and vote for their favorite new releases. Annotated lists of the final selections are offered for three age levels: beginning readers (grades K–2), young readers (grades 3 and 4), and advanced readers (grades 5 and 6). Free access to these booklists and downloadable bookmarks are available on ILA's website (www.reading.org/resources/booklists/childrenschoices.aspx).

Notable Children's Books in the English Language Arts

The written text of books for children can delight and inspire, fostering a lifelong love of literature. Sponsored by CLA, this booklist (www.childrensliteratureassembly .org/notables.html) identifies quality books for grades K–8 that explore wordplay and/or word origin, display uniqueness in style, and invite readers to respond or participate. Annotated booklists are presented at the NCTE and ILA annual conferences.

Notable Books for a Global Society

Literature can be a wonderful way for children to learn about other people, cultures, and the world around them. Each year, the CL/R committee selects 25 books that help young people read and understand other people and cultures. This booklist (clrsig.org/nbgs_books.php) includes a wide range of cultures, topics, and formats, providing welcome additions to cultural studies units.

Notable Children's Books

In addition to including the many books that receive ALA's major awards, the Association for Library Service to Children identifies other books of note published throughout the year. This booklist seeks to recognize books that push boundaries in the realm of creativity for readers from birth through 14 years of age. Given the numerous titles that are included from varied awards, this booklist is particularly useful in capturing the best of the best. Free access to annotated booklists is provided on the website (www.ala.org/alsc/awardsgrants/notalists/ncb).

Notable Tradebooks for Young People

Compiled by NCSS and CBC, this annual list (www.social studies.org/resources/notable) identifies books that help children explore topics in the social studies in creative, new ways; special attention is given to including works from many groups, cultures, and perspectives. Use of books from this list can help teachers avoid flat, repetitious, and limited explorations of common events or themes in history. Annotated lists online offer teachers a rich variety of books to recommend for research projects and to supplement instruction.

USBBY Outstanding International Books List

International books can and should be part of every child's elementary school experience. In fact, if students have read *Charlie and the Chocolate Factory* by Roald Dahl (1964) or any of the Harry Potter series books by J.K. Rowling (1998–2007), these types of books already are. Encouraging students to read both fiction and nonfiction written by authors from outside the United States invites students to compare multiple perspectives, a goal set forth by the Common Core. USBBY committee members prepare an annual list of the best international books that can help teachers and students explore some of these fascinating gems. This booklist is published each year in the *School Library Journal* and then posted on USBBY's website (www.usbby.org/list_oibl.html).

Gateway Websites: One-Stop Shopping for Booklists and Awards

Because there as dozens of awards and booklists that might be of interest, finding a gateway website that provides a single access point to individual resources worldwide is invaluable! The following websites are some of the more comprehensive ones.

Notable Children's Books

ALA offers an alphabetized list of major awards in book, print, and media with direct hotlinks. Their annual Notable Children's Books list, discussed previously, includes major awards as well as other titles selected by the committee, thus serving as a fairly comprehensive annual resource. Open access is provided online to award and booklist links.

Reading Rockets

Reading Rockets (www.readingrockets.org), a multimedia project sponsored by public television station WETA of Washington, DC, provides a rich variety of online resources for literature and literacy, with particular emphasis on issues related to meeting Common Core mandates. In particular, the themed booklist offer over 100 suggestions ranging from monsters to magic, science to social studies, plus dozens of special interest categories. If you're looking for 10 great bedtime stories, you'll find suggestions here, with open access and no membership required.

Goodreads

Goodreads (www.goodreads.com) has become an Internet phenomenon in the world of books and reading, using the power of social media to connect books to readers. Launched in 2007, Goodreads (2014) describes itself as "the world's largest site for readers and book recommendations" (para. 1). More than 30 million members share reviews, engage in discussions, and contribute to an aggregate data source that uses technology to provide individual recommendations based on personal reading tastes and experiences. Now it's even easier to help students find a book that might be of interest. Membership is free.

Commercial Booksellers

Commercial booksellers such as Amazon (www.amazon.com) and AbeBooks (www.abebooks.com) have long offered powerful search engines for finding books. In recent years, they've expanded their links to noted awards. The editors' selections of the top 50 or 100 books for kids are of interest.

Database of Award-Winning Children's Literature

Individual initiatives by teachers and librarians can offer surprising resources! Reference librarian Lisa Bartle at California State University, San Bernardino, started the Database of Award-Winning Children's Literature (www.dawcl.com), a searchable, open access tool that's useful for learning about awards and winners.

Literature in Action: Lesson Plans, Ideas, and Resources

The Internet seems to provide endless suggestions for books, lessons, and other activities, but sorting through them can be overwhelming. In this section, I note some of the most useful websites for teachers interested in exploring creative ways to use children's literature in the classroom. In addition to the websites highlighted in this section, Table 14.1 notes other resources that offer support for instruction and planning in math, science, and social studies.

The Teaching Channel

This website (https://www.teachingchannel.org) teaches through video, presenting some of the best practices in education through free, streaming videos. Clips often include real classroom settings that show teachers and students interacting with

Table 14.1. Additional Content Area Links of Interest to Teachers

Math	Science	Social Studies
AAA Math: www.aaamath.com	Edheads: www.edheads.org	History Globe: www.historyglobe.com
Coolmath.com: www.coolmath.com	Exploratorium's Snacks: www.exploratorium.edu/snacks/index.html	Library of Congress: www.loc.gov
Illuminations: illuminations.nctm.org	FOSSweb: www.fossweb.com	National Geographic Kids: kids.nationalgeographic.com
Math Playground: www.mathplayground.com	NASA: www.nasa.gov	the.News: www.pbs.org/newshour/spc/thenews
National Library of Virtual Manipulatives: nlvm.usu.edu/en/nav/vlibrary.html	NASA Kids' Club: www.nasa.gov/audience/forkids/kidsclub/flash/index.html#.VD_ypflSYbI	Our Documents: www.ourdocuments.gov
Real World Math: www.realworldmath.org	National Science Digital Library: nsdl.org	PBS: www.pbs.org
	PhET: phet.colorado.edu	Smithsonian: www.si.edu
	Science Kids: www.sciencekids.co.nz	Smithsonian's History Explorer: historyexplorer.si.edu
	Wonderville: www.wonderville.ca	The Statue of Liberty–Ellis Island Foundation: www.libertyellisfoundation.org
		Teachinghistory.org: www.teachinghistory.org
		ThinkQuest: https://gitso-outage.oracle.com/thinkquest
		Time For Kids: www.timeforkids.com

literature. The searchable database offers nearly 1,000 downloadable segments, including hundreds in the English language arts, illustrating some of the best practices in classroom instruction. For example, Jennifer Ochoa demonstrates the use of text graffiti with her language arts class, modeling an excellent way to preview complex tests (Newell, 2011). Support is provided on the website for grades K–8 and beyond. Access is free, but additional resources are only available to those who register.

Google Lit Trips

When reading about a particular setting in a story, have you ever wondered what that place is really like? How does the mental image you have from the story compare with real life? Or, for literature that uses the journey motif, such as *The Watsons Go to Birmingham—1963* by Christopher Paul Curtis (1995), how long would it really take to go from Michigan to Alabama, and what would you see along the way? These questions are natural ones inspired by literature that promotes inquiry and investigation. Google Lit Trips (www.googlelittrips.com) offers a visually rich, interactive way for students to make real-world connections to literature of all genres, supporting Common Core objectives of fostering close reading. The website offers examples such as Holly Doe's project for her first graders, an exploration of marine life and geography inspired by David Wiesner's (2006) wordless picture book *Flotsam*. Other projects using *Esperanza Rising* by Pam Muñoz Ryan (2002), *Fever 1793* by Laurie Halse Anderson (2002), and *Sugar Changed the World: A Story of Magic, Spice, Slavery, Freedom, and Science* by Marc Aronson and Marina Budhos (2010) show how global mapping technology can bring both nonfiction and historical fiction to life. This is a free resource with support for grades K–8 and beyond.

Digital Storytelling

For today's students accustomed to high-powered graphics and technological wizardry, the rise of online digital storytelling provides fascinating new ways to engage learners. Digital storytelling uses open-access online programs that allow the user to format text with all types of graphics (e.g., photos, drawings, clip art, computer-generated). Projects range from comic strips to Ken Burns–style visuals with voice overlay, animated cartoons to movies, and more. Remarkably, these programs are fairly simple to use yet result in rather sophisticated products. Offering new takes on projects such as Readers Theatre, story extensions, book talks, and creative writing, this technology can be used in countless ways to deepen and extend the reading/writing experience, bringing text alive for learners in the digital age. Moreover, the close reading necessary for summarization, rewriting, and artistic representation of text supports 21st-century literacy skills.

Teachers need not be technological experts to use these tools in class, as most programs offer simple tutorials with examples to inspire student creativity. Projects can be viewed on-screen, projected, sent electronically, or printed. Animato (www.animato.com) provides a free version of their product that's ideal for combining music with text and images. The website 50+ Web Ways to Tell a Story (50ways.wikispaces.com) is a superb gateway, with links to programs that help students create imaginative slideshows, storybooks, comics, collages, maps, and more.

ReadWriteThink

Online searches for lesson and unit plans often lead to materials of mixed quality or ones that require costly membership fees. A partnership of ILA and NCTE, ReadWriteThink's (www.readwritethink.org) mission is clear: to promote best practices in reading and language arts instruction by providing access to the best free materials. A searchable database supports K–12 teachers; classroom apps and professional development resources are all free. The Student Interactives section of the website offers dozens of ways for students to engage and respond through technology.

Science NetLinks

The American Association for the Advancement of Science provides support for teachers seeking to achieve literacy goals in content areas. Its Science NetLinks website (sciencenetlinks.com) shows how to use great nonfiction (and even some fiction) trade books to teach and engage learners. Specific collections include "Inventors and Inventions" and "STEM and the Common Core."

Math Maven's Mysteries

This free teacher resource from Scholastic (teacher.scholastic.com/maven) offers short, online mysteries to solve using math and logical reasoning. It's great for warm-ups and bell-ringer activities.

Additional Language Arts Websites

The Write-n-ator!

The Write-n-ator! (writenator.nhptv.org), sponsored by New Hampshire Public Television, offers a collection of free video clips that provide the background for writing challenges to build targeted skills.

Starfall

Starfall (www.starfall.com) offers an entertaining way for children to learn phonics through games and activities.

KidsReads

KidsReads (www.kidsreads.com) provides a free network to share reviews, commentaries, and discussions about books. It's ideal for helping students share their views and find books they'll enjoy.

Websites for Children's Poetry

All Poetry

All Poetry (allpoetry.com) introduces itself as "the world's largest poetry community." It's ideal for quick research on famous poets and poems, plus it provides young poets with access to writing groups, competitions, and opportunities for virtual publication.

Poets.org

Poets.org (www.poets.org), sponsored by the Academy of American Poets, is glad to e-mail you a fresh, unpublished poem each day (if you desire!). Browse their virtual collection of poems or check out their teaching resources for great ideas on how to include poetry in your lesson plans.

Poetry4kids.com

Poetry4kids.com (www.poetry4kids.com) is the Web presence of the Poetry Foundation's Children's Poet Laureate, Kenn Nesbitt. He offers teachers everything from games, contests, and lesson-planning tips to an online rhyming dictionary, video clips, and podcasts.

Giggle Poetry

Giggle Poetry (www.gigglepoetry.com) is dedicated to making both poetry and learning fun. The Poetry Theater section of the website offers downloadable scripts that give teachers and students a new take on Readers Theatre. The Poetry Class section gives students quick, independent instruction on how to write poems in a variety of formats.

Free, Free, Free: E-Books at No Cost

International Children's Digital Library

The International Children's Digital Library (en.childrenslibrary.org) is a hidden gem. Reading the art and stories of other cultures is fascinating, yet access to international picture books can be difficult and expensive. This free resource offers a searchable database of more than 4,600 digitized picture books from dozens of countries in dozens of languages.

Project Gutenberg

Project Gutenberg (www.gutenberg.org) provides searchable access to more than 46,000 free e-books, many in other languages, too.

ManyBooks.net

ManyBooks.net is a database of nearly 30,000 e-books available at no cost. This website (manybooks.net) is searchable, with browsing features by author, title, genre, and language.

Grants and Scholarships: Funding to Support Your Journey

The organizations and resources discussed throughout this chapter are excellent sources for funding to help you get involved with the children's literature community, both nationally and internationally. You may be surprised at the number of opportunities that exist! Most importantly, there are many programs that are directed toward classroom teachers.

Check the websites of these organizations, as each has a section for awards and grants that provides the most updated information about funding amounts, application qualifications, and procedures. The following awards and grants are just a few of the opportunities available.

ILA Regie Routman Teacher Recognition Grant

Funded by leading literacy educator Regie Routman, this $2,500 grant (www.reading.org/resources/awardsandgrants/teachers_routman.aspx) honors K–6 classroom teachers working in high-needs districts who are committed to improving reading and writing across the curriculum.

Bonnie Campbell Hill National Literacy Leader Award

Administered by CLA, this award (www.childrensliteratureassembly.org/teacher-leader-award.html) offers two $2,500 grants each year plus $150 in professional books for professional development in children's literature and literacy in grades K–8.

ALA

ALA has a comprehensive grants webpage (www.ala.org/awardsgrants) that lists awards ranging from single-event tickets at their annual convention to larger travel grants and funding for special projects.

REFERENCES

Goodreads. (2014). *About us*. Retrieved from www.goodreads.com/about/us

Newell, B. (Producer). (2011). *Text graffiti: Previewing challenging topics* [Video]. Washington, DC: Teaching Channel. Retrieved from https://www.teachingchannel.org/videos/preview-challenging-topics

Traditional print book production dipped slightly in 2013. (2014). *Bowker*. Retrieved from www.bowker.com/en-US/aboutus/press_room/2014/pr_08052014.shtml

CHILDREN'S LITERATURE CITED

Anderson, L.H. (2002). *Fever 1793*. New York, NY: Aladdin.

Ansberry, K., & Morgan, E. (2005–2013). Picture-perfect science lessons [Series]. Arlington, VA: National Science Teachers Association.

Aronson, M., & Budhos, M. (2010). *Sugar changed the world: A story of magic, spice, slavery, freedom, and science*. Boston, MA: Clarion.

Comenius, J.A. (1887). *Orbis pictus* [*The world in pictures*] (9th ed.; C.W. Bardeen, Ed.; C. Hoole, Trans.). Syracuse, NY: C.W. Bardeen.

Curtis, C.P. (1995). *The Watsons go to Birmingham—1963*. New York, NY: Yearling.

Dahl, R. (1964). *Charlie and the chocolate factory*. New York, NY: Alfred A. Knopf.

O'Dell, S. (1960). *Island of the blue dolphins*. New York, NY: Houghton Mifflin.

Lindgren, A. (1950–2001). Pippi Longstocking [Series]. New York, NY: Viking.

Rowling, J.K. (1998–2007). Harry Potter [Series]. New York, NY: Arthur A. Levine.

Ryan, P.M. (2002). *Esperanza rising*. New York, NY: Scholastic.

Wiesner, D. (2006). *Flotsam*. New York, NY: Clarion.

ABOUT THE AUTHOR

 James W. Stiles is an assistant professor of elementary education and childhood studies at Plymouth State University, New Hampshire, USA, with expertise in language arts, children's literature, teaching methodologies, and cross-cultural studies. His research explores the dynamics of fostering active literacy through critical inquiry, children's literature, and performance. An international educator for more than 20 years, James has organized and led programs for high school and college students in the United States, Europe, Africa, and Asia. He is a board member of USBBY (2012–2015) and served as president (2012–2014) of the Children's Literature Assembly of the National Council of Teachers of English. James can be contacted at jwstiles@live.com.

INDEX

Note. Page numbers followed by *f* or *t* indicate figures or tables, respectively.

CHILDREN'S LITERATURE AUTHOR INDEX

Note. Page numbers followed by *f* or *t* indicate figures or tables, respectively.

CHILDREN'S LITERATURE TITLE INDEX

Note. Page numbers followed by *f* or *t* indicate figures or tables, respectively.